Departme

ONE WEEK LOAN

Cc

Menta

Published pursuant to section 118 of the Act

London: TSO

Front cover
Title: Three Layers of Life by Annette Zink

www.artinminds.org.uk

Art in Minds (AIMs) came into being as a project of Shrub Hill Workshop,
Worcestershire Mental Health Partnership NHS Trust, to celebrate World Mental
Health Day by showcasing the wealth of untapped and largely unrecognised
talent that exists in the mental health arena.

information & publishing solutions

Published by TSO (The Stationery Office) and available from:

Online
www.tsoshop.co.uk

Mail, Telephone, Fax & E-mail
TSO
PO Box 29, Norwich NR3 1GN
Telephone orders/general enquiries: 0870 600 5522
Fax orders: 0870 600 5533
E-mail: customer.services@tso.co.uk
Textphone: 0870 240 3701

TSO Shops
16 Arthur Street, Belfast BT1 4GD
028 9023 8451 Fax 028 9023 5401
71 Lothian Road, Edinburgh EH3 9AZ
0870 606 5566 Fax 0870 606 5588

TSO@Blackwell and other Accredited Agents

Printed in the United Kingdom for The Stationery Office
5939430 C75 10/08 19585 410290

Foreword

Since the Code of Practice for the Mental Health Act 1983 was last revised in 1999, we have seen a transformation in the way that mental health services are provided in England. That transformation is continuing.

Through the Mental Health Act 2007, the Government has updated the 1983 Act to ensure it keeps pace with the changes in the way that mental health services are – and need to be – delivered.

It is important that we have a modern legal framework within which clinicians can intervene where necessary to protect people with mental disorders themselves and, sometimes, to protect other people as well. But with the power to intervene compulsorily comes the responsibility to do so only where it is right and to the highest standards possible.

That is why we have comprehensively revised this Code of Practice, following wide consultation with the people who provide and receive services under the Mental Health Act.

Many individuals and organisations read and commented on earlier drafts of the Code of Practice. I am grateful to all of them for sharing their ideas and their practical experience.

I am confident that together we have achieved a new Code of Practice that will meet the needs of those who use it.

Secretary of State for Health
Alan Johnson

Contents

Introduction

i   This revised Code of Practice ("the Code") has been prepared in accordance with section 118 of the Mental Health Act 1983 ("the Act") by the Secretary of State for Health after consulting such bodies as appeared to him to be concerned, and laid before Parliament. The Code will come into force on 3 November 2008.

Purpose and legal status of the Code of Practice

ii   The Code provides guidance to registered medical practitioners ("doctors"), approved clinicians, managers and staff of hospitals, and approved mental health professionals on how they should proceed when undertaking duties under the Act.

iii   It also gives guidance to doctors and other professionals about certain aspects of medical treatment for mental disorder more generally.

iv   While the Act does not impose a legal duty to comply with the Code, the people listed above to whom the Code is addressed must have regard to the Code. The reasons for any departure should be recorded. Departures from the Code could give rise to legal challenge, and a court, in reviewing any departure from the Code, will scrutinise the reasons for the departure to ensure that there is sufficiently convincing justification in the circumstances.

v   The Code should also be beneficial to the police and ambulance services and others in health and social services (including the independent and voluntary sectors) involved in providing services to people who are, or may become, subject to compulsory measures under the Act.

vi   It is intended that the Code will also be helpful to patients, their representatives, carers, families and friends, and others who support them.

Presentation of this Code

vii   Throughout this Code, the Mental Health Act 1983 is referred to as "the Act". Where there is reference to sections of other acts, the relevant act is clearly indicated. Where the Code refers to "the regulations", it means regulations made under the Act.

viii   The Code is intended to offer guidance on the operation of the Act, and does not set out to explain each and every aspect of the Act and the regulations, orders and directions which go with it.

ix   To guide readers to more detailed information and explanation, references are given in the margins of the Code to relevant legislation and to other reference material.

x   A list of relevant material is also provided at the end of each chapter, where appropriate. These references do not form part of the Code and do not attract the same legal status. The information is provided for assistance only.

> References in the margins of this edition to "sections" are to sections of the Mental Health Act 1983 itself. References to chapters and paragraphs of the "Reference Guide" are to the Mental Health Act Reference Guide produced by the Department of Health. They do not form part of the Code itself.

Scenarios – applying the principles

xi   In a number of the chapters of the Code, scenarios have been included which are intended to illustrate the way in which the guiding principles set out in **chapter 1** might be applied to decisions which people have to take under the Act. The scenarios are not intended to provide a template for decisions in applying the principles in similar situations. The scenarios themselves are only illustrative and do not form part of the Code.

References to patients, children and young people

xii The Code refers throughout to "patients" when it means people who are, or appear to be, suffering from a mental disorder. This use of the term is not a recommendation that the term "patient" should be used in practice in preference to other terms such as "service users", "clients" or similar. It is simply a reflection of the terminology used in the Act itself.

xiii When the Code refers to "children" it means people under the age of 16. When it refers to "young people" it means people aged 16 or 17.

References to the Commission and Tribunal

xiv The Code refers in a number of places to the Commission which is responsible for monitoring the operation of the Act. At the time of publication, this is the Mental Health Act Commission (MHAC). However, legislation is currently before Parliament which will abolish the MHAC and transfer its functions to the Care Quality Commission, a new integrated health and adult social care regulator, bringing together existing health and social care regulators into one body. Subject to Parliament, it is expected that the new Commission will be established in April 2009.

xv Similarly, the Code refers frequently to the Tribunal which has the power to discharge patients from detention and other compulsory measures under the Act. At the time of publication, this means the Mental Health Review Tribunal (MHRT). However, subject to Parliament, the MHRT is intended to be replaced in England by a new First Tier Tribunal established under the Tribunals, Courts and Enforcement Act 2007.

Mental Capacity Act 2005

xvi There are many references throughout this Code to the Mental Capacity Act 2005 (MCA). The Code assumes that its readers are familiar with the main provisions of the MCA as it relates to the care and treatment of people with mental disorders who lack the capacity to take particular decisions for themselves, and does not attempt to explain them.

xvii It will be difficult for professionals involved in providing care for people with mental health problems to carry out their work (including their responsibilities under the Act) without an understanding of key concepts in the MCA.

xviii In particular, they will need to be familiar with the principles of the MCA to understand what it means to lack capacity and to know when decisions can be taken in the best interests of people who lack capacity to take those decisions themselves, the steps to be taken before doing so, and the principles to be applied. They will also need to be familiar with the concepts of advance decisions to refuse treatment, lasting powers of attorney and donees of such powers ("attorneys"), court-appointed deputies and independent mental capacity advocates.

xix Although patients' capacity to consent to treatment does not by itself determine whether they can or ought to be detained under the Act, people involved in deciding whether patients should be detained under the Act will also need to understand the circumstances in which deprivation of liberty in hospitals and care homes may be authorised under the deprivation of liberty safeguards added to the MCA by the Mental Health Act 2007, and the procedures for so doing.[1]

[1] The deprivation of liberty safeguards are expected to be in force in April 2009.

CHAPTER 1
Statement of guiding principles

1.1   This chapter provides a set of guiding principles which should be considered when making decisions about a course of action under the Act.

Guiding principles

Purpose principle

1.2   Decisions under the Act must be taken with a view to minimising the undesirable effects of mental disorder, by maximising the safety and wellbeing (mental and physical) of patients, promoting their recovery and protecting other people from harm.

Least restriction principle

1.3   People taking action without a patient's consent must attempt to keep to a minimum the restrictions they impose on the patient's liberty, having regard to the purpose for which the restrictions are imposed.

Respect principle

1.4   People taking decisions under the Act must recognise and respect the diverse needs, values and circumstances of each patient, including their race, religion, culture, gender, age, sexual orientation and any disability. They must consider the patient's views, wishes and feelings (whether expressed at the time or in advance), so far as they are reasonably ascertainable, and follow those wishes wherever practicable and consistent with the purpose of the decision. There must be no unlawful discrimination.

Participation principle

1.5   Patients must be given the opportunity to be involved, as far as is practicable in the circumstances, in planning, developing and reviewing their own treatment and care to help ensure that it is delivered in a way that is as appropriate and effective for them as possible. The involvement of carers, family members and other people who have an interest in the patient's welfare should be encouraged (unless there are particular reasons to the contrary) and their views taken seriously.

Effectiveness, efficiency and equity principle

1.6   People taking decisions under the Act must seek to use the resources available to them and to patients in the most effective, efficient and equitable way, to meet the needs of patients and achieve the purpose for which the decision was taken.

Using the principles

1.7   All decisions must, of course, be lawful and informed by good professional practice. Lawfulness necessarily includes compliance with the Human Rights Act 1998.

1.8   The principles inform decisions, they do not determine them. Although all the principles must inform every decision made under the Act, the weight given to each principle in reaching a particular decision will depend on the context.

1.9   That is not to say that in making a decision any of the principles should be disregarded. It is rather that the principles as a whole need to be balanced in different ways according to the particular circumstances of each individual decision.

Related material

- Human Rights Act 1998

  This material does not form part of the Code. It is provided for assistance only.

CHAPTER 2 Information for patients, nearest relatives and others

2.1   This chapter gives guidance on the information that must be given to patients and their nearest relatives. It also gives guidance on communication with patients and others generally.

Communication with patients

2.2   Effective communication is essential in ensuring appropriate care and respect for patients' rights. It is important that the language used is clear and unambiguous and that people giving information check that the information that has been communicated has been understood.

2.3   Everything possible should be done to overcome barriers to effective communication, which may be caused by any of a number of reasons – for example, if the patient's first language is not English. Patients may have difficulty in understanding technical terms and jargon or in maintaining attention for extended periods. They may have a hearing or visual impairment or have difficulty in reading or writing. A patient's cultural background may also be very different from that of the person speaking to them.

2.4   Those with responsibility for the care of patients need to identify how communication difficulties affect each patient individually, so that they can assess the needs of each patient and address them in the most appropriate way. Hospitals and other organisations should make people with specialist expertise (eg in sign language or Makaton) available as required.

2.5   Where an interpreter is needed, every effort should be made to identify who is appropriate to the patient, given the patient's gender, religion, language, dialect, cultural background and age. The patient's relatives and friends should only exceptionally be used as intermediaries or interpreters. Interpreters (both professional and non-professional) must respect the confidentiality of any personal information they learn about the patient through their involvement.

2.6   Independent advocates[1] engaged by patients can be invaluable in helping patients to understand the questions and information being presented to them and in helping them to communicate their views to staff. (See **chapter 20.**)

2.7   Wherever possible, patients should be engaged in the process of reaching decisions which affect their care and treatment under the Act. Consultation with patients involves assisting them in understanding the issue, their role and the roles of others who are involved in taking the decision. Ideally decisions should be agreed with the patient. Where a decision is made that is contrary to the patient's wishes, that decision and the authority for it should be explained to the patient using a form of communication that the patient understands.

Sections 132 and 132A Reference Guide chapters 12 (detention) and 15 (SCT)

Information for detained patients and patients on supervised community treatment

2.8   The Act requires hospital managers to take steps to ensure that patients who are detained in hospital under the Act, or who are on supervised community treatment (SCT), understand important information about how the Act applies to them. This must be done as soon as practicable after the start of the patient's detention or SCT. This information must also be given to SCT patients who are recalled to hospital.

2.9   Information must be given to the patient both orally and in writing. These are not alternatives. Those providing information to patients should ensure that all relevant information is conveyed in a way that the patient understands.

[1] Independent mental health advocacy services under the Act are expected to be introduced in April 2009.

CHAPTER

2

Information
for patients,
nearest
relatives and
others

2.10   It would not be sufficient to repeat what is already written on an information leaflet as a way of providing information orally.

Information about detention and SCT

2.11   Patients must be informed:

- of the provisions of the Act under which they are detained or on SCT, and the effect of those provisions;

- of the rights (if any) of their nearest relative to discharge them (and what can happen if their responsible clinician does not agree with that decision); and

- for SCT patients, of the effect of the community treatment order, including the conditions which they are required to keep to and the circumstances in which their responsible clinician may recall them to hospital.

2.12   As part of this, they should be told:

- the reasons for their detention or SCT;

- the maximum length of the current period of detention or SCT;

- that their detention or SCT may be ended at any time if it is no longer required or the criteria for it are no longer met;

- that they will not automatically be discharged when the current period of detention or SCT ends; and

- that their detention or SCT will not automatically be renewed or extended when the current period of detention or SCT ends.

2.13   Patients should also be told the essential legal and factual grounds for their detention or SCT. For the patient to be able to effectively challenge the grounds for their detention or SCT, should they wish, they should be given the full facts rather than simply the broad reasons. This should be done promptly and clearly.

2.14   In addition, a copy of the detention or SCT documentation should be made available to the patient, unless the hospital managers are of the opinion (based on the advice of the authors of the documents) that the information disclosed would adversely affect the health or wellbeing of the patient or others. It may be necessary to remove any personal information about third parties.

2.15   Where the section of the Act under which the patient is being detained changes, they must be provided with the above information to reflect the new situation. This also applies where a detained patient becomes an SCT patient, where an SCT patient's community treatment order is revoked, or where a conditionally discharged patient is recalled to hospital.

Information about consent to treatment

2.16   Patients must be told what the Act says about treatment for their mental disorder. In particular they must be told:

- the circumstances (if any) in which they can be treated without their consent – and the circumstances in which they have the right to refuse treatment;

- the role of second opinion appointed doctors (SOADs) and the circumstances in which they may be involved; and

- (where relevant) the rules on electro-convulsive therapy (ECT).

Information about seeking a review of detention or SCT

2.17   Patients must be informed:

- of the right of the responsible clinician and the hospital managers to discharge them (and, for restricted patients, that this is subject to the agreement of the Secretary of State for Justice);

- of their right to ask the hospital managers to discharge them;

CHAPTER

2

Information
for patients,
nearest
relatives and
others

- that the hospital managers must consider discharging them when their detention is renewed or their SCT extended;

- (for NHS patients in independent hospitals) of the power of the relevant NHS body to discharge them;

- of their rights to apply to the Tribunal;

- of the rights (if any) of their nearest relative to apply to the Tribunal on their behalf;

- about the role of the Tribunal; and

- how to apply to the Tribunal.

2.18 Hospital managers should ensure that patients are offered assistance to request a hospital managers' hearing or make an application to the Tribunal. They should also be told:

- how to contact a suitably qualified legal representative (and should be given assistance to do so if required);

- that free legal aid may be available; and

- how to contact any other organisation which may be able to help them make an application to the Tribunal.

2.19 It is particularly important that patients on SCT who may not have daily contact with people who could help them make an application to the Tribunal are informed and supported in this process.

2.20 SCT patients whose community treatment orders are revoked, and conditionally discharged patients recalled to hospital, should be told that their cases will be referred automatically to the Tribunal.

Information about the Commission

2.21 Patients must be informed about the role of the Commission and of their right to meet visitors appointed by the Commission in private. Patients should be told when the Commission is to visit their hospital and be reminded of the Commission's role.

2.22   Patients may also make a complaint to the Commission, and they should be informed of the process for this. Support should be made available to patients to do this, if required. Patients should also be given information about the hospital's own complaints system and how to use it.

Information about withholding of correspondence

2.23   Detained patients must be told that post sent by them may be withheld if the person to whom it is addressed asks the hospital managers to do so. Patients in high security psychiatric hospitals must be told about the other circumstances in which their correspondence may be withheld, the procedures that will be followed and their right to ask the Commission to review the decisions taken.

Keeping patients informed of their rights

2.24   Those with responsibility for patient care should ensure that patients are reminded from time to time of their rights and the effects of the Act. It may be necessary to convey the same information on a number of different occasions or in different formats and to check regularly that the patient has fully understood it. Information given to a patient who is unwell may need to be repeated when their condition has improved.

2.25   A fresh explanation of the patient's rights should be considered in particular where:

- the patient is considering applying to the Tribunal, or when the patient becomes eligible again to apply to the Tribunal;

- the patient requests the hospital managers to consider discharging them;

- the rules in the Act about their treatment change (for example, because three months have passed since they were first given medication, or because they have regained capacity to consent to treatment – see **chapters 23 and 24**);

CHAPTER

2

Information
for patients,
nearest
relatives and
others

- any significant change in their treatment is being considered;

- there is to be a Care Programme Approach review (or its equivalent);

- renewal of their detention or extension of their SCT is being considered; or

- a decision is taken to renew their detention or to extend their SCT.

2.26 When a patient is discharged from detention or SCT, or the authority for their detention or SCT expires, this fact should be made clear to them. The patient should also be given an explanation of what happens next, including any section 117 after-care or other services which are to be provided.

Information for nearest relatives

Section 133

2.27 The Act also requires hospital managers to take such steps as are practicable to give the patient's nearest relative a copy of any information given to the patient in writing, unless the patient requests otherwise. The information should be given to the nearest relative when the information is given to the patient, or within a reasonable time afterwards.

2.28 When a patient detained under the Act or on SCT is given information, they should be told that the written information will also be supplied to their nearest relative, so that they have a chance to object.

2.29 The nearest relative should also be told of the patient's discharge from detention or SCT (where practicable), unless either the patient or the nearest relative has requested that information about discharge should not be given. This includes discharge from detention onto SCT. If practicable, the information should be given at least seven days in advance of the discharge.

2.30   In addition, regulations require nearest relatives to be informed of various other events, including the renewal of a patient's detention, extension of SCT and transfer from one hospital to another.

2.31   These duties to inform nearest relatives are not absolute. In almost all cases, information is not to be shared if the patient objects.

2.32   In addition, there will occasionally be cases where these duties do not apply because disclosing information about the patient to the nearest relative cannot be considered practicable, on the grounds that it would have a detrimental impact on the patient that is disproportionate to any advantage to be gained from informing the nearest relative. This would therefore be a breach of the patient's right to privacy under the European Convention on Human Rights. The risk of this is greatest where the nearest relative is someone whom the patient would not have chosen themselves.

2.33   Before disclosing information to nearest relatives without a patient's consent, the person concerned must consider whether the disclosure would be likely to:

- put the patient at risk of physical harm or financial or other exploitation;

- cause the patient emotional distress or lead to a deterioration in their mental health; or

- have any other detrimental effect on their health or wellbeing, and if so whether the advantages to the patient and the public interest of the disclosure outweigh the disadvantages to the patient, in the light of all the circumstances of the case.

Communication with other people nominated by the patient

2.34   Patients may want to nominate one or more people who they would wish to be involved in, or notified of, decisions related to their care and treatment.

CHAPTER

2

Information
for patients,
nearest
relatives and
others

2.35   Patients may nominate an independent mental health advocate, another independent advocate or a legal professional. But they may also nominate a relative, friend or other informal supporter.

2.36   The involvement of such friends, relatives or other supporters can have significant benefits for the care and treatment of the patient. It can provide reassurance to the patient, who may feel distrustful of professionals who are able to impose compulsory measures on them, or are relatively unfamiliar and unknown to the patient. People who know the patient well can provide knowledge of the patient and perspectives that come from long-standing and intimate involvement with the patient prior to (and during) their involvement with mental health services. They can provide practical assistance in helping the patient to convey information and views and may have knowledge of advance decisions or statements made by the patient (see **chapter 17**).

2.37   Professionals should normally agree to a patient's request to involve relatives, friends or other informal supporters. They should tell the patient whenever such a request will not be, or has not been, granted. Where a patient's request is refused, it is good practice to record this in the patient's notes, giving reasons for the refusal. It may not always be appropriate to involve another person as requested by the patient, for example where:

- contacting and involving the person would result in a delay to the decision in question that would not be in the patient's best interests;

- the involvement of the person is contrary to the best interests of the patient; or

- that person has requested that they should not be involved.

2.38 Professionals should also take steps to find out whether patients who lack capacity to take particular decisions for themselves have an attorney or deputy with authority to take the decision on their behalf. Where there is such a person, they act as the agent of the patient, and should be informed in the same way as the patient themselves about matters within the scope of their authority.

Involvement of carers

2.39 Carers frequently play a vital role in helping to look after relatives and friends who have mental disorders. It is important to identify all individuals who provide regular and substantial care for patients, to ensure that health and social services assess those carers' needs and, where relevant, provide services to meet them.

2.40 Unless there are reasons to the contrary, patients should be encouraged to agree to their carers being involved in decisions under the Act and to them being kept informed. If patients lack capacity to consent to this, it may be appropriate to involve and inform carers if it is in the patient's best interests – although that decision must always be made in the light of the specific circumstances of the case.

2.41 In order to ensure that carers can, where appropriate, participate fully in decision-making, it is important that they have access to:

- practical and emotional help and support to help them to participate; and

- timely access to comprehensive, up-to-date and accurate information.

2.42 Even if carers cannot be given detailed information about the patient's case, where appropriate they should be offered general information which may help them understand the nature of mental disorder, the way it is treated, and the operation of the Act.

CHAPTER

2

Information
for patients,
nearest
relatives and
others

Information for patients' children

2.43 In considering the kind and amount of information which
children and young people (especially young carers)
should receive about a parent's condition or treatment,
the people giving the information will need to balance the
interests of the child or young person against the patient's
right to privacy and their wishes and feelings. Any such
information should be appropriate to the age and
understanding of the child or young person.

Hospital managers' information policy

2.44 The formal duty to ensure that detained and SCT patients
and their nearest relatives have been informed about their
legal situation and rights falls to the hospital managers.
In practice, it would usually be more appropriate for
professionals working with the patient to provide them
with the information. In order to fulfil their statutory
duties hospital managers should have policies in place
to ensure that:

- the correct information is given to patients and their
nearest relatives;

- information is given in accordance with the requirements
of the legislation, at a suitable time and in an accessible
format, where appropriate with the aid of assistive
technologies and interpretative and advocacy services;

- people who give the information have received
sufficient training and guidance;

- a record is kept of the information given, including
how, when, where and by whom it was given, and an
assessment made of how well the information was
understood by the recipient; and

- a regular check is made that information has been
properly given to each patient and understood
by them.

Information for informal hospital in-patients

2.45   Although the Act does not impose any duties to give
information to informal patients, these patients should
be made aware of their legal position and rights. Local
policies and arrangements about movement around the
hospital and its grounds must be clearly explained to the
patients concerned. Failure to do so could lead to a
patient mistakenly believing that they are not allowed
freedom of movement, which could result in an unlawful
deprivation of their liberty.

Reference Guide
chapter 19 ## Information for those subject to guardianship

2.46   Responsible local social service authorities (LSSAs) are
required to take steps to ensure that guardianship patients
understand their rights to apply to the Tribunal and the
rights of their nearest relatives. The same information
must also normally be given to nearest relatives. More
generally, LSSAs (and private guardians) should do what
they can to ensure that patients understand why they
have been made subject to guardianship and what it
means for them.

CHAPTER 3
Mental disorder

3.1   This chapter gives guidance on the definition of mental disorder for the purposes of the Act.

Definition of mental disorder

3.2   Mental disorder is defined for the purposes of the Act as "any disorder or disability of the mind". Relevant professionals should determine whether a patient has a disorder or disability of the mind in accordance with good clinical practice and accepted standards of what constitutes such a disorder or disability.

Section 1(2)

3.3   Examples of clinically recognised conditions which could fall within this definition are given in the following box.

Clinically recognised conditions which could fall within the Act's definition of mental disorder

- affective disorders, such as depression and bipolar disorder

- schizophrenia and delusional disorders

- neurotic, stress-related and somatoform disorders, such as anxiety, phobic disorders, obsessive compulsive disorders, post-traumatic stress disorder and hypochondriacal disorders

- organic mental disorders such as dementia and delirium (however caused)

- personality and behavioural changes caused by brain injury or damage (however acquired)

- personality disorders

- mental and behavioural disorders caused by psychoactive substance use (but see **paragraphs 3.8-3.12**)

- eating disorders, non-organic sleep disorders and non-organic sexual disorders

- learning disabilities (but see **paragraphs 3.13-3.15**)

- autistic spectrum disorders (including Asperger's syndrome) (but see **paragraphs 3.16-3.17**)

- behavioural and emotional disorders of children and adolescents

(Note: this list is not exhaustive.)

3.4   The fact that someone has a mental disorder is never sufficient grounds for any compulsory measure to be taken under the Act. Compulsory measures are permitted only where specific criteria about the potential consequences of a person's mental disorder are met. There are many forms of mental disorder which are unlikely ever to call for compulsory measures.

3.5   Care must always be taken to avoid diagnosing, or failing to diagnose, mental disorder on the basis of preconceptions about people or failure to appreciate cultural and social differences. What may be indicative of mental disorder in one person, given their background and individual circumstances, may be nothing of the sort in another person.

3.6   Difference should not be confused with disorder. No-one may be considered to be mentally disordered solely because of their political, religious or cultural beliefs, values or opinions, unless there are proper clinical grounds to believe that they are the symptoms or manifestations of a disability or disorder of the mind. The same is true of a person's involvement, or likely involvement, in illegal, anti-social or "immoral" behaviour. Beliefs, behaviours or actions which do not result from a disorder or disability of the mind are not a basis for compulsory measures under the Act, even if they appear unusual or cause other people alarm, distress or danger.

3.7   A person's sexual orientation towards people of the same gender (or both the same and the other gender) is not a mental disorder for any purpose.

Dependence on alcohol or drugs

3.8   Section 1(3) of the Act states that dependence on alcohol or drugs is not considered to be a disorder or disability of the mind for the purposes of the definition of mental disorder in the Act.

3.9   This means that there are no grounds under the Act for detaining a person in hospital (or using other compulsory measures) on the basis of alcohol or drug dependence alone. Drugs for these purposes may be taken to include solvents and similar substances with a psychoactive effect.

3.10   Alcohol or drug dependence may be accompanied by, or associated with, a mental disorder which does fall within the Act's definition. If the relevant criteria are met, it is therefore possible (for example) to detain people who are suffering from mental disorder, even though they are also dependent on alcohol or drugs. This is true even if the mental disorder in question results from the person's alcohol or drug dependence.

3.11   The Act does not exclude other disorders or disabilities of the mind related to the use of alcohol or drugs. These disorders – for example, withdrawal state with delirium or associated psychotic disorder, acute intoxication and organic mental disorders associated with prolonged abuse of drugs or alcohol – remain mental disorders for the purposes of the Act.

3.12   Medical treatment for mental disorder under the Act (including treatment with consent) can include measures to address alcohol or drug dependence if that is an appropriate part of treating the mental disorder which is the primary focus of the treatment.

Reference Guide
1.12-1.15 ## Learning disabilities and autistic spectrum disorders

3.13   Learning disabilities and autistic spectrum disorders are forms of mental disorder as defined in the Act.

3.14   However, someone with a learning disability and no other form of mental disorder may not be detained for treatment or made subject to guardianship or supervised community treatment unless their learning disability is accompanied by abnormally aggressive or seriously irresponsible conduct on their part.

Section 1(2A) and (2B) 3.15   This "learning disability qualification" applies only to specific sections of the Act. In particular, it does not apply to detention for assessment under section 2 of the Act.

3.16   The learning disability qualification does not apply to autistic spectrum disorders (including Asperger's syndrome). It is possible for someone with an autistic spectrum disorder to meet the criteria for compulsory measures under the Act without having any other form of mental disorder, even if their autistic spectrum disorder is not associated with abnormally aggressive or seriously irresponsible behaviour. While experience suggests that this is likely to be necessary only very rarely, the possibility should never automatically be discounted.

3.17   For further guidance on particular issues relating to people with learning disabilities or autistic spectrum disorders (including further guidance on the learning disability qualification), see **chapter 34**.

Personality disorders

3.18   Apart from the learning disability qualification described above, the Act does not distinguish between different forms of mental disorder. The Act therefore applies to personality disorders (of all types) in exactly the same way as it applies to mental illness and other mental disorders.

3.19　No assumptions should be made about the suitability of using the Act – or indeed providing services without using the Act – in respect of personality disorders or the people who have them. The factors which should inform decisions are the needs of the individual patient, the risks posed by their disorder and what can be done to address those needs and risks, in both the short and longer term (see **chapter 35** for further guidance on personality disorders).

CHAPTER 4 Applications for detention in hospital

Reference Guide chapter 2 4.1   This chapter gives guidance on the making of applications for detention in hospital under Part 2 of the Act.

Grounds for making an application for detention

4.2   An application for detention may only be made where the grounds in either section 2 or section 3 of the Act are met (see box below).

Criteria for applications

A person can be detained for assessment under section 2 only if both the following criteria apply:

- the person is suffering from a mental disorder of a nature or degree which warrants their detention in hospital for assessment (or for assessment followed by treatment) for at least a limited period; and

- the person ought to be so detained in the interests of their own health or safety or with a view to the protection of others.

A person can be detained for treatment under section 3 only if all the following criteria apply:

- the person is suffering from a mental disorder of a nature or degree which makes it appropriate for them to receive medical treatment in hospital;

- it is necessary for the health or safety of the person or for the protection of other persons that they should receive such treatment and it cannot be provided unless the patient is detained under this section; and

- appropriate medical treatment is available.

4.3   The criteria require consideration of both the nature and degree of a patient's mental disorder. Nature refers to the particular mental disorder from which the patient is suffering, its chronicity, its prognosis, and the patient's previous response to receiving treatment for the disorder. Degree refers to the current manifestation of the patient's disorder.

4.4   Before it is decided that admission to hospital is necessary, consideration must be given to whether there are alternative means of providing the care and treatment which the patient requires. This includes consideration of whether there might be other effective forms of care or treatment which the patient would be willing to accept, and of whether guardianship would be appropriate instead.

4.5   In all cases, consideration must be given to:

- the patient's wishes and view of their own needs;

- the patient's age and physical health;

- any past wishes or feelings expressed by the patient;

- the patient's cultural background;

- the patient's social and family circumstances;

- the impact that any future deterioration or lack of improvement in the patient's condition would have on their children, other relatives or carers, especially those living with the patient, including an assessment of these people's ability and willingness to cope; and

- the effect on the patient, and those close to the patient, of a decision to admit or not to admit under the Act.

Factors to consider – the health or safety of the patient

4.6   Factors to be considered in deciding whether patients should be detained for their own health or safety include:

- the evidence suggesting that patients are at risk of:
  - suicide;
  - self-harm;
  - self-neglect or being unable to look after their own health or safety; or
  - jeopardising their own health or safety accidentally, recklessly or unintentionally;

  or that their mental disorder is otherwise putting their health or safety at risk;

- any evidence suggesting that the patient's mental health will deteriorate if they do not receive treatment;

- the reliability of such evidence, including what is known of the history of the patient's mental disorder;

- the views of the patient and of any carers, relatives or close friends, especially those living with the patient, about the likely course of the disorder and the possibility of it improving;

- the patient's own skills and experience in managing their condition;

- the potential benefits of treatment, which should be weighed against any adverse effects that being detained might have on the patient's wellbeing; and

- whether other methods of managing the risk are available.

Factors to consider – protection of others

4.7   In considering whether detention is necessary for the protection of other people, the factors to consider are the nature of the risk to other people arising from the patient's mental disorder, the likelihood that harm will result and the severity of any potential harm, taking into account:

- that it is not always possible to differentiate risk of harm to the patient from the risk of harm to others;

- the reliability of the available evidence, including any relevant details of the patient's clinical history and past behaviour, such as contact with other agencies and (where relevant) criminal convictions and cautions;

- the willingness and ability of those who live with the patient and those who provide care and support to the patient to cope with and manage the risk; and

- whether other methods of managing the risk are available.

4.8 Harm to other people includes psychological as well as physical harm.

Alternatives to detention – patients with capacity to consent to admission

4.9 When a patient needs to be in hospital, informal admission is usually appropriate when a patient who has the capacity to do so consents to admission. (See **chapter 36** for guidance on when parents might consent to admission on behalf of children and young people.)

4.10 However, this should not be regarded as an absolute rule, especially if the reason for considering admission is that the patient presents a clear danger to themselves or others because of their mental disorder.

4.11 Compulsory admission should, in particular, be considered where a patient's current mental state, together with reliable evidence of past experience, indicates a strong likelihood that they will have a change of mind about informal admission, either before or after they are admitted, with a resulting risk to their health or safety or to the safety of other people.

4.12 The threat of detention must not be used to induce a patient to consent to admission to hospital or to treatment (and is likely to invalidate any apparent consent).

Alternatives to detention – patients who lack capacity to consent to admission or treatment

4.13 In deciding whether it is necessary to detain patients, doctors and approved mental health professionals (AMHPs) must always consider the alternative ways of providing the treatment or care they need.

4.14 The fact that patients cannot consent to the treatment they need, or to being admitted to hospital, does not automatically mean that the Act must be used. It may be possible to rely instead on the provisions of the Mental Capacity Act 2005 (MCA) to provide treatment in the best interests of patients who are aged 16 or over and who lack capacity to consent to treatment.

4.15 This may be possible even if the provision of treatment unavoidably involves depriving patients of their liberty. Deprivation of liberty for the purposes of care or treatment in a hospital or care home can be authorised in a person's best interests under the deprivation of liberty safeguards in the MCA if the person is aged 18 or over.[1]

4.16 If admission to hospital for assessment or treatment for mental disorder is necessary for a patient who lacks capacity to consent to it, an application under the Mental Health Act should be made if:

- providing appropriate care or treatment for the patient will unavoidably involve depriving them of their liberty and the MCA deprivation of liberty safeguards cannot be used; or[2]

- for any other reason, the assessment or treatment the patient needs cannot be safely or effectively delivered by relying on the MCA alone.

[1] The deprivation of liberty safeguards are expected to be in force from April 2009. It is also possible for the Court of Protection to authorise deprivation of liberty under the MCA, but doctors and AMHPs are not required to apply to the Court before considering whether the use of the Mental Health Act is necessary.
[2] The version of the Code presented to Parliament also included the words "there is no attorney or deputy willing to consent to admission and treatment on their behalf" – but, in fact, those words are redundant because attorneys or deputies may not consent to deprivation of liberty.

4.17　The MCA deprivation of liberty safeguards can be used
only if the six qualifying requirements summarised in the
table below are met.

**Summary of qualifying requirements in the MCA's deprivation
of liberty safeguards**

Age requirement	The person is at least 18 years old.
Mental health requirement	The person has a mental disorder.
Mental capacity requirement	The person lacks capacity to decide whether to be in a hospital or care home for the proposed treatment or care.
Best interests requirement	The proposed deprivation of liberty is in the person's best interests and it is a necessary and proportionate response to the risk of them suffering harm.
Eligibility requirement	The person is not subject, or potentially subject, to specified provisions of the Mental Health Act in a way that makes them ineligible.
No refusals requirement	There is no advance decision, or decision of an attorney or deputy which makes the proposed deprivation of liberty impossible.

4.18　The key points when considering whether an application
for detention should be made under the Mental Health
Act instead of relying on the MCA's deprivation of liberty
safeguards are that those safeguards cannot be used if:

- the patient is aged under 18;

- the patient has made a valid and applicable advance
decision refusing a necessary element of the treatment
for which they are to be admitted to hospital
(see **chapter 17**);

- the use of the safeguards would conflict with a decision of the person's attorney or deputy or of the Court of Protection; or

- the patient meets the criteria in section 2 or section 3 of the Mental Health Act and is objecting to being admitted to (or remaining in) hospital for mental health treatment (unless an attorney or deputy consents on their behalf).[3]

4.19   In that last case, whether a patient is objecting has to be considered in the round, taking into account all the circumstances, so far as they are reasonably ascertainable. The decision to be made is whether the patient objects to treatment – the reasonableness of that objection is not the issue. In many cases the patient will be perfectly able to state their objection. But in other cases doctors and AMHPs will need to consider the patient's behaviour, wishes, feelings, views, beliefs and values, both present and past, so far as they can be ascertained. If there is reason to think that a patient would object, if able to do so, then the patient should be taken to be objecting.

4.20   Even if providing appropriate care or treatment will not unavoidably involve a deprivation of liberty, it may be necessary to detain a patient under the Mental Health Act rather than relying on the MCA because:

- the patient has, by means of a valid and applicable advance decision, refused a necessary element of the treatment required; or

- the patient lacks capacity to make decisions on some elements of the care and treatment they need, but has capacity to decide about a vital element – eg admission to hospital – and either has already refused it or is likely to do so.

4.21   Whether or not the deprivation of liberty safeguards could be used, other reasons why it may not be possible to rely on the MCA alone include the following:

[3]The final words in brackets were omitted by mistake from the version of the Code presented to Parliament.

- the patient's lack of capacity to consent is fluctuating or temporary and the patient is not expected to consent when they regain capacity. This may be particularly relevant to patients having acute psychotic, manic or depressive episodes;

- a degree of restraint needs to be used which is justified by the risk to other people but which is not permissible under the MCA because, exceptionally, it cannot be said to be proportionate to the risk to the patient personally; and

- there is some other specific identifiable risk that the person might not receive the treatment they need if the MCA is relied on and that either the person or others might potentially suffer harm as a result.

4.22   Otherwise, if the MCA can be used safely and effectively to assess or treat a patient, it is likely to be difficult to demonstrate that the criteria for detaining the patient under the Mental Health Act are met.

4.23   For further information on the MCA deprivation of liberty safeguards, see the addendum to the MCA Code of Practice.

4.24   For the different considerations which apply to children and young people, see **chapter 36**.

Section 2 or section 3

4.25   An application for detention can be made under either section 2 or section 3 of the Mental Health Act.

4.26   Section 2 should be used if:

- the full extent of the nature and degree of a patient's condition is unclear;

- there is a need to carry out an initial in-patient assessment in order to formulate a treatment plan, or to reach a judgement about whether the patient will accept treatment on a voluntary basis following admission; or

- there is a need to carry out a new in-patient assessment in order to re-formulate a treatment plan, or to reach a judgement about whether the patient will accept treatment on a voluntary basis.

4.27 Section 3 should be used if:

- the patient is already detained under section 2 (detention under section 2 cannot be renewed by a new section 2 application); or

- the nature and current degree of the patient's mental disorder, the essential elements of the treatment plan to be followed and the likelihood of the patient accepting treatment on a voluntary basis are already established.

The assessment process

4.28 An application for detention may be made by an AMHP or the patient's nearest relative. An AMHP is usually a more appropriate applicant than a patient's nearest relative, given an AMHP's professional training and knowledge of the legislation and local resources, together with the potential adverse effect that an application by the nearest relative might have on their relationship with the patient.

4.29 An application must be supported by two medical recommendations given in accordance with the Act.

4.30 Doctors who are approached directly by a nearest relative about making an application should advise the nearest relative that it is preferable for an AMHP to consider the need for a patient to be admitted under the Act and for the AMHP to make any consequent application. Doctors should also advise the nearest relative of their right to require a local social services authority (LSSA) to arrange for an AMHP to consider the patient's case. Doctors should never advise a nearest relative to make an application themselves in order to avoid involving an AMHP in an assessment.

Objective of the assessment

4.31   The objective of the assessment is to determine whether
the criteria for detention are met and, if so, whether an
application for detention should be made.

4.32   Because a proper assessment cannot be carried out
without considering alternative means of providing care
and treatment, AMHPs and doctors should, as far as
possible in the circumstances, identify and liaise with
services which may potentially be able to provide
alternatives to admission to hospital. That could include
crisis and home treatment teams.

Responsibilities of local social services authorities

4.33   LSSAs are responsible for ensuring that sufficient AMHPs
are available to carry out their roles under the Act,
including assessing patients to decide whether an
application for detention should be made. To fulfil their
statutory duty, LSSAs must have arrangements in place in
their area to provide a 24-hour service that can respond
to patients' needs.

4.34   Section 13 of the Act places a specific duty on LSSAs to
arrange for an AMHP to consider the case of any patient
who is within their area if they have reason to believe that
an application for detention in hospital may need to be
made in respect of the patient. LSSAs must make such
arrangements if asked to do so by (or on behalf of) the
nearest relative.

4.35   If a patient is already detained under section 2 as the
result of an application made by an AMHP, the LSSA on
whose behalf that AMHP was acting is responsible for
arranging for an AMHP to consider the patient's case
again if the LSSA has reason to believe that an application
under section 3 may be necessary. This applies even if the
patient has been detained outside that LSSA's area.

4.36   These duties do not prevent any other LSSA from
arranging for an AMHP to consider a patient's case if
that is more appropriate.

Setting up the assessment

4.37 Local arrangements should, as far as possible, ensure that assessments are carried out by the most appropriate AMHP and doctors in the particular circumstances.

4.38 Where a patient is known to belong to a group for which particular expertise is desirable (eg they are aged under 18 or have a learning disability), at least one of the professionals involved in their assessment should have expertise in working with people from that group, wherever possible.

4.39 If this is not possible, at least one of the professionals involved in the person's assessment should, if at all possible, consult with one or more professionals who do have relevant expertise and involve them as closely as the circumstances of the case allow.

4.40 Unless different arrangements have been agreed locally between the relevant authorities, AMHPs who assess patients for possible detention under the Act have overall responsibility for co-ordinating the process of assessment. In doing so, they should be sensitive to the patient's age, gender (and gender identity), social, cultural, racial and religious background and sexual orientation. They should also consider how any disability the patient has may affect the way the assessment needs to be carried out.

4.41 Given the importance of good communication, it is essential that those professionals who assess patients are able to communicate with the patient effectively and reliably to prevent potential misunderstandings. AMHPs should establish, as far as possible, whether patients have particular communication needs or difficulties and take steps to meet them, for example by arranging a signer or a professional interpreter. AMHPs should also be in a position, where appropriate, to supply suitable equipment to make communication easier with patients who have impaired hearing, but who do not have their own hearing aid.

4.42   See **paragraphs 4.106-4.110** for specific guidance in
        relation to the assessment of people who are deaf. For
        further guidance on specific issues that may arise when
        assessing people who have a learning disability or an
        autistic spectrum disorder, or who have a personality
        disorder, see **chapter 34** and **chapter 35** respectively.

4.43   Doctors and AMHPs undertaking assessments need to
        apply professional judgement and reach decisions
        independently of each other, but in a framework of
        co-operation and mutual support.

4.44   Unless there is good reason for undertaking separate
        assessments, patients should, where possible, be seen
        jointly by the AMHP and at least one of the two doctors
        involved in the assessment.

4.45   While it may not always be feasible for the patient to be
        examined by both doctors at the same time, they should
        both discuss the patient's case with the person considering
        making an application for the patient's detention.

4.46   Everyone involved in an assessment should be alert to
        the need to provide support for colleagues, especially
        where there is a risk of the patient causing physical harm.
        People carrying out assessments should be aware of
        circumstances in which the police should be asked to
        provide assistance, in accordance with arrangements
        agreed locally with the police, and of how to use that
        assistance to maximise the safety of everyone involved
        in the assessment.

4.47   Locally agreed arrangements on the involvement of the
        police should include a joint risk assessment tool to help
        determine the level of risk, what (if any) police assistance
        may be required and how quickly it is needed. In cases
        where no warrant for the police to enter premises under
        section 135 of the Act is being applied for (see **chapter 10**),
        the risk assessment should indicate the reasons for this
        and explain why police assistance is nonetheless necessary.

The role of approved mental health professionals

Section 13(1A) and (2) 4.48 AMHPs may make an application for detention only if they:

- have interviewed the patient in a suitable manner;

- are satisfied that the statutory criteria for detention are met; and

- are satisfied that, in all the circumstances of the case, detention in hospital is the most appropriate way of providing the care and medical treatment the patient needs.

4.49 Once AMHPs have decided that an application should be made, they must then decide whether it is necessary or proper for them to make the application themselves. If they decide it is, having considered any views expressed by the patient's relatives and all the other relevant circumstances, AMHPs must make the application.

4.50 At the start of an assessment, AMHPs should identify themselves to the person being assessed, members of the person's family, carers or friends and the other professionals present. AMHPs should ensure that the purpose of the visit, their role and that of the other professionals are explained. They should carry documents with them at all times which identify them as AMHPs and which specify both the LSSA which approved them and the LSSA on whose behalf they are acting.

4.51 Although AMHPs act on behalf of a LSSA, they cannot be told by the LSSA or anyone else whether or not to make an application. They must exercise their own judgement, based on social and medical evidence, when deciding whether to apply for a patient to be detained under the Act. The role of AMHPs is to provide an independent decision about whether or not there are alternatives to detention under the Act, bringing a social perspective to bear on their decision.

4.52   If patients want someone else (eg a familiar person or an advocate) to be present during the assessment and any subsequent action that may be taken, then ordinarily AMHPs should assist in securing that person's attendance, unless the urgency of the case makes it inappropriate to do so. Patients may feel safer or more confident with a friend or other person they know well in attendance. Equally, an advocate can help to reassure patients. Some patients may already be receiving help from an advocate.

4.53   Patients should usually be given the opportunity of speaking to the AMHP alone. However, if AMHPs have reason to fear physical harm, they should insist that another professional is present.

4.54   It is not desirable for patients to be interviewed through a closed door or window, and this should be considered only where other people are at serious risk. Where direct access to the patient is not possible, but there is no immediate risk of physical danger to the patient or to anyone else, AMHPs should consider applying for a warrant under section 135 of the Act, allowing the police to enter the premises (see **chapter 10**).

4.55   Where patients are subject to the short-term effects of alcohol or drugs (whether prescribed or self-administered) which make interviewing them difficult, the AMHP should either wait until the effects have abated before interviewing the patient or arrange to return later. If it is not realistic to wait, because of the patient's disturbed behaviour and the urgency of the case, the assessment will have to be based on whatever information the AMHP can obtain from reliable sources. This should be made clear in the AMHP's record of the assessment.

The AMHP and the nearest relative

4.56   AMHPs are required by the Act to attempt to identify the patient's nearest relative as defined in section 26 of the Act.

Section 11(3) 4.57 When AMHPs make an application for detention under section 2, they must take such steps as are practicable to inform the nearest relative that the application is to be (or has been) made and of the nearest relative's power to discharge the patient.

Section 11(4) 4.58 Before making an application for detention under section 3, AMHPs must consult the nearest relative, unless it is not reasonably practicable or would involve unreasonable delay.

4.59 Circumstances in which the nearest relative need not be informed or consulted include those where:

- it is not practicable for the AMHP to obtain sufficient information to establish the identity or location of the nearest relative, or where to do so would require an excessive amount of investigation involving unreasonable delay; and

- consultation is not possible because of the nearest relative's own health or mental incapacity.

4.60 There may also be cases where, although physically possible, it would not be reasonably practicable to inform or consult the nearest relative because there would be a detrimental impact on the patient which would result in infringement of the patient's right to respect for their privacy and family life under article 8 of the European Convention on Human Rights and which could not be justified by the benefit of the involvement of the nearest relative.[4] Detrimental impact may include cases where patients are likely to suffer emotional distress, deterioration in their mental health, physical harm, or financial or other exploitation as a result of the consultation.

4.61 Consulting and notifying the nearest relative is a significant safeguard for patients. Therefore decisions not to do so on these grounds should not be taken lightly. AMHPs should consider all the circumstances of the case, including:

[4]See in particular R. (on the application of E) v Bristol City Council [2005] EWHC 74 (Admin).

- the benefit to the patient of the involvement of their nearest relative;

- the patient's wishes (taking into account whether they have the capacity to decide whether they would want their nearest relative involved and any statement of their wishes they have made in advance);

- any detrimental effect that involving the nearest relative would have on the patient's health and wellbeing; and

- whether there is any good reason to think that the patient's objection may be intended to prevent information relevant to the assessment being discovered.

4.62 AMHPs may also consider the degree to which the nearest relative has been willing to be involved on previous occasions, but unwillingness to act previously should not automatically be taken to imply current unwillingness.

4.63 If they do not consult or inform the nearest relative, AMHPs should record their reasons. Consultation must not be avoided purely because it is thought that the nearest relative might object to the application.

4.64 When consulting nearest relatives AMHPs should, where possible:

- ascertain the nearest relative's views about both the patient's needs and the nearest relative's own needs in relation to the patient;

- inform the nearest relative of the reasons for considering an application for detention and what the effects of such an application would be; and

- inform the nearest relative of their role and rights under the Act.

4.65 If the nearest relative objects to an application being made for admission for treatment under section 3, the application cannot be made. If it is thought necessary to proceed with the application to ensure the patient's safety and the nearest relative cannot be persuaded to agree, the AMHP will need to consider applying to the county court for the nearest relative's displacement under section 29 of the Act (see **chapter 8**).

Consultation with other people

4.66   Although there are specific requirements to consult the nearest relative, it is important to recognise the value of involving other people, particularly the patient's carers and family, in the decision-making process as well. Carers and family members are often able to provide a particular perspective on the patient's circumstances. Insofar as the urgency of the case allows, AMHPs should consider consulting with other relevant relatives, carers or friends and should take their views into account.

4.67   Where patients are under 18, AMHPs should in particular consider consulting with the patient's parents (or other people who have parental responsibility for the patient), assuming they are not the patient's nearest relative anyway.

4.68   In deciding whether it is appropriate to consult carers and other family members, AMHPs should consider:

   • the patient's wishes;

   • the nature of the relationship between the patient and the person in question, including how long the relationship has existed; and

   • whether the patient has referred to any hostility between them and the person in question, or there is other evidence of hostility, abuse or exploitation.

4.69   AMHPs should also consult wherever possible with other people who have been involved with the patient's care. These could include people working for statutory, voluntary or independent mental health services and other service providers who do not specialise in mental health services but have contact with the patient. For example, the patient may be known to services for older people or substance misuse services.

4.70   Some patients may have an attorney or deputy appointed under the MCA who has authority to make decisions about their personal welfare. Where such a person is known to exist, AMHPs should take reasonable steps to contact them and seek their opinion. Where attorneys or deputies have the power to consent or refuse treatment for mental disorder on the patient's behalf, they should also be given the opportunity to talk directly to the doctors assessing the patient, where practicable.

Medical examination by doctors as part of the assessment

4.71   A medical examination must involve:

- direct personal examination of the patient and their mental state; and

- consideration of all available relevant clinical information, including that in the possession of others, professional or non-professional.

4.72   If direct physical access to the patient is not immediately possible and it is not desirable to postpone the examination in order to negotiate access, consideration should be given to requesting that an AMHP apply for a warrant under section 135 of the Act (see **paragraph 4.54**).

4.73   Where practicable, at least one of the medical recommendations must be provided by a doctor with previous acquaintance with the patient. Preferably, this should be a doctor who has personally treated the patient. But it is sufficient for the doctor to have had some previous knowledge of the patient's case.

4.74   It is preferable that a doctor who does not have previous acquaintance with the patient be approved under section 12 of the Act. The Act requires that at least one of the doctors must be so approved.

4.75   If the doctors reach the opinion that the patient needs to be admitted to hospital, it is their responsibility to take the necessary steps to secure a suitable hospital bed. It is not the responsibility of the applicant, unless it has been agreed locally between the LSSA and the relevant NHS bodies that this will be done by any AMHP involved in the assessment. Primary care trusts are responsible for commissioning mental health services to meet the needs of their areas. They should ensure that procedures are in place through which beds can be identified where required.

4.76   Doctors must give reasons for the opinions stated in their recommendations. When giving a clinical description of the patient's mental disorder as part of these reasons, doctors should include a description of the patient's symptoms and behaviour, not merely a diagnostic classification.

4.77   When making recommendations for detention under section 3, doctors are required to state that appropriate medical treatment is available for the patient (see chapter 6). Preferably, they should know in advance of making the recommendation the name of the hospital to which the patient is to be admitted. But, if that is not possible, their recommendation may state that appropriate medical treatment will be available if the patient is admitted to one or more specific hospitals (or units within a hospital).

Communicating the outcome of the assessment

4.78   Having decided whether or not to make an application for detention, AMHPs should inform the patient, giving their reasons. Subject to the normal considerations of patient confidentiality, AMHPs should also give their decision and the reasons for it to:

- the patient's nearest relative;
- the doctors involved in the assessment;
- the patient's care co-ordinator (if they have one); and
- the patient's GP, if they were not one of the doctors involved in the assessment.

4.79 An AMHP should, when informing the nearest relative that they not do intend to make an application, advise the nearest relative of their right to do so instead. If the nearest relative wishes to pursue this, the AMHP should suggest that they consult with the doctors involved in the assessment to see if they would be prepared to provide recommendations anyway.

4.80 Where the AMHP has considered a patient's case at the request of the nearest relative, the reasons for not applying for the patient's detention must be given to the nearest relative in writing. Such a letter should contain, as far as possible, sufficient details to enable the nearest relative to understand the decision while at the same time preserving the patient's right to confidentiality.

Section 13(4)

Action when it is decided not to apply for detention

4.81 There is no obligation on an AMHP or nearest relative to make an application for detention just because the statutory criteria are met.

4.82 Where AMHPs decide not to apply for a patient's detention they should record the reasons for their decision. The decision should be supported, where necessary, by an alternative framework of care and treatment. AMHPs must decide how to pursue any actions which their assessment indicates are necessary to meet the needs of the patient. That might include, for example, referring the patient to social, health or other services.

4.83 The steps to be taken to put in place any new arrangements for the patient's care and treatment, and any plans for reviewing them, should be recorded in writing and copies made available to all those who need them (subject to the normal considerations of patient confidentiality).

4.84 It is particularly important that the patient's care co-ordinator (if they have one) is fully involved in decisions about meeting the patient's needs.

4.85 Arrangements should be made to ensure that information about assessments and their outcome is passed to professional colleagues where appropriate, for example where an application for detention is not immediately necessary but might be in the future. This information will need to be available at short notice at any time of day or night.

4.86 More generally, making out-of-hours services aware of situations that are ongoing – such as when there is concern over an individual but no assessment has begun, or when a person has absconded before an assessment could start or be completed – assists out-of-hours services in responding accordingly.

Action when it is decided to make an application

Sections 6(1) and 11(5)

4.87 Most compulsory admissions require prompt action. However, applicants have up to 14 days (depending on when the patient was last examined by a doctor as part of the assessment) in which to decide whether to make the application, starting with the day they personally last saw the patient. There may be cases where AMHPs conclude that they should delay taking a final decision, in order to see whether the patient's condition changes, or whether successful alternatives to detention can be put in place in the interim.

4.88 Before making an application, AMHPs should ensure that appropriate arrangements are in place for the immediate care of any dependent children the patient may have and any adults who rely on the patient for care. Their needs should already have been considered as part of the assessment.

4.89   Where relevant, AMHPs should also ensure that practical
        arrangements are made for the care of any pets and for
        the LSSA to carry out its other duties under the National
        Assistance Act 1948 to secure the patient's home and
        protect their property.

4.90   Applications for detention must be addressed to the
        managers of the hospital where the patient is to be
        detained. An application must state a specific hospital.
        An application cannot, for example, be made to an NHS
        trust without specifying which of the trust's hospitals the
        patient is to be admitted to.

4.91   Where units under the management of different bodies
        exist on the same site (or even in the same building), they
        will be separate hospitals for the purposes of the Act,
        because one hospital cannot be under the control of two
        sets of managers. Where there is potential for confusion,
        the respective hospital managers should ensure that there
        are distinct names for the units. In collaboration with
        LSSAs, they should take steps to ensure that information
        is available to AMHPs who are likely to be making
        relevant applications to enable them effectively to
        distinguish the different hospitals on the site and to
        describe them correctly in applications.

4.92   Once an application has been completed, the patient
        should be conveyed to the hospital as soon as possible,
        if they are not already in the hospital. But patients should
        not be moved until it is known that the hospital is willing
        to accept them.

4.93   A properly completed application supported by the   Section 6(1)
        necessary medical recommendations provides the
        applicant with the authority to convey the patient to
        hospital even if the patient does not wish to go. That
        authority lasts for 14 days from the date when the patient
        was last examined by one of the doctors with a view to
        making a recommendation to support the application.
        See **chapter 11** for further guidance on conveyance.

4.94 The AMHP should provide an outline report for the hospital at the time the patient is first admitted or detained, giving reasons for the application and details of any practical matters about the patient's circumstances which the hospital should know. Where possible, the report should include the name and telephone number of the AMHP or a care co-ordinator who can give further information. LSSAs should consider the use of a standard form on which AMHPs can make this outline report.

4.95 Where it is not realistic for the AMHP to accompany the patient to the hospital – for example, where the admitting hospital is some distance from the area in which the AMHP operates – it is acceptable for them to provide the information outlined above by telephone or fax or other means compatible with transferring confidential information. If providing the information by telephone, the AMHP should ensure that a written report is sent to the admitting hospital as soon as possible.

4.96 An outline report does not take the place of the full report which AMHPs are expected to complete for their employer or the LSSA on whose behalf they are acting (if different).

4.97 If the patient is a restricted patient, the AMHP should ensure that the Mental Health Unit of the Ministry of Justice is notified of the detention as soon as possible. A duty officer is available at all times to receive this information, which should not be left until office hours.[5]

4.98 An application cannot be used to admit a patient to any hospital other than the one stated in the application (although once admitted a patient may be transferred to another hospital – see **chapter 30**).

4.99 In exceptional circumstances, if patients are conveyed to a hospital which has agreed to accept them, but there is no longer a bed available, the managers and staff of that hospital should assist in finding a suitable alternative for the patient. This may involve making a new application to a different hospital. If the application is under section 3, new medical recommendations will be required, unless the

[5] At the time of publication the telephone number is 020 7035 4848.

original recommendations already state that appropriate medical treatment is available in the proposed new hospital. The hospital to which the original application was made should assist in securing new medical recommendations if they are needed. A situation of this sort should be considered a serious failure and should be recorded and investigated accordingly.

Resolving disagreements

4.100 Sometimes there will be differences of opinion between professionals involved in the assessment. There is nothing wrong with disagreements: handled properly they offer an opportunity to safeguard the interests of the patient by widening the discussion on the best way of meeting their needs. Doctors and AMHPs should be ready to consult other professionals (especially care co-ordinators and others involved with the patient's current care), while themselves retaining the final responsibility for their decision. Where disagreements do occur, professionals should ensure that they discuss these with each other.

4.101 Where there is an unresolved dispute about an application for detention, it is essential that the professionals do not abandon the patient. Instead, they should explore and agree an alternative plan – if necessary on a temporary basis. Such a plan should include a risk assessment and identification of the arrangements for managing the risks. The alternative plan should be recorded in writing, as should the arrangements for reviewing it. Copies should be made available to all those who need them (subject to the normal considerations of patient confidentiality).

Responsibilities of strategic health authorities for doctors approved under section 12

Reference Guide
chapter 32

4.102 The Secretary of State has delegated to strategic health authorities (SHAs) the task of approving medical practitioners under section 12(2) of the Act. Medical practitioners who are approved clinicians under the Act are automatically treated as being approved under section 12 as well.

4.103 SHAs should:

- take active steps to encourage sufficient doctors, including GPs and those working in prison health services and the police service, to apply for approval;

- ensure that arrangements are in place for 24-hour on-call rotas of approved doctors (or an equivalent arrangement) sufficient to cover each area for which they are responsible;

- ensure that regularly updated lists of approved doctors are maintained which indicate how they can be contacted and the hours that each is available; and

- ensure that the up-to-date list of approved doctors and details of 24-hour on-call rotas (or the equivalent arrangement) are available to all those who may need them, including GPs, providers of hospital and community mental health services and social services.

Co-operation between local agencies

4.104 NHS bodies and LSSAs should co-operate in ensuring that there are opportunities for regular communication between professionals involved in mental health assessments, in order to promote understanding and to provide a forum for clarification of their respective roles and responsibilities. NHS bodies and LSSAs should also keep in mind the interface with the criminal justice agencies, including the probation service and the police.

4.105 Opportunities should also be sought to involve and learn directly from people with experience of being assessed.

Patients who are deaf

4.106 AMHPs and doctors assessing a deaf person should, wherever possible, have had deaf awareness training, including basic training in issues relating to mental health and deafness. Where required, they should also seek assistance from specialists with appropriate expertise in mental health and deafness. This may be available from one of the specialist hospital units for deafness and mental health. Contact with such units may, in particular, help to prevent deaf people being wrongly assessed as having a learning disability or another mental disorder.

4.107 Unless different arrangements have been agreed locally, the AMHP involved in the assessment should be responsible for booking and using registered qualified interpreters with expertise in mental health interpreting, bearing in mind that the interpretation of thought-disordered language requires particular expertise. Relay interpreters (interpreters who relay British Sign Language (BSL) to hands-on BSL or visual frame signing or close signing) may be necessary, such as when the deaf person has a visual impairment, does not use BSL to sign or has minimal language skills or a learning disability.

4.108 Reliance on unqualified interpreters or health professionals with only limited signing skills should be avoided. Family members may (subject to the normal considerations about patient confidentiality) occasionally be able to assist a professional interpreter in understanding a patient's idiosyncratic use of language. However, family members should not be relied upon in place of a professional interpreter, even if the patient is willing for them to be involved.

4.109 Pre-lingual deafness may cause delayed language acquisition, which may in turn influence social behaviour. People carrying out assessments of deaf people under the Act should have an awareness and knowledge of how mental health problems present in pre-lingually deaf people.

4.110 Cultural issues need to be taken into account, for instance in people who are pre-lingually deaf, as they have a visual perspective of the world and may consider themselves to be part of a cultural and linguistic minority. This means that they may behave in ways which are misperceived as evidence of mental disorder. For example, animated signing may be misunderstood as aggression, while touching a hearing person to talk to them may be misunderstood as an assault. Deaf people's spoken or written English may be poor, giving rise to a false assumption of thought disorder.

Related material

- Mental Capacity Act 2005
- *Mental Capacity Act 2005 Code of Practice,* TSO, 2007
- *Deprivation of Liberty Safeguards,* Addendum to the *Mental Capacity Act 2005 Code of Practice*[6]
- National Assistance Act 1948

  This material does not form part of the Code. It is provided for assistance only.

[6]To be published later in 2008.

CHAPTER 5 Emergency applications for detention

5.1 This chapter gives guidance on the making of emergency applications for detention in hospital under section 4 of the Act.

Reference Guide
2.46-2.54

Applications for detention for assessment in an emergency

5.2 The Act permits an application for detention for assessment to be made under section 4 on the basis of a single medical recommendation, but only in very limited circumstances. An application for detention under section 4 may be made only when:

- the criteria for detention for assessment under section 2 are met;

- the patient's detention is required as a matter of urgent necessity; and

- obtaining a second medical recommendation would cause undesirable delay.

5.3 An application under section 4 may be made only if the applicant has seen the patient personally within the previous 24 hours. Otherwise, the duties of approved mental health professionals (AMHPs) in respect of applications are the same as for applications under section 2. The guidance given in **chapter 4** about the way in which assessments should be carried out applies equally to applications under section 4 (except, of course, that there will be only one doctor involved).

Urgent necessity

5.4 Section 4 should be used only in a genuine emergency, where the patient's need for urgent assessment outweighs the desirability of waiting for a second doctor.

5.5   Section 4 should never be used for administrative convenience. So, for example, patients should not be detained under section 4 merely because it is more convenient for the second doctor to examine the patient in, rather than outside, hospital.

5.6   An emergency may arise where the patient's mental state or behaviour presents problems which those involved cannot reasonably be expected to manage while waiting for a second doctor. To be satisfied that an emergency has arisen, the person making the application and the doctor making the supporting recommendation should have evidence of:

- an immediate and significant risk of mental or physical harm to the patient or to others;

- danger of serious harm to property; or

- a need for physical restraint of the patient.

Availability of second medical recommendation

5.7   It is the responsibility of primary care trusts (and other NHS commissioners) to ensure that doctors are available in a timely manner to examine patients under the Act when requested to do so by AMHPs and in other cases where such an examination is necessary.

5.8   If AMHPs find themselves having to consider making emergency applications because of difficulties in securing a second doctor, they should report that fact to the local social services authority (LSSA) on whose behalf they are acting (or in accordance with locally agreed arrangements, if they are different).

5.9   Hospital managers and LSSAs should monitor the use of section 4 to ensure that it is not misused and to allow action to be taken to rectify any problems with the availability of doctors.

Detention under section 4

5.10 The authority to convey a patient to hospital and to start their detention there on the basis of an emergency application lasts only for 24 hours from the last time at which the doctor examined the patient for the purposes of the application, or from the time the application is made, whichever is the earlier. A patient may then be detained only for a maximum of 72 hours unless a second medical recommendation is provided to the hospital managers in accordance with the Act. Section 6(1)

5.11 Patients detained under section 4 should be examined by an appropriate second doctor as soon as possible, to decide whether they should continue to be detained. If the doctor who made the recommendation for the section 4 application was not a doctor approved under section 12, the Act requires the doctor making the second recommendation to be so approved.

5.12 Patients detained on the basis of emergency applications may not be treated without their consent under Part 4 of the Act unless or until the second medical recommendation is received. Until then they are in exactly the same position in respect of consent to treatment as patients who are not detained under the Act. Section 56

5.13 An application for detention for treatment under section 3 of the Act may be made while a patient is detained under section 4 – but two fresh medical recommendations would be required.

CHAPTER 6 The appropriate medical treatment test

6.1   This chapter gives guidance on the application of the appropriate medical treatment test in the criteria for detention and supervised community treatment (SCT) under the Act.

Purpose of medical treatment for mental disorder

Section 145(1)   6.2   For the purposes of the Act, medical treatment also includes nursing, psychological intervention and specialist mental health habilitation, rehabilitation and care. Habilitation means equipping someone with skills and abilities they have never had, whereas rehabilitation means helping them recover skills and abilities they have lost.

Section 145(4)   6.3   In the Act, medical treatment for mental disorder means medical treatment which is for the purpose of alleviating, or preventing a worsening of, a mental disorder or one or more of its symptoms or manifestations.

6.4   Purpose is not the same as likelihood. Medical treatment may be for the purpose of alleviating, or preventing a worsening of, a mental disorder even though it cannot be shown in advance that any particular effect is likely to be achieved.

6.5   Symptoms and manifestations include the way a disorder is experienced by the individual concerned and the way in which the disorder manifests itself in the person's thoughts, emotions, communication, behaviour and actions. But it should be remembered that not every thought or emotion, or every aspect of the behaviour, of a patient suffering from a mental disorder will be a manifestation of that disorder.

CHAPTER

6

The
appropriate
medical
treatment
test

6.6   Even if particular mental disorders are likely to persist or
       get worse despite treatment, there may well be a range of
       interventions which would represent appropriate medical
       treatment. It should never be assumed that any disorders,
       or any patients, are inherently or inevitably untreatable.
       Nor should it be assumed that likely difficulties in
       achieving long-term and sustainable change in a person's
       underlying disorder make medical treatment to help
       manage their condition and the behaviours arising from
       it either inappropriate or unnecessary.

Appropriate medical treatment test

6.7   The purpose of the appropriate medical treatment test is
       to ensure that no-one is detained (or remains detained)
       for treatment, or is an SCT patient, unless they are
       actually to be offered medical treatment for their mental
       disorder.

6.8   This medical treatment must be appropriate, taking into
       account the nature and degree of the person's mental
       disorder and all their particular circumstances, including
       cultural, ethnic and religious considerations. By definition,
       it must be treatment which is for the purpose of
       alleviating or preventing a worsening of the patient's
       mental disorder or its symptoms or manifestations.

6.9   The appropriate medical treatment test requires a
       judgement about whether an appropriate package
       of treatment for mental disorder is available for the
       individual in question. Where the appropriate medical
       treatment test forms part of the criteria for detention,
       the medical treatment in question is treatment for mental
       disorder in the hospital in which the patient is to be
       detained. Where it is part of the criteria for SCT it refers
       to the treatment for mental disorder that the person will
       be offered while on SCT.

Applying the appropriate medical treatment test

6.10 The test requires a judgement about whether, when looked at in the round, appropriate medical treatment is available to the patient, given:

- the nature and degree of the patient's mental disorder; and

- all the other circumstances of the patient's case.

In other words, both the clinical appropriateness of the treatment and its appropriateness more generally must be considered.

6.11 The other circumstances of a patient's case might include factors such as:

- the patient's physical health – how this might impact on the effectiveness of the available medical treatment for the patient's mental disorder and the impact that the treatment might have in return;

- any physical disabilities the patient has;

- the patient's culture and ethnicity;

- the patient's age;

- the patient's gender, gender identity and sexual orientation;

- the location of the available treatment;

- the implications of the treatment for the patient's family and social relationships, including their role as a parent;

- its implications for the patient's education or work; and

- the consequences for the patient, and other people, if the patient does not receive the treatment available. (For mentally disordered offenders about to be sentenced for an offence, the consequence will sometimes be a prison sentence.)

CHAPTER

6

The
appropriate
medical
treatment
test

6.12 Medical treatment need not be the most appropriate treatment that could ideally be made available. Nor does it need to address every aspect of the person's disorder. But the medical treatment available at any time must be an appropriate response to the patient's condition and situation.

6.13 Medical treatment must actually be available to the patient. It is not sufficient that appropriate treatment could theoretically be provided.

6.14 What is appropriate will vary greatly between patients. It will depend, in part, on what might reasonably be expected to be achieved given the nature and degree of the patient's disorder.

6.15 Medical treatment which aims merely to prevent a disorder worsening is unlikely, in general, to be appropriate in cases where normal treatment approaches would aim (and be expected) to alleviate the patient's condition significantly. For some patients with persistent mental disorders, however, management of the undesirable effects of their disorder may be all that can realistically be hoped for.

6.16 Appropriate medical treatment does not have to involve medication or individual or group psychological therapy – although it very often will. There may be patients whose particular circumstances mean that treatment may be appropriate even though it consists only of nursing and specialist day-to-day care under the clinical supervision of an approved clinician, in a safe and secure therapeutic environment with a structured regime.

6.17 Simply detaining someone – even in a hospital – does not constitute medical treatment.

6.18   A patient's attitude towards the proposed treatment may be relevant in determining whether the appropriate medical treatment test is met. But an indication of unwillingness to co-operate with treatment generally, or with a specific aspect of treatment, does not make such treatment inappropriate.

6.19   In particular, psychological therapies and other forms of medical treatments which, to be effective, require the patient's co-operation are not automatically inappropriate simply because a patient does not currently wish to engage with them. Such treatments can potentially remain appropriate and available as long as it continues to be clinically suitable to offer them and they would be provided if the patient agreed to engage.

6.20   People called on to make a judgement about whether the appropriate medical treatment test is met do not have to be satisfied that appropriate treatment will be available for the whole course of the patient's detention or SCT. What is appropriate may change over time, as the patient's condition changes or clinicians obtain a greater understanding of the patient's case. But they must satisfy themselves that appropriate medical treatment is available for the time being, given the patient's condition and circumstances as they are currently understood.

CHAPTER 7
Conflicts of interest

7.1 This chapter is concerned with the circumstances in which applications by approved mental health professionals (AMHPs) for a person to be admitted under the Act to hospital or guardianship, or provision of medical recommendations by doctors for the purpose of such applications, must not be made because of potential conflicts of interest. It also discusses some other potential conflicts.

Conflict of Interest Regulations

Reference Guide 2.55-2.59 (detention) and 19.42-19.46 (guardianship)

7.2 The Mental Health (Conflict of Interest) (England) Regulations 2008 set out the circumstances in which a potential conflict of interest prevents an AMHP making an application for a patient's detention or guardianship and a doctor making a recommendation supporting the application. AMHPs and these doctors are collectively referred to as "assessors" in this chapter.

7.3 These potential conflicts of interest may concern the relationship of AMHPs and doctors to each other, to the patient, to the nearest relative or to the hospital where the patient is to be admitted. They concern potential conflicts of interest for financial, business, professional and personal reasons.

Financial conflict

7.4 Where the patient is to be admitted to an independent hospital and the doctor providing one of the medical recommendations is on the staff of that hospital, the other medical recommendation must be given by a doctor who is not on the staff of that hospital. That is, there will be a potential conflict if both doctors giving recommendations are on the staff of the independent hospital.

7.5 There will be no potential conflict of interest for financial reasons just because both doctors are on the staff of an NHS hospital to which the patient will be admitted.

7.6 An assessor will have a conflict of interest for financial reasons if the assessor stands to make a financial benefit (or loss) from their decision. There will not be a potential conflict of interest for financial reasons where an assessor is paid a fee for making an application or giving a medical recommendation if it is paid regardless of the outcome of the assessment.

Business conflict

7.7 An assessor will have a potential conflict of interest if both that assessor and one of the other assessors, the patient or the nearest relative (if the nearest relative is the applicant) are closely involved in the same business venture. Being closely involved is not defined in the regulations, but examples could include being a partner in a partnership, being a director or other office-holder of a company, or being a major shareholder in it. This will apply even if the business venture is not associated with the provision of services for the care and treatment of persons with a mental disorder.

7.8 Business ventures include any form of commercial enterprise from which the person concerned stands to profit. Such people include: directors and major investors in a company (of any size) which provides goods or services for profit; partners in a GP practice; partners in a business established as a limited liability partnership. Involvement in a business venture does not include involvement in societies and similar organisations which are essentially non-commercial, and from which the people concerned do not stand to profit.

Professional conflict

7.9 Regulations set out that a conflict of interest for professional reasons will occur where:

- the assessor is in a line management or employment relationship with one of the other assessors or the patient or the nearest relative (where the nearest relative is the applicant);

- the assessor is a member of the same team as the patient; or

- where there are three assessors, all of them are members of the same team.

7.10 A line management relationship will exist whether an assessor manages, or is managed by, one of the other assessors, the patient or the nearest relative (where the nearest relative is the applicant). Similarly an employment relationship will exist whether the assessor employs, or is employed by, one of the other assessors, the patient or the nearest relative (where the nearest relative is the applicant).

7.11 For the purposes of the regulations a team is defined as a group of professionals who work together for clinical purposes on a routine basis. That might include a community mental health team, a crisis resolution or home treatment team, or staff on an in-patient unit (but not necessarily the staff of an entire hospital).

Urgent necessity

7.12 If there is a case of urgent necessity all three assessors may be from the same team. However, this should happen only in a genuine emergency, where the patient's need for urgent assessment outweighs the desirability of waiting for another assessor who has no potential conflict of interest. Any decisions made to proceed despite a potential conflict of interest should be recorded, with reasons, in case notes.

7.13   In a case of urgent necessity it is preferable to proceed with three assessors, despite a potential conflict of interest, rather than make the application under section 4 of the Act with only two assessors (one doctor and one AMHP). (See **paragraphs 5.4-5.6.**)

7.14   There are no other circumstances in which potential conflicts of interest can be set aside because of urgent necessity.

Other potential conflicts

7.15   There may be circumstances not covered by these regulations where the assessor feels, nonetheless, that there is (or could be seen to be) a potential conflict of interest. Assessors should work on the principle that in any situation where they believe that the objectivity or independence of their decision is (or could be seen to be) undermined, they should not become involved or should withdraw.

7.16   These regulations do not cover potential conflicts of interest relating to supervised community treatment (SCT). However, the responsible clinician and the AMHP responsible for making the decision as to whether to place a patient on SCT, or any decision to revoke a community treatment order, should not have any financial interest in the outcome of the decision. Similarly, neither the responsible clinician nor the AMHP should be a relative of the patient or of each other.

7.17   The Act requires an AMHP to take an independent decision about whether or not to make an application under the Act. If an AMHP believes that they are being placed under undue pressure to make, or not make, an application, they should raise this through the appropriate channels. Local arrangements should be in place to deal with such circumstances.

CHAPTER 8
The nearest relative

8.1 This chapter gives guidance on the identification, appointment and displacement of nearest relatives under the Act.

Reference Guide chapter 33

Identification of the nearest relative

8.2 Section 26 of the Act defines "relative" and "nearest relative" for the purposes of the Act. It is important to remember that the nearest relative for the purposes of the Act may not be the same person as the patient's next of kin. The identity of the nearest relative may also change with the passage of time (eg if the patient enters into a marriage or civil partnership). (See **paragraphs 4.56-4.65**.)

8.3 Patients remanded to hospital under sections 35 and 36 of the Act and people subject to interim hospital orders under section 38 do not have nearest relatives (as defined by the Act). Nor do patients subject to special restrictions under Part 3 of the Act (restricted patients).

Delegation of nearest relative functions

8.4 A nearest relative is not obliged to act as such. They can authorise, in writing, another person to perform the functions of the nearest relative on their behalf. The procedure for doing this is set out in the Mental Health (Hospital, Guardianship and Treatment) (England) Regulations 2008.

Where there is no nearest relative

8.5 Where an approved mental health professional (AMHP) discovers, when assessing a patient for possible detention or guardianship under the Act (or at any other time), that the patient appears to have no nearest relative, the

AMHP should advise the patient of their right to apply to the county court for the appointment of a person to act as their nearest relative.

Sections 29 and 30

Displacement of nearest relatives and appointment of acting nearest relatives by the county court

Grounds for displacement and appointment

8.6 An acting nearest relative can be appointed by the county court on the grounds that:

- the nearest relative is incapable of acting as such because of illness or mental disorder;

- the nearest relative has objected unreasonably to an application for admission for treatment or a guardianship application;

- the nearest relative has exercised the power to discharge a patient without due regard to the patient's health or wellbeing or the safety of the public;

- the nearest relative is otherwise not a suitable person to act as such; or

- the patient has no nearest relative within the meaning of the Act, or it is not reasonably practicable to ascertain whether the patient has a nearest relative or who that nearest relative is.

8.7 The effect of a court order appointing an acting nearest relative is to displace the person who would otherwise be the patient's nearest relative.

8.8 However, as an alternative to an order by the court, it may sometimes be enough for the actual nearest relative to delegate their role to someone else (see **paragraph 8.4**).

Who can make an application to the court?

8.9   An application to displace the nearest relative may be made by any of the following people:

- the patient;

- any relative of the patient;

- anyone with whom the patient is residing (or was residing prior to admission); or

- an AMHP.

Applications to the court by AMHPs

8.10   AMHPs will need to consider making an application for displacement or appointment if:

- they believe that a patient should be detained in hospital under section 3 of the Act, or should become a guardianship patient, but the nearest relative objects; or

- they believe that the nearest relative is likely to discharge a patient from detention or guardianship unwisely.

8.11   They should also consider doing so if they think that:

- a patient has no identifiable nearest relative or their nearest relative is incapable of acting as such; or

- they have good reasons to think that a patient considers their nearest relative unsuitable and would like them to be replaced;

and it would not be reasonable in the circumstances to expect the patient, or anyone else, to make an application.

8.12   AMHPs should bear in mind that some patients may wish to apply to displace their nearest relative but may be deterred from doing so by the need to apply to the county court.

8.13   It is entirely a matter for the court to decide what constitutes "suitability" of a person to be a nearest relative. But factors which an AMHP might wish to consider when deciding whether to make an application to displace a nearest relative on grounds of unsuitability, and when providing evidence in connection with an application, could include:

- any reason to think that the patient has suffered, or is suspected to have suffered, abuse at the hands of the nearest relative (or someone with whom the nearest relative is in a relationship), or is at risk of suffering such abuse;

- any evidence that the patient is afraid of the nearest relative or seriously distressed by the possibility of the nearest relative being involved in their life or their care; and

- a situation where the patient and nearest relative are unknown to each other, there is only a distant relationship between them, or their relationship has broken down irretrievably.

This is not an exhaustive list.

8.14 In all cases, the decision to make an application lies with the AMHP personally.

8.15 Before making an application for displacement, AMHPs should consider other ways of achieving the same end, including:

- whether the nearest relative will agree to delegate their role as the patient's nearest relative to someone else; or

- providing or arranging support for the patient (or someone else) to make an application themselves. This could include support from an independent mental health advocate.[1]

[1] Independent mental health advocacy services under the Act are expected to be introduced in April 2009.

8.16   Local social services authorities (LSSAs) should provide
clear practical guidance to help AMHPs decide whether
to make an application and how to proceed. Before
producing such guidance, LSSAs should consult with the
county court. LSSAs should ensure that they have access
to the necessary legal advice and support.

Making an application

8.17   People making an application to the county court will
need to provide the court with the facts that will help it
make a decision on the application. Exactly what will be
required will depend on the type of application and the
specific circumstances of the case.

8.18   When applying to displace a nearest relative, AMHPs
should nominate someone to become the acting nearest
relative in the event that the application is successful.
Wherever practicable, they should first consult the patient
about the patient's own preferences and any concerns
they have about the person the AMHP proposes to
nominate. AMHPs should also seek the agreement of the
proposed nominee prior to an application being made,
although this is not a legal requirement.

8.19   LSSAs should provide clear practical guidance to help the
AMHP decide who it is appropriate to nominate when
making an application to displace a nearest relative.

8.20   If the patient has any concerns that any information
given to the court on their views on the suitability of
the nearest relative may have implications for their own
safety, an application can be made to the court seeking
its permission not to make the current nearest relative a
party to the proceedings. The reasons for the patient's
concerns should be set out clearly in the application.

8.21   Hospital managers should provide support to detained
patients to enable them to attend the court, if they wish,
subject to the patient being granted leave under section
17 for this purpose.

8.22   If, exceptionally, the court decides to interview the patient (as the applicant), the court has the discretion to decide where and how this interview may take place and whether it should take place in the presence of, or separate from, other parties.

8.23   If the court decides that the nearest relative should be displaced and finds the proposed replacement to be suitable, and that person is willing to act as nearest relative, then the court will appoint them.

CHAPTER 9
Attorneys and deputies

9.1   This chapter gives guidance on the effect of the Mental Health Act on the powers of donees of lasting power of attorney (attorneys) and deputies appointed under the Mental Capacity Act 2005 (MCA).

Powers of attorneys and deputies

9.2   In general, the fact that a person is subject to the Mental Health Act does not affect the validity of any lasting power of attorney (LPA), nor the scope of the authority of an attorney or deputy (or the Court of Protection) to make decisions on their behalf.

9.3   Attorneys and deputies can take any decisions in relation to the welfare, property or affairs of a person subject to the Act that they are otherwise authorised to take, with two exceptions:

- they will not be able to consent on the patient's behalf to treatment which is regulated by Part 4 of the Mental Health Act, including neurosurgery for mental disorder and other treatments under section 57 (see **chapter 23**); and

- they will not be able to take decisions about where a patient subject to guardianship is to live, nor take other decisions which conflict with decisions that a guardian has a legal right to make (see **chapter 26**).

9.4   Being subject to compulsory measures under the Mental Health Act does not prevent people creating new LPAs under the MCA if they have the capacity to do so. Nor does it prevent the Court of Protection from appointing a deputy to take decisions for them which they lack the capacity to make themselves.

9.5   In certain cases, conditions can be imposed on patients subject to the Mental Health Act in relation to leave of absence from hospital, supervised community treatment (SCT) or conditional discharge. If an attorney or deputy takes a decision on the patient's behalf which goes against one of these conditions, the patient will be taken to have gone against the condition. In SCT and conditional discharge cases, this might result in the patient's recall to hospital being considered.

9.6   Attorneys and deputies are able to exercise a patient's rights under the Mental Health Act on their behalf, if they have the relevant authority under the LPA or the order of the court appointing them and the patient concerned lacks the capacity to do so themselves. In particular, personal welfare attorneys and deputies may be able to exercise the patient's various rights to apply to the Tribunal for discharge from detention, guardianship or SCT.

9.7   It is good practice, where practicable, for clinicians and others involved in the assessment or treatment of patients under the Act to try to find out whether the person has an attorney or deputy and to establish effective means of communication to ensure that the attorney or deputy is informed and, where relevant, consulted about the patient's care.

Relationship between the powers of attorneys and deputies and the role of nearest relatives

9.8   The rights of the nearest relative are not affected just because a patient has an attorney or deputy.

9.9   Attorneys and deputies may not exercise the rights of the nearest relative, unless they are themselves the nearest relative (because the rights belong to the nearest relative, not the patient).

9.10   There may sometimes be a disagreement between a
nearest relative and an attorney or deputy (eg over
whether the attorney or deputy should exercise the
patient's right to apply to the Tribunal, or whether the
nearest relative should make a discharge order). If so, it
may be helpful for the two to discuss the issue, perhaps
with the assistance of one of the professionals involved in
the patient's case. But ultimately they have different roles,
and each must act as they think best. Specifically, an
attorney or deputy must act in accordance with their
authority and in the patient's best interests.

Related material

- Mental Capacity Act 2005

- *Mental Capacity Act 2005 Code of Practice*, TSO, 2007

  This material does not form part of the Code. It is provided for
  assistance only.

CHAPTER 10 Police powers and places of safety

Reference Guide chapter 30

10.1 This chapter deals with entry to premises under the Act and powers temporarily to remove people who appear to be suffering from a mental disorder to a place of safety.

Section 135: warrant to search for and remove patients

10.2 A police officer may use powers of entry under section 135(1) of the Act when it is necessary to gain access to premises to remove a person who is believed to have a mental disorder and is not receiving proper care. This requires a magistrate's warrant. A magistrate may issue a warrant under section 135(1) in response to an application from an approved mental health professional (AMHP).

10.3 The warrant gives any police officer the right to enter the premises, by force if necessary. When acting on the warrant, the officer must be accompanied by an AMHP and a doctor. It may be helpful if the doctor who accompanies the police officer is approved for the purposes of section 12(2) of the Act. The police officer may then remove the person to a place of safety, where they can be detained for up to 72 hours from the time of their arrival.

10.4 Following entry under section 135(1), the AMHP and doctor between them should, if feasible, carry out a preliminary assessment of the person to determine whether they need to be assessed further for an application under the Act or for other arrangements for care or treatment. It may be possible to carry out any such further assessment in the premises themselves.

10.5   Section 135(2) provides for the issue of a warrant by a magistrate authorising entry by the police to remove a patient who is liable to be taken or returned to hospital or any other place or into custody under the Act. It enables a police officer to enter the premises and remove the patient so that they can be taken or returned to where they ought to be. Such a warrant may be used, for example, to help return a patient who has absconded, or who needs to be conveyed to hospital, if access to the premises where they are staying has been refused or is likely to be refused. (See **chapter 22** for detailed guidance on patients who are absent from hospital without leave.)

10.6   When a warrant issued under section 135(2) is being used, it is good practice for the police officer to be accompanied by a person with authority from the managers of the relevant hospital (or local social services authority (LSSA), if applicable) to take the patient into custody and to take or return them to where they ought to be. For patients on supervised community treatment (SCT) it is good practice for this person to be, if possible, a member of the multi-disciplinary team responsible for the patient's care.

10.7   LSSAs should ensure that guidance is available to AMHPs on how and when to apply for a warrant.

10.8   LSSAs and hospital managers should ensure that there are procedures in place for obtaining warrants, both during and outside court hours. These should describe the necessary processes, the evidence which individuals may be reasonably expected to produce, and the documents that should be prepared to help the process run smoothly.

10.9   Where a section 135 warrant is used, the AMHP, the hospital managers or the LSSA (as appropriate) should ensure that an ambulance or other transport is available to take the person to the place of safety or to the place where they ought to be, in accordance with a locally agreed policy on the transport of patients under the Act (see **chapter 11**).

10.10 Magistrates have to be satisfied that it is appropriate to issue a warrant. They are likely to ask applicants why they are applying for a warrant, whether reasonable attempts to enter without a warrant have been made and, if not, why not. Applicants should provide documented reasons for seeking a warrant if they have not already tried to gain access.

10.11 Thought should be given to the choice of the place of safety before a warrant is applied for under section 135(1). Proper planning should mean that it is almost never necessary to use a police station as a place of safety for people removed under section 135(1).

Section 136: mentally disordered people found in public places

10.12 Section 136 allows for the removal to a place of safety of any person found in a place to which the public have access (by payment or otherwise) who appears to a police officer to be suffering from mental disorder and to be in immediate need of care or control.

10.13 Removal to a place of safety may take place if the police officer believes it necessary in the interests of that person, or for the protection of others.

10.14 The purpose of removing a person to a place of safety in these circumstances is only to enable the person to be examined by a doctor and interviewed by an AMHP, so that the necessary arrangements can be made for the person's care and treatment. It is not a substitute for an application for detention under the Act, even if it is thought that the person will need to be detained in hospital only for a short time. It is also not intended to substitute for or affect the use of other police powers.

10.15 The maximum period a person may be detained under section 136 is 72 hours. The imposition of consecutive periods of detention under section 136 is unlawful.

Local policies on the use of police powers and places of safety

10.16 It is important to ensure that a jointly agreed local policy is in place governing all aspects of the use of sections 135 and 136. Good practice depends on a number of factors. For example:

- LSSAs, hospitals, NHS commissioners, police forces and ambulance services should ensure that they have a clear and jointly agreed policy for use of the powers under sections 135 and 136, as well as the operation of agreed places of safety within their localities;

- all professionals involved in implementation of the powers should understand them and their purpose, and the roles and responsibilities of other people involved, and should follow the local policy;

- professionals involved in implementation of the powers should receive the necessary training; and

- the parties to the local policy should meet regularly to discuss its effectiveness in the light of experience.

10.17 The policy should define responsibilities for:

- commissioning and providing secure places of safety in healthcare settings;

- identifying and agreeing the most appropriate place of safety in individual cases;

- providing prompt assessment and, where appropriate, admission to hospital for further assessment or treatment;

- securing the attendance of police officers, where appropriate for the patient's health or safety or the protection of others;

- the safe, timely and appropriate conveyance of the person to and between places of safety (bearing in mind that hospital or ambulance transport will generally be preferable to police transport, which should be used exceptionally, such as in cases of extreme urgency or where there is a risk of violence);

- deciding whether it is appropriate to transfer the person from the place of safety to which they have been taken to another place of safety (see **paragraphs 10.34-10.39**);

- dealing with people who are also under the effects of alcohol or drugs;

- dealing with people who are behaving, or have behaved, violently;

- arranging access to a hospital accident and emergency department for assessment, where necessary;

- record keeping (see **paragraphs 10.40-10.41**) and monitoring (see **paragraphs 10.42-10.44**) and audit of practice against policy; and

- the release, transport and follow-up of people assessed under section 135 or 136 who are not then admitted to hospital or immediately accommodated elsewhere.

10.18 Responsibilities should be allocated to those who are best placed to discharge them, bearing in mind the different purposes for which health and social services and the police service exist. Local policies should ensure that police officers know whom to contact prior to the removal of a person to a place of safety under section 136.

10.19 Such policies may be best maintained by the establishment of a liaison committee, which might also take responsibility for examining the processes in place for other multi-agency tasks, such as conveyance of persons under the Act and policies in respect of patients who go absent without leave.

Places of safety

10.20 The process for identifying the most appropriate place of safety to which a particular person is to be removed should be clearly outlined in the local policy.

10.21 A police station should be used as a place of safety only on an exceptional basis. It may be necessary to do so because the person's behaviour would pose an unmanageably high risk to other patients, staff or users of a healthcare setting. It is preferable for a person thought to be suffering from a mental disorder to be detained in a hospital or other healthcare setting where mental health services are provided (subject, of course, to any urgent physical healthcare needs they may have).

10.22 A police station should not be assumed to be the automatic second choice if the first choice place of safety is not immediately available. Other available options, such as a residential care home or the home of a relative or friend of the person who is willing to accept them temporarily, should also be considered.

10.23 If a police station is used, health and social care agencies should work with the police in arranging, where appropriate, the transfer of the person to a more suitable place of safety. In defining responsibility for providing a prompt assessment, the locally agreed policy should set out the time within which it would be reasonable to expect the appropriate health and social care professionals to attend the police station to assess the person or to assist in arranging to transfer them.

10.24 In identifying the most appropriate place of safety for an individual, consideration should be given to the impact that the proposed place of safety (and the journey to it) may have on the person and on their examination and interview. It should always be borne in mind that the use of a police station can give the impression that the person detained is suspected of having committed a crime. This may cause distress and anxiety to the person concerned and may affect their co-operation with, and therefore the effectiveness of, the assessment process.

10.25 Where an individual is removed to a place of safety by the police, the following recommendations apply:

- where the place of safety is a hospital, the police should make immediate contact with both the hospital and the LSSA (or the people arranging AMHP services on its behalf), and this contact should take place prior to the person's arrival at the place of safety. This will allow arrangements to be made for the person to be interviewed and examined as soon as possible. Where a warrant has been issued under section 135, these arrangements should, wherever possible, have been made in advance by the AMHP, the hospital or any other organisation responsible for the person;

- where a hospital is used as a place of safety, it is a local decision whether the person is admitted to a bed on arrival or whether that happens only after they have been interviewed and examined; and

- where a police station is to be used as the place of safety, contact should be quickly made with the LSSA (or its AMHP service) and with an appropriate doctor. This will enable the examination and interview to be conducted as quickly as possible, thus ensuring that the person spends no longer than necessary in police custody before being released or taken to hospital. Early assessment will also allow consideration to be given to the possibility of a transfer to an alternative place of safety as soon as this is considered to be safe and appropriate in all the circumstances.

Assessment at a place of safety

10.26 The same care should be taken in examining and interviewing people in places of safety as in any other assessment. No assumptions should be made about them simply because the police have been involved, nor should they be assumed to be in any less need of support and assistance during the assessment. The guidance on assessment in **chapter 4** applies in these circumstances as in any others.

10.27 Doctors examining patients should, wherever possible, be approved under section 12 of the Act. Where the examination has to be conducted by a doctor who is not approved under section 12, the doctor concerned should record the reasons for that.

10.28 Assessment by the doctor and AMHP should begin as soon as possible after the arrival of the individual at the place of safety. Where possible, the assessment should be undertaken jointly by the doctor and the AMHP.

10.29 It is desirable for either a consultant psychiatrist in learning disabilities or an AMHP with knowledge and experience of working with people with learning disabilities to be available to make the assessment where it appears that the detained person has a learning disability.

10.30 Similarly, where the person detained is under the age of 18, or is known to have moved recently to adult mental health services, either a child and adolescent mental health services (CAMHS) consultant or an AMHP with knowledge and experience of caring for this age group should undertake the assessment, if possible.

10.31 The authority to detain a person under section 135(1) or 136 ends as soon as it has been decided to make no application in respect of them under Part 2 of the Act or other arrangements for their treatment or care. This means that where a doctor has completed an examination of such a person prior to the arrival of the AMHP and concludes that the person is not mentally disordered, the person can no longer be detained and must immediately be released.

10.32 In no case may a patient continue to be detained in a police station under section 136 once a custody officer deems that detention is no longer appropriate.

10.33 If the doctor sees the person first and concludes that they have a mental disorder and that, while compulsory admission to hospital is not necessary, they may still need treatment or care (whether in or out of hospital), the person should still be seen by an AMHP. The AMHP should consult the doctor about any arrangements that might need to be made for the person's treatment or care.

Transfer between places of safety

10.34 A person removed to a place of safety under section 135 or section 136 may be moved to a different place of safety before the end of the maximum 72-hour period for which they may be detained. The maximum period of detention begins from the time of the person's arrival at the first place of safety to which they are taken and cannot be extended if the person is transferred to another place of safety.

10.35 The person may be taken to the second or subsequent place of safety by a police officer, an AMHP or a person authorised by either a police officer or an AMHP.

10.36 A person may be transferred before their assessment has begun, while it is in progress or after it is completed and they are waiting for any necessary arrangements for their care or treatment to be put in place. If it is unavoidable, or it is in the person's interests, an assessment begun by one AMHP or doctor may be taken over and completed by another, either in the same location or at another place to which the person is transferred.

10.37 Although it may be helpful for local policies to outline circumstances in which a person is usually to be transferred between places of safety, the decision in each case should reflect the individual circumstances, including the person's needs and the level of risk. For example, where the purpose of the transfer would be to move a person from a police station to a more appropriate healthcare setting, the benefit of that move needs to be weighed against any delay it might cause in the person's assessment and any distress that the journey might cause them.

10.38 Someone with the authority to effect a transfer should proceed by agreement wherever possible. Unless it is an emergency, a person should not be transferred without the agreement of an AMHP, a doctor or another healthcare professional who is competent to assess whether the transfer would put the person's health or safety (or that of other people) at risk. It is for those professionals to decide whether they first need to see the person themselves.

10.39 Unless it is unavoidable, a person should never be moved from one place of safety to another unless it has been confirmed that the new place of safety is willing and able to accept them.

Record keeping

10.40 A record of the person's time of arrival must be made immediately when they reach the place of safety. As soon as detention in a place of safety under section 135 or 136 ends, the individual must be told that they are free to leave by those who are detaining them. The organisation responsible for the place of safety (where there is one) should ensure that proper records are kept of the end of the person's detention under these sections.

10.41 Given that the maximum period of detention at a place of safety is not affected by any subsequent transfer to a different place of safety (see **paragraph 10.34**), it is very important to ensure that the time of detention at the first place of safety is recorded clearly. This information should be shared between the transferring and receiving place of safety in the event of a transfer.

Monitoring the use of the Act to remove people

10.42 The locally agreed policy should include arrangements for the use of section 136 (in particular) to be monitored effectively so that:

- a check can be made of how, in what circumstances and with what outcome it is being used, including its use in relation to people from black and minority ethnic communities and children and young people; and

- the parties to the policy can consider any changes to the mental health services or police operations or any other matters that might result in a reduction in its use.

10.43 The local policy should address who is responsible for collecting, analysing and disseminating the information required for monitoring purposes. It should also set target times for the commencement of assessment at a place of safety, and the relevant NHS bodies and LSSAs should review local practice against these targets.

10.44 Although information systems (and definitions) may differ between organisations, efforts should be made to ensure that the most important data for monitoring purposes is collected in a way that allows it to be analysed so that is of use to all the parties to the policy.

Rights of persons detained in places of safety

10.45 A person removed under section 136 is deemed to be "arrested" for the purposes of the Police and Criminal Evidence Act 1984 (PACE). This means that police officers have the power to search a person they detain under section 136, as they would in the case of a person arrested for an offence. Under section 54 of PACE, the custody officer at the police station has the power to ascertain what items the person has on them, to remove items (where permitted) and to search the person as necessary for those purposes.

10.46 Where a hospital is used as a place of safety, the managers must ensure that the provisions of section 132 (giving of information) are complied with. In addition, access to legal advice should be facilitated whenever it is requested.

10.47 If a person is detained in a police station as a place of safety, they have a right of access to legal advice under PACE. The conditions of detention and treatment of the person must be in accordance with PACE Code of Practice C. Among other things, this requires that the person must be notified of their rights and entitlements, both orally and in writing. This will be achieved by handing the person a copy of the Notice of Rights and Entitlements.

10.48 In all cases, the person detained should be told that the maximum period of detention is 72 hours.

Places of safety and consent to treatment

10.49 Detaining a patient in a place of safety under section 135 or 136 does not confer any power under the Act to treat them without their consent. In other words, they are in exactly the same position in respect of consent to treatment as patients who are not detained under the Act.

Making necessary arrangements following assessment

10.50 Once the assessment has been concluded, it is the responsibility of the doctors and AMHPs involved to make any necessary further arrangements for the person's treatment and care.

10.51 Where compulsory admission is indicated, the AMHP should arrange for a second doctor to examine the patient in accordance with the Act (unless it has been agreed locally that someone else should make such arrangements).

10.52 It is unlikely that an emergency application will be justified in these circumstances. If there is an urgent need to secure the transfer of the patient to hospital, the power of transfer between places of safety can be used.

10.53 A person who is detained in hospital under section 135 or 136 pending completion of their assessment should not have their detention extended by use of section 5(2) or section 5(4).

10.54 It should also be borne in mind that a person who is removed to a place of safety may already be on SCT or conditional discharge or may be on leave of absence from detention in hospital and that their recall to hospital may need to be considered. If it becomes apparent that this is the case, the professionals assessing the patient should make an effort to contact the patient's responsible clinician as soon as possible.

10.55 Where the person is known to be on SCT and compulsory admission is indicated, the recall power should be used. An application for detention cannot be made in respect of a person who is known to be on SCT.

Related material

- *Police and Criminal Evidence Act 1984 (PACE) Code C: Code of Practice for the Detention, Treatment and Questioning of Persons by Police Officers,* Home Office, 2008

This material does not form part of the Code. It is provided for assistance only.

APPLYING THE PRINCIPLES

This scenario is not intended to provide a template for decisions in applying the principles in similar situations. The scenario itself is only illustrative and does not form part of the Code itself.

TRANSFER BETWEEN PLACES OF SAFETY

Following an incident in the street, Fred has been detained under section 136 and taken to a police station as a place of safety. The police have contacted the local mental health services to make arrangements for a mental health assessment.

Fred is in an agitated state, but settles slightly after arriving at the police station. He advises that he is 17 years old and lives some distance away with his mother. The local mental health service confirms that he is known to CAMHS in his local area and that there is a place of safety in the local hospital where he could be assessed.

Neither the AMHP nor the doctor are specialists working with young people, and with the police they need to consider whether they should move Fred to the place of safety in his home area. In making this determination, the guiding principles of this Code should be considered. This could include thinking about the following questions.

Purpose principle
- Would transferring Fred be to his benefit?

- Would transferring Fred create a risk to the public?

- Would assessing him where he is help him or protect other people?

Least restriction principle
- Is there anything to choose between the police station and the local place of safety in terms of Fred's freedom of action, or how he might feel about being detained?

- If the local place of safety would be less restrictive, what about the restrictions that would have to be placed on him to get him there?

Respect principle

- Does Fred have any views about whether he would rather see the clinical team that knows him?

- If he cannot focus on the question of where he would rather be, is he expressing any concerns about seeing the assessing AMHP or doctors, or about being seen by people he does not know?

- Has this situation arisen before (as far as anyone can easily discover)? If so, how was it handled previously? Was it successfully managed?

- Fred is strong and young – are we sure we are not making any unwarranted assumptions about the risk his behaviour poses, or about his ability to know and say what he wants?

Participation principle

- Can we explain the options to Fred and ask him for his views?

- If he were to be transferred, would he want to go before or after he had eaten or slept?

- Can his family be contacted? Does Fred want his family to be contacted? What do they want – and what do they think he would want?

Effectiveness, efficiency and equity principle

- If the assessment is carried out in the police station by people who do not know him, is it effectively going to have to be carried out again very shortly anyway by the team that does?

- Could someone from that team come and see him in the police station?

- Which option would serve Fred's best interests, balancing these against any risk to the public?

- What would the implications be for that team's ability to serve its other patients?

- Does the custody officer at the police station have any view about what should happen?

CHAPTER 11
Conveyance of patients

11.1 This chapter provides guidance on the conveyance of patients under the Act.

General considerations

11.2 Patients should always be conveyed in the manner which is most likely to preserve their dignity and privacy consistent with managing any risk to their health and safety or to other people.

11.3 This applies in all cases where patients are compulsorily conveyed under the Act, including:

- taking patients to hospital to be detained for assessment or treatment;

- transferring patients between hospitals;

- returning patients to hospital if they are absent without leave;

- taking supervised community treatment (SCT) patients or patients who have been conditionally discharged to hospital on recall;

- taking and returning patients who are subject to guardianship to the place their guardian requires them to live;

- taking patients to and between places of safety; and

- taking patients to and from court.

11.4 When deciding on the most appropriate method for conveying a patient, factors to be taken into account include:

- the availability of different transport options;

- the distance to be travelled;

- the wishes and views of the patient, including any relevant statement of those views or wishes made in advance;

- the patient's age;

- any physical disability the patient has;

- any risks to the health and safety of the patient and any need for support, supervision and clinical care or monitoring during the journey. This is particularly important where sedation has been, or may be, used;

- the nature of the patient's mental disorder and their current state of mind;

- the likelihood of the patient behaving in a violent or dangerous manner;

- the health and safety of the people conveying the patient and anyone else accompanying them;

- the likelihood that the patient may attempt to abscond and the risk of harm to the patient or other people were that to happen;

- the impact that any particular method of conveying the patient will have on the patient's relationship with the community to which they will return;

- the effect on the patient of who accompanies them, for example, whether the presence of the approved mental health professional (AMHP) or one of the doctors involved in the decision to detain them may have a detrimental effect; and

- the availability of transport to return those who accompany the patient.

11.5   Patients who have been sedated before being conveyed should always be accompanied by a health professional who is knowledgeable in the care of such patients, is able to identify and respond to any physical distress which may occur and has access to the necessary emergency equipment to do so.

Local protocols

11.6   It is for primary care trusts (PCTs) to commission
ambulance and patient transport services to meet the
needs of their areas. This includes services for transporting
patients to and from hospital (and other places) under
the Act.

11.7   PCTs should ensure, through their contracts, that
appropriate transport will be made available in a timely
manner where it is needed to convey patients under
the Act. It is for service providers, whoever they are, to
provide those services in accordance with their contracts.

11.8   However, if the patient is a private patient in an
independent hospital, it is for the managers of that
hospital to make arrangements for any necessary transport.

11.9   The respective responsibilities of different agencies and
service providers for conveying patients in different
circumstances should be clearly established locally and
communicated to the professionals who need to know.

11.10   In particular, it is essential to have clear agreements in
place so that people who need assistance in conveying
patients under the Act can secure it without delay.
Authorities, including NHS bodies responsible for
hospitals, ambulance services and the police, should agree
joint local policies and procedures. These should include,
in particular:

- a clear statement of the respective roles and obligations
of each agency and service provider (and their staff);

- the form of any authorisation to be given by AMHPs
(and others) when authorising people to convey
patients on their behalf;

- the assistance that managers and staff of hospitals will
provide to AMHPs to make necessary arrangements for
the conveyance of patients who are to be admitted to
their hospital;

- guidance and training on legal powers in relation to conveying patients;

- a clear statement of how risk assessment and management should be conducted and how the outcomes will influence decisions in relation to the conveyance of patients;

- agreement on the appropriate use of different methods of restraint in conveying patients and how decisions on their use will be made in any given case;

- any special arrangements where patients need to be conveyed outside the local area; and

- processes for reviewing and monitoring the involvement of the different agencies, including standards against which delivery will be monitored.

11.11 Policies should ensure that AMHPs (in particular) are not left to negotiate arrangements with providers of transport services on an ad hoc basis, in the absence of clear expectations about the responsibilities of all those involved.

11.12 Policies should also be consistent with those agreed in relation to the use of the police powers in sections 135 and 136 of the Act (see **chapter 10**).

Section 6
Reference Guide
2.66-2.69

Conveying patients to hospital on the basis of an application for detention

11.13 A properly completed application for detention under the Act, together with the required medical recommendations, gives the applicant (the AMHP or nearest relative) the authority to convey the patient to the hospital named in the application.

11.14 Where AMHPs are the applicant, they have a professional responsibility to ensure that all the necessary arrangements are made for the patient to be conveyed to hospital.

11.15 If the nearest relative is the applicant, any AMHP and other professionals involved in the assessment of the patient should give advice and assistance. But they should not assist in a patient's detention unless they believe it is justified and lawful.

11.16 AMHPs should make decisions on which method of transport to use in consultation with the other professionals involved, the patient and (as appropriate) their carer, family or other supporters. The decision should be made following a risk assessment carried out on the basis of the best available information.

11.17 If the patient is likely to be unwilling to be moved, the applicant should provide the people who are to convey the patient (including any ambulance staff or police officers involved) with authority to convey the patient. It is that authorisation which confers on them the legal power to transport the patient against their will, using reasonable force if necessary, and to prevent them absconding en route.

11.18 If the patient's behaviour is likely to be violent or dangerous, the police should be asked to assist in accordance with locally agreed arrangements. Where practicable, given the risk involved, an ambulance service (or similar) vehicle should be used even where the police are assisting.

11.19 The locally agreed arrangements should set out what assistance the police will provide to AMHPs and health services in transporting patients safely, and what support ambulance or other health services will be expected to provide where patients are, exceptionally, transported in police vehicles.

11.20 Where it is necessary to use a police vehicle because of the risk involved, it may be necessary for the highest qualified member of an ambulance crew to ride in the same vehicle with the patient, with the appropriate equipment to deal with immediate problems. In such cases, the ambulance should follow directly behind to provide any further support that is required.

11.21 AMHPs should not normally agree to a patient being conveyed by car unless satisfied that it would not put the patient or other people at risk of harm and that it is the most appropriate way of transporting the patient. In these circumstances there should be an escort for the patient other than the driver.

11.22 People authorised by the applicant to convey patients act in their own right and not as the agent of the applicant. They may act on their own initiative to restrain patients and prevent them absconding, if necessary. However, when they are the applicant, AMHPs retain a professional responsibility to ensure that the patient is conveyed in a lawful and humane manner and should give guidance to those asked to assist.

11.23 Patients may be accompanied by another person, provided that the AMHP and the person in charge of the vehicle are satisfied that this will not increase the risk of harm to the patient or others.

11.24 Before patients are moved, the applicant should ensure that the receiving hospital is expecting the patient and has been told the likely time of arrival. If possible, the name of the person who will be formally receiving the patient and their admission documents should be obtained in advance.

11.25 Where the applicant is not travelling in the same vehicle as the patient, the application form and medical recommendations should be given to the person authorised to convey the patient, with instructions for them to be presented to the member of hospital staff receiving the patient.

Conveying patients between hospitals and returning patients who abscond

11.26 Where a patient requires transport between hospitals, it is for the managers of the hospitals concerned to make sure that appropriate arrangements are put in place. The managers of the hospital from which the patient is being transferred remain responsible for the patient until the patient is admitted to the new hospital.

11.27 Where a patient who is absent without leave from a hospital is taken into custody by someone working for another organisation, the managers of the hospital from which the patient is absent are responsible for making sure that any necessary transport arrangements at put in place for the patient's return.

11.28 However, the organisation which temporarily has custody of the patient is responsible for them in the interim and should therefore assist in ensuring that the patient is returned in a timely and safe manner.

11.29 When making arrangements for the return of patients temporarily held in police custody, hospital managers should bear in mind that police transport to return them to hospital will not normally be appropriate. Decisions about the kind of transport to be used should be taken in the same way as for patients being detained in hospital for the first time.

Conveying SCT patients who are recalled to hospital

Reference Guide
15.66

11.30 A notice of recall, properly completed by the responsible clinician and served on the patient in accordance with regulations, provides the authority to convey an SCT patient to hospital compulsorily, if necessary (see **paragraphs 25.47-25.64**).

11.31 Unless it has been agreed otherwise locally, the responsible clinician has responsibility for co-ordinating the recall process. The factors outlined above at **paragraph 11.4**, and the urgency of the situation, will need to be considered in deciding the best way to transport the patient to hospital. The guidance in **paragraphs 11.13-11.25** about taking patients to hospital when they are first to be detained applies here as well, except that an AMHP will not necessarily be involved.

11.32 An SCT patient who has been recalled can be conveyed by any officer on the staff of the hospital to which the patient is recalled, any police officer, any AMHP or any other person authorised in writing by the responsible clinician or the managers of that hospital. Who the most appropriate person to convey the patient is will depend on the individual circumstances.

CHAPTER 12
Holding powers

12.1 This chapter provides guidance on the use of holding powers available to doctors and approved clinicians under section 5(2) of the Act and to certain nurses under section 5(4).

Reference Guide
2.71-2.85

Holding power of doctors and approved clinicians under section 5(2)

Nature of the power

12.2 The power can be used where the doctor or approved clinician in charge of the treatment of a hospital in-patient (or their nominated deputy) concludes that an application for detention under the Act should be made. It authorises the detention of the patient in the hospital for a maximum of 72 hours so that the patient can be assessed with a view to such an application being made.

12.3 The identity of the person in charge of a patient's medical treatment at any time will depend on the particular circumstances. But a professional who is treating the patient under the direction of another professional should not be considered to be in charge.

12.4 There may be more than one person who could reasonably be said to be in charge of a patient's treatment, for example where a patient is already receiving treatment for both a physical and a mental disorder. In a case of that kind, the psychiatrist or approved clinician in charge of the patient's treatment for the mental disorder is the preferred person to use the holding power, if necessary.

12.5 The period of detention starts at the moment the doctor's or approved clinician's report is furnished to the hospital managers (eg when it is handed to an officer who is authorised by the managers to receive it, or when it is put in the hospital's internal mail system).

12.6　In this context, a hospital in-patient means any person who is receiving in-patient treatment in a hospital, except a patient who is already liable to be detained under section 2, 3 or 4 of the Act, or who is a supervised community treatment patient. It includes patients who are in hospital by virtue of a deprivation of liberty authorisation under the Mental Capacity Act 2005[1] (see **chapter 4**). It does not matter whether or not the patient was originally admitted for treatment primarily for a mental disorder.

12.7　The power cannot be used for an out-patient attending a hospital's accident and emergency department, or any other out-patient. Patients should not be admitted informally with the sole intention of then using the holding power.

12.8　Section 5(2) should only be used if, at the time, it is not practicable or safe to take the steps necessary to make an application for detention without detaining the patient in the interim. Section 5(2) should not be used as an alternative to making an application, even if it is thought that the patient will only need to be detained for 72 hours or less.

12.9　Doctors and approved clinicians should use the power only after having personally examined the patient.

12.10　Sometimes a report under section 5(2) may be made in relation to a patient who is not at the time under the care of a psychiatrist or an approved clinician. In such cases, the doctor invoking the power should make immediate contact with a psychiatrist or an approved clinician to obtain confirmation of their opinion that the patient needs to be detained. If possible, the doctor should seek such advice before using the power.

Nomination of deputies

12.11　Section 5(3) allows the doctor or approved clinician in charge of an in-patient's treatment to nominate a

[1] The deprivation of liberty safeguards are expected to be in force from April 2009.

deputy to exercise the holding power in their absence. The deputy will then act on their own responsibility.

12.12 Only a doctor or approved clinician on the staff of the same hospital may be a nominated deputy (although the deputy does not have to be a member of the same profession as the person nominating them). Only one deputy may be authorised at any time for any patient, and it is unlawful for a nominated deputy to nominate another.

12.13 Doctors should not be nominated as a deputy unless they are competent to perform the role. If nominated deputies are not approved clinicians (or doctors approved under section 12 of the Act), they should wherever possible seek advice from the person for whom they are deputising, or from someone else who is an approved clinician or section 12 approved doctor, before using section 5(2). Hospital managers should see that arrangements are in place to allow nominated deputies to do this.

12.14 Nominated deputies should report the use of section 5(2) to the person for whom they are deputising as soon as practicable.

12.15 It is permissible for deputies to be nominated by title, rather than by name – for example, the junior doctor on call for particular wards – provided that there is only one nominated deputy for any patient at any time and it can be determined with certainty who that nominated deputy is.

12.16 Hospital managers should ensure that ward staff know who the nominated deputy for a particular patient is at any given time.

12.17 Doctors and approved clinicians may leave instructions with ward staff to contact them (or their nominated deputy) if a particular patient wants or tries to leave. But they may not leave instructions for their nominated deputy to use section 5, nor may they complete a section 5 report in advance to be used in their absence.

Assessment for admission while a patient is detained under section 5(2)

12.18 Arrangements for an assessment to consider an application under section 2 or section 3 of the Act should be put in place as soon as the section 5(2) report is furnished to the hospital managers.

Ending section 5(2)

12.19 Although the holding power lasts for a maximum of 72 hours, it should not be used to continue to detain patients after:

- the doctor or approved clinician decides that, in fact, no assessment for a possible application needs to be carried out; or

- a decision is taken not to make an application for the patient's detention.

12.20 Patients should be informed immediately that they are no longer detained under the holding power and are free to leave the hospital, unless the patient is to be detained under some other authority, such as an authorisation under the deprivation of liberty safeguards in the Mental Capacity Act 2005 (see **chapter 4**).

Holding power of nurses under section 5(4)

Nature of the power

12.21 Nurses of the "prescribed class" may invoke section 5(4) of the Act in respect of a hospital in-patient who is already receiving treatment for mental disorder.[2]

12.22 This power may be used only where the nurse considers that:

- the patient is suffering from mental disorder to such a degree that it is necessary for the patient to be immediately prevented from leaving the hospital either for the patient's health or safety or for the protection of other people; and

[2] The prescribed classes at the time of publication are nurses registered in sub-parts 1 or 2 of the register maintained by the Nursing and Midwifery Council whose entry in the register indicates that their field of practice is either mental health nursing or learning disability nursing.

- it is not practicable to secure the attendance of a doctor or approved clinician who can submit a report under section 5(2).

It can be used only when the patient is still on the hospital premises.

12.23 The use of the holding power permits the patient's detention for up to six hours or until a doctor or approved clinician with the power to use section 5(2) arrives, whichever is the earlier. It cannot be renewed.

12.24 The patient may be detained from the moment the nurse makes the necessary record. The record must then be sent to the hospital managers.

12.25 The decision to invoke the power is the personal decision of the nurse, who cannot be instructed to exercise the power by anyone else.

12.26 Hospital managers should ensure that suitably qualified, experienced and competent nurses are available to all wards where there is a possibility of section 5(4) being invoked, particularly acute psychiatric admission wards and wards where there are patients who are acutely unwell or who require intensive nursing care. Where nurses may have to apply the power to patients from outside their specialist field, it is good practice for hospital managers to arrange suitable training in the use of the power in such situations.

Assessment before invoking section 5(4)

12.27 Before using the power, nurses should assess:

- the likely arrival time of the doctor or approved clinician, as against the likely intention of the patient to leave. It may be possible to persuade the patient to wait until a doctor or approved clinician arrives to discuss the matter further; and

- the consequences of a patient leaving the hospital before the doctor or approved clinician arrives – in other words, the harm that might occur to the patient or others.

12.28 In doing so, nurses should consider:

- the patient's expressed intentions;

- the likelihood of the patient harming themselves or others;

- the likelihood of the patient behaving violently;

- any evidence of disordered thinking;

- the patient's current behaviour and, in particular, any changes in their usual behaviour;

- whether the patient has recently received messages from relatives or friends;

- whether the date is one of special significance for the patient (eg the anniversary of a bereavement);

- any recent disturbances on the ward;

- any relevant involvement of other patients;

- any history of unpredictability or impulsiveness;

- any formal risk assessments which have been undertaken (specifically looking at previous behaviour); and

- any other relevant information from other members of the multi-disciplinary team.

12.29 Nurses should be particularly alert to cases where patients suddenly decide to leave or become determined to do so urgently.

12.30 Nurses should make as full an assessment as possible in the circumstances before using the power, but sometimes it may be necessary to invoke the power on the basis of only a brief assessment.

Action once section 5(4) is used

12.31 The reasons for invoking the power should be entered in the patient's notes. Details of any patients who remain subject to the power at the time of a shift change should be given to staff coming on duty.

12.32   The use of section 5(4) is an emergency measure, and the doctor or approved clinician with the power to use section 5(2) in respect of the patient should treat it as such and arrive as soon as possible. The doctor or approved clinician should not wait six hours before attending simply because this is the maximum time allowed.

12.33   If the doctor or approved clinician arrives before the end of the six hour maximum period, the holding power lapses on their arrival. But if the doctor or approved clinician then uses their own holding power, the maximum period of 72 hours runs from when the nurse first made the record detaining the patient under section 5(4).

12.34   If no doctor or approved clinician able to make a report under section 5(2) has attended within six hours, the patient is no longer detained and may leave if not prepared to stay voluntarily. This should be considered as a serious failing, and should be reported and investigated locally as such.

General points about using section 5

Recording the end of detention

12.35   The time at which a patient ceases to be detained under section 5(2) or 5(4) should be recorded, preferably using a standardised system established by the hospital managers for the purpose. The reason why the patient is no longer detained under the power should also be recorded, as well as what then happened to the patient (eg the patient remained in hospital voluntarily, was discharged, or was detained under a different power).

12.36   Detention under section 5(2) or 5(4) cannot be renewed, but that does not prevent it being used again on a future occasion if necessary.

Monitoring use

12.37   Hospital managers should monitor the use of section 5, including:

- how quickly patients are assessed for detention and discharged from the holding power;

- the attendance times of doctors and approved clinicians following the use of section 5(4); and

- the proportion of cases in which applications for detention are, in fact, made following use of section 5.

Information

12.38 Hospital managers must ensure that patients detained under section 5 are given information about their position and their rights, as required by section 132 of the Act.

Section 56 ## Medical treatment of patients

12.39 Detaining patients under section 5 does not confer any power under the Act to treat them without their consent. In other words, they are in exactly the same position in respect of consent to treatment as patients who are not detained under the Act.

Transfer to other hospitals

12.40 It is not possible for patients detained under section 5 to be transferred to another hospital under section 19 (because they are not detained by virtue of an application made under Part 2 of the Act).

Related material

- Mental Capacity Act 2005
- *Mental Capacity Act 2005 Code of Practice*, TSO, 2007
- *Deprivation of Liberty Safeguards*, Addendum to the *Mental Capacity Act 2005 Code of Practice*[3]

This material does not form part of the Code. It is provided for assistance only.

[3]To be published later in 2008.

CHAPTER 13 **Receipt and scrutiny of documents**

13.1   This chapter provides guidance on the receipt and scrutiny of documents under the Act.

Statutory forms

13.2   Regulations require specific statutory forms to be used for certain applications, recommendations, decisions, reports and records under the Act. The forms are set out in the regulations themselves.

13.3   If no hard copies of the statutory forms are available, photocopies of the original blank forms can be completed instead, as can computer-generated versions. However, the wording of the forms must correspond to the current statutory versions of the forms set out in the regulations.

Applications for detention in hospital and supporting medical recommendations

Reference Guide 2.86-2.110

13.4   Regulations say that applications for detention under the Act must be delivered to a person who is authorised by the hospital managers to receive them.

13.5   People who sign applications and make the supporting medical recommendations must take care to comply with the requirements of the Act. People who act on the authority of these documents should also make sure that they are in the proper form, as an incorrectly completed or indecipherable form may not constitute authority for a patient's detention.

13.6   This chapter distinguishes between receiving admission documents and scrutinising them. For these purposes, receipt involves physically receiving documents and checking that they appear to amount to an application that has been duly made (since that is sufficient to give the managers the power to detain the patient). Scrutiny involves more detailed checking for omissions, errors and other defects and, where permitted, taking action to have the documents rectified after they have already been acted on.

13.7   Hospital managers should formally delegate their duties to receive and scrutinise admission documents to a limited number of officers, who may include clinical staff on wards. Someone with the authority to receive admission documents should be available at all times at which patients may be admitted to the hospital. A manager of appropriate seniority should take overall responsibility on behalf of the hospital managers for the proper receipt and scrutiny of documents.

13.8   Hospitals should have a checklist for the guidance of people delegated to receive documents ("receiving officers"), to help them detect those errors which fundamentally invalidate an application and which cannot be corrected at a later stage in the procedure.

13.9   When a patient is being admitted on the application of an approved mental health professional (AMHP), the receiving officer should go through the documents and check their accuracy with the AMHP.

13.10 Receiving officers should have access to a manager for advice outside office hours, especially at night.

13.11 Where the receiving officer is not also authorised by the hospital managers to agree to the rectification of a defective admission document, the documents must be scrutinised by a person who is authorised to do so. This scrutiny should happen at the same time as the documents are received or as soon as possible afterwards (and certainly no later than the next working day).

13.12 Documents should be scrutinised for accuracy and completeness and to check that they do not reveal any failure to comply with the procedural requirements of the Act in respect of applications for detention. Medical recommendations should also be scrutinised by someone with appropriate clinical expertise to check that the reasons given appear sufficient to support the conclusions stated in them.

13.13 If admission documents reveal a defect which fundamentally invalidates the application and which cannot, therefore, be rectified under section 15 of the Act, the patient can no longer be detained on the basis of the application. Authority for the patient's detention can be obtained only through a new application (or, in the interim, by the use of the holding powers under section 5 if the patient has already been admitted to the hospital).

Guardianship applications and supporting medical recommendations

Reference Guide
19.56-19.59

13.14 Where a guardianship application is made, the person receiving the documents on behalf of the local social services authority (LSSA) should check them for inaccuracies and defects with the AMHP or nearest relative making the application.

13.15 LSSAs should prepare a checklist for the guidance of those delegated to receive guardianship applications on their behalf. That checklist should identify those errors which can be rectified and those which cannot.

Supervised community treatment documentation

13.16 There are no provisions in the Act for community treatment orders and related documents to be rectified once made. Hospital managers should nonetheless ensure that arrangements are in place to check that documents have been properly completed. Significant errors or inadequacies in community treatment orders themselves may render patients' supervised community treatment (SCT) invalid, and errors in recall notices or revocations may invalidate hospital managers' authority to detain.

13.17 To avoid errors being made, hospital managers should ensure that responsible clinicians have access to advice about how the relevant forms should be completed and the opportunity (where practicable) to have them checked in advance by someone else familiar with what the Act requires.

Audit

13.18 Hospital managers are responsible for ensuring that patients are lawfully detained or on SCT. LSSAs are responsible for ensuring that guardianship is lawful.

13.19 Hospital managers and LSSAs should ensure that the people they authorise to receive and scrutinise statutory documents on their behalf are competent to perform these duties, understand the requirements of the Act and receive suitable training.

13.20 Hospital managers and LSSAs should also ensure that arrangements are in place to audit the effectiveness of receipt and scrutiny of documents on a regular basis.

CHAPTER 14 **Allocating or changing a responsible clinician**

14.1　This chapter deals with the identification of responsible clinicians for patients being assessed and treated under the Act.

Allocating a responsible clinician

14.2　The responsible clinician is the approved clinician who will have overall responsibility for the patient's case.

Reference Guide
12.36-12.38
and 15.5

14.3　Hospital managers should have local protocols in place for allocating responsible clinicians to patients. This is particularly important when patients move between hospitals or from the hospital to the community and vice versa. The protocols should:

- ensure that the patient's responsible clinician is the available approved clinician with the most appropriate expertise to meet the patient's main assessment and treatment needs;

- ensure that it can be easily determined who a particular patient's responsible clinician is;

- ensure that cover arrangements are in place when the responsible clinician is not available (eg during non-working hours, annual leave etc);

- include a system for keeping the appropriateness of the responsible clinician under review.

14.4　To ensure that the most appropriate available clinician is allocated as the patient's responsible clinician, hospital managers should keep a register of approved clinicians to treat patients for whom they are responsible.

14.5　The selection of the appropriate responsible clinician should be based on the individual needs of the patient concerned. For example, where psychological therapies are central to the patient's treatment, it may be appropriate for a professional with particular expertise in this area to act as the responsible clinician. There are special considerations for patients aged under 18. (See **chapter 36**.)

14.6   Even if the patient's main treatment needs are not immediately clear, it will be necessary to allocate a responsible clinician promptly upon the patient's detention in hospital.

Change of responsible clinician

14.7   As the needs of the patient may change over time, it is important that the appropriateness of the responsible clinician is kept under review through the care planning process. It may be appropriate for the patient's responsible clinician to change during a period of care and treatment, if such a change enables the needs of the patient to be met more effectively. However, in considering such a change it is also important to take account of the need for continuity and continuing engagement with, and knowledge of, the patient.

14.8   Where a patient's treatment and rehabilitation require movement between different hospitals or to the community, successive responsible clinicians need to be identified in good time to enable movement to take place The existing responsible clinician is responsible for overseeing the patient's progress through the system. If movement to another hospital is indicated, responsible clinicians should take the lead in identifying their successors, and hospital managers should respond promptly to requests to assist in this process.

14.9   There may be circumstances where the responsible clinician is qualified with respect to the patient's main assessment and treatment needs but is not appropriately qualified to be in charge of a subsidiary treatment needed by the patient (eg medication which the responsible clinician is not qualified to prescribe). In such situations, the responsible clinician will maintain their overarching responsibility for the patient's case, but another appropriately qualified professional will take responsibility for a specific treatment or intervention.

14.10 Where the person in charge of a particular treatment is not the patient's responsible clinician, the person in charge of the treatment should ensure that the responsible clinician is kept informed about the treatment and that treatment decisions are discussed with the responsible clinician in the context of the patient's overall case. Guidance should be available locally on the procedures to follow, including when to seek a second opinion, if there are unresolved differences of opinion.

APPLYING THE PRINCIPLES

This scenario is not intended to provide a template for decisions in applying the principles in similar situations. The scenario itself is only illustrative and does not form part of the Code itself.

ALLOCATING THE RESPONSIBLE CLINICIAN

Frank is a 24 year old man; he was admitted to hospital having presented himself at A&E. He was seen by the crisis team and was admitted under section 2; this is his first admission to hospital under the Act. On admission, the duty team saw him and a psychiatrist was allocated as responsible clinician for his case.

Frank was subsequently placed on section 3 and has been in hospital for four months. Over this time, his needs have changed and the multi-disciplinary team arranges a review to determine the most appropriate available approved clinician to be the responsible clinician in charge of his care. In making this determination, the guiding principles should be considered. This could include thinking about the following questions.

Purpose principle

- What are Frank's main assessment treatment needs? Which approved clinician has the expertise to best meet these needs, in order to maximise Frank's wellbeing and minimise risk of harm to Frank and others?

- Is the choice of responsible clinician likely to affect Frank's wellbeing in any other way?

- Which professional may be best suited to acting as Frank's responsible clinician?

Least restriction principle

- Are there any reasons to think that the choice of responsible clinician will affect Frank's freedom within the hospital? (Eg might having a responsible clinician who is only available at specific times interrupt Frank's routine on the ward in a way he would find distressing?)

Respect principle

- Does Frank have any views about who should be his responsible clinician?

- Is there any reason to think that Frank would prefer a male rather than a female clinician (or vice versa)?

Participation principle

- What is the best way of explaining the options to Frank and asking for his view?

- Are there any paid, or unpaid, carers, family members or friends whose views ought to be sought? Does Frank have any view about whether to involve these people?

- Has Frank been reminded of his right to an independent mental health advocate (IMHA) to assist him?[1]

Effectiveness, efficiency and equity principle

- If Frank does have views about a particular professional being allocated as his responsible clinician, and such a clinician is appropriate, is the particular clinician available?

- Could Frank's wishes be accommodated without there being a disproportionate effect on resources available to other patients?

[1] Independent mental health advocacy services under the Act are expected to be introduced in April 2009.

CHAPTER 15 Safe and therapeutic responses to disturbed behaviour

15.1   The guidance in this chapter covers a range of interventions which may be considered for the safe and therapeutic management of hospital patients whose behaviour may present a particular risk to themselves or to others, including those charged with their care. Except where otherwise stated, this guidance applies to all patients presenting such behaviour, whether or not they are detained under the Act.

15.2   Nationally recognised guidelines, such as those of the National Institute for Health and Clinical Excellence (NICE), complement the guidance provided in this chapter.

Assessment and management of disturbed behaviour

15.3   On admission, all patients should be assessed for immediate and potential risks of going missing, suicide, self-harm and possible harm to others, and individual care plans should be developed including actions to be taken should any of these occur.

15.4   Individuals in need of care and treatment for mental disorder may, as a consequence of their disorder, present particular risks to themselves or others. These might include hyperactivity, leaving the ward without permission, self-harming, aggressive and threatening behaviour towards others, physical violence and drug or alcohol abuse. Staff should also be aware of other risks that may not be so apparent, such as self-neglect.

CHAPTER

15

Safe and
therapeutic
responses
to disturbed
behaviour

15.5 Factors which may contribute to disturbed behaviour
include:

- boredom and lack of environmental stimulation;

- too much stimulation, noise and general disruption;

- excessive heating, overcrowding and lack of access to
external space;

- personal frustrations associated with being in a
restricted environment;

- difficulties in communication;

- emotional distress, eg following bereavement;

- antagonism, aggression or provocation on the part
of others;

- the influence of alcohol or drugs;

- physical illness; and

- an unsuitable mix of patients.

15.6 All hospitals should have a policy on the recognition and
prevention of disturbed, or violent behaviour, as well as
risk assessment and management, including the use of
de-escalation techniques, enhanced observation, physical
intervention, rapid tranquilisation and seclusion. Local
policies should suit the needs of the particular groups of
patients who may be treated in the hospital.

15.7 The primary focus of any policy for managing patients
who may present with disturbed or violent behaviour
(or both) should be the establishment of a culture which
focuses on early recognition, prevention and de-escalation
of potential aggression, using techniques that minimise
the risk of its occurrence.

15.8 Interventions such as physical restraint, rapid tranquilisation, seclusion and observation should be used only where de-escalation alone proves insufficient, and should always be used in conjunction with further efforts at de-escalation; they must never be used as punishment or in a punitive manner.

15.9 Any such intervention must be used in a way that minimises any risk to the patient's health and safety and that causes the minimum interference to their privacy and dignity, while being consistent with the need to protect the patient and other people.

15.10 Staff must try to gain the confidence of patients so that they can learn to recognise potential danger signs. Staff should understand when to intervene to prevent harm from occurring. Continuity of staffing is an important factor in both the development of professional skills and consistency in managing patients.

15.11 Patients who are identified as being at risk of disturbed or violent behaviour should be given the opportunity to have their views and wishes recorded, in the form of an advance statement. They should be encouraged to identify as clearly as possible what interventions they would and would not wish to be used. Patients should be encouraged to review their wishes with staff from time to time, and any changes should be recorded. Guidance on advance statements of wishes and feelings can be found in **chapter 17**.

15.12 Services and their staff should demonstrate and encourage respect for racial and cultural diversity and recognise the need for privacy and dignity. These are essential values that must be engendered and asserted in all policy, educational material, training, and practice initiatives related to the safe and therapeutic management of patients.

CHAPTER

15

Safe and
therapeutic
responses
to disturbed
behaviour

15.13   Patients' behaviour should be seen in context.
Professionals should not categorise behaviour as disturbed
without taking account of the circumstances under which
it occurs. While it is an important factor in assessing
current risk, they should not assume that a previous
history of disturbance means that a patient will necessarily
behave in the same way in the immediate future.

15.14   Particular care needs to be taken to ensure that negative
and stigmatising judgements about certain diagnoses,
behaviours or personal characteristics do not obscure a
rigorous assessment of the degree of risk which may be
presented – or the potential benefits of appropriate
treatment to people in severe distress.

15.15   Wherever practicable, the circumstances (if any) in which
medication is to be used as a response to episodes of
particularly disturbed behaviour should be established
in advance in each patient's treatment plan. The use of
medication as an unplanned response to disturbed
behaviour should be exceptional. Medication should
never be used to manage patients as a substitute for
adequate staffing.

15.16   Individual care plans are fundamental to the appropriate
management of disturbed behaviour. In addition,
problems may be minimised by promoting the therapeutic
culture of the ward or other environment and by
identifying and managing problem areas. Among such
general measures are:

- engaging patients and keeping them fully informed,
  in a way they can understand, of what is happening
  and why;

- developing a therapeutic relationship between each
  patient and a key worker or nurse;

- seeking patients' co-operation, and encouraging their participation in the general running of the ward;

- ensuring an appropriate mix of patients;

- ensuring an appropriate mix of staff to meet patients' needs;

- identifying those patients most at risk and implementing appropriate risk management plans;

- involving patients in identification of their own trigger factors and early warning signs of disturbed or violent behaviour and in how to respond to them;

- organising the ward to provide, for example, quiet rooms, recreation rooms, single-sex areas, separate visitors' rooms and access to fresh air;

- giving each patient a defined personal space and a secure locker for the safe keeping of possessions;

- ensuring access to open space;

- ensuring that patients are able to make telephone calls in private, wherever possible;

- providing appropriate activities for all patients, including exercise, and encouraging patients to take part in activities appropriate to them;

- providing training for staff in the management of disturbed behaviour, including prevention and de-escalation; and

- ensuring that patients' complaints are dealt with quickly and fairly.

Interventions where de-escalation is insufficient

15.17 Interventions such as physical restraint, seclusion or rapid tranquillisation should be considered only if de-escalation and other strategies have failed to calm the patient.

CHAPTER

15

Safe and
therapeutic
responses
to disturbed
behaviour

15.18 The most common reasons for needing to consider such interventions are:

- physical assault;

- dangerous, threatening or destructive behaviour;

- self-harm or risk of physical injury by accident;

- extreme and prolonged over-activity that is likely to lead to physical exhaustion; and

- attempts to abscond (where the patient is detained under the Act).

15.19 The method chosen must balance the risk to others with the risk to the patient's own health and safety and must be a reasonable, proportionate and justifiable response to the risk posed by the patient.

15.20 The purposes of interventions where de-escalation has failed are to:

- take immediate control of a dangerous situation;

- end or reduce significantly the danger to the patient or others around them; and

- contain or limit the patient's freedom for no longer than is necessary.

Policy on physical restraint

15.21 Hospitals' policies on the management of disturbed behaviour should include clear written policies on the use of restraint and physical interventions, and all relevant staff should be aware of the policies. The policies should include provisions for post-incident reviews.

15.22 Any physical restraint used should:

- be reasonable, justifiable and proportionate to the risk posed by the patient;

- be used for only as long as is absolutely necessary;

- involve a recognised technique that does not depend on the deliberate application of pain (the application of pain should be used only for the immediate relief or rescue of staff where nothing else will suffice); and

- be carried out by those who have received appropriate training in the use of restraint techniques.

15.23 Managing aggressive behaviour by using physical restraint should be done only as a last resort and never as a matter of course. It should be used in an emergency when there seems to be a real possibility that harm would occur if no intervention is made.

15.24 Any initial attempt to restrain aggressive behaviour should, as far as the situation allows, be non-physical – for example, assistance should be sought by the call system or by verbally summoning help. A single member of staff should assume control of the incident. The patient should be approached, where possible, and agreement sought to stop the behaviour. The special needs of patients with sensory impairments should be taken into consideration – approaches to deaf or hearing-impaired patients should be made within their visual field. Where possible, an explanation should be given to the patient of the consequences of refusing the request from staff to desist.

CHAPTER

15

Safe and
therapeutic
responses
to disturbed
behaviour

15.25 Verbal de-escalation should continue throughout the intervention, and negotiations with the patient to comply with requests to stop the behaviour should continue, where appropriate.

15.26 A member of staff should take the lead in caring for other patients and moving them away from the area of disturbance. Staff not involved in the use of physical restraint should leave the area quietly.

15.27 Throughout the period when physical restraint is being used:

- a doctor should be quickly available to attend an alert by staff members;

- staff should continue to employ de-escalation;

- staff should be alert to the risk of any respiratory or cardiac distress;

- emergency resuscitation devices should be readily available in the area where the restraint is taking place; and

- the patient's physical and psychological wellbeing should be monitored.

15.28 Where physical restraint is used staff should:

- record the decision and the reasons for it; and

- document and review every episode of physical restraint, which should include a detailed account of the restraint.

15.29 Hospitals should have in place a system of post-incident support and review which allows the organisation to learn from experience of using physical restraint and which caters for the needs of the patient who has been restrained, any other patients in the area where the restraint occurred, the staff involved in the incident, the restrained patient's carers and family (where appropriate) and any visitors who witnessed the incident.

15.30 After physical restraint has been used, staff should reassess the patient's care plan and help them reintegrate into the ward environment. They should also give the patient an opportunity to write their account of the episode, which will be filed in their notes.

Use of mechanical restraint

15.31 Mechanical restraint is not a first-line response or standard means of managing disturbed or violent behaviour in acute mental health settings. Its use should be exceptional. If any forms of mechanical restraint are to be employed a clear policy should be in place governing their use. Restraint which involves tying (whether by means of tape or by using a part of the patient's garments) to some part of a building or its fixtures should never be used.

Restraint in order to administer medication

15.32 Restraint is also used in order to administer medication (or other forms of treatment) to an unwilling patient, where there is legal authority to treat the patient without consent. It should not be used unless there is such legal authority (whether under the Mental Health Act, the Mental Capacity Act 2005 (MCA) or otherwise). In particular, restraint may not be used to treat an informal patient who has the capacity to refuse treatment and who has done so.

CHAPTER

15

Safe and
therapeutic
responses
to disturbed
behaviour

15.33 The use of restraint to administer treatment in non-emergency circumstances should be avoided wherever possible, but may sometimes be necessary, especially if not administering the treatment would increase the likelihood of an emergency situation occurring. The decision to use restraint should first be discussed with the clinical team and should be properly documented in the patient's notes, along with the justification for it.

Restraint as an indicator of the need for detention under the Act

15.34 If a patient is not detained, but restraint in any form has been deemed necessary (whether as an emergency or as part of the patient's treatment plan), consideration should be given to whether formal detention under the Act is appropriate (subject to the criteria being met).

15.35 Where a patient is deprived of liberty in a hospital for mental health treatment under the deprivation of liberty safeguards in the MCA,[1] the use of restraint may well indicate that the patient objects to treatment or to being in hospital and is therefore no longer eligible to be held under those safeguards. If so, consideration will need to be given to whether the patient can and should be detained under the Mental Health Act instead.

Training

15.36 All hospitals should have a policy on training of staff who work in areas where they may be exposed to aggression or violence, or who may need to become involved in the restraint of patients. The policy should specify who will receive what level of training (based on training needs analysis), how often they will be trained and the techniques in which they will be trained. The training should be delivered during the induction period of new staff members or as soon as is practicably possible thereafter.

---

[1]The deprivation of liberty safeguards are expected to be in force from April 2009.

15.37 All staff who practise physical intervention in the management of disturbed behaviour should also be competent in physical monitoring and emergency resuscitation techniques to ensure the safety of patients following administration of rapid tranquillisation and during periods of restraint or seclusion.

15.38 All clinical staff who undertake training in the recognition, prevention and management of violence and aggression and associated physical skills training (formerly known as control and restraint training) should attend periodic refresher or update education and training programmes.

15.39 Training should be specifically designed for healthcare settings.

Observation

15.40 Increased levels of observation may be used both for the short-term management of disturbed behaviour and to prevent suicide or serious self-harm.

15.41 Staff must balance the potentially distressing effects on the patient of increased levels of observation, particularly if these levels of observation are proposed for many hours or days, against the identified risk of self-injury. Levels of observation and risk should be regularly reviewed and a record made of agreed decisions in relation to increasing or decreasing the observation.

15.42 All hospitals should have clear written policies on the use of observation.

Seclusion

15.43 Seclusion is the supervised confinement of a patient in a room, which may be locked. Its sole aim is to contain severely disturbed behaviour which is likely to cause harm to others.

15.44 Alternative terminology such as "therapeutic isolation", "single-person wards" and "enforced segregation" should not be used to deprive patients of the safeguards

CHAPTER

15

Safe and
therapeutic
responses
to disturbed
behaviour

established for the use of seclusion. All episodes which meet the definition in the previous paragraph must be treated as seclusion, regardless of the terminology used.

15.45 Seclusion should be used only as a last resort and for the shortest possible time. Seclusion should not be used as a punishment or a threat, or because of a shortage of staff. It should not form part of a treatment programme. Seclusion should never be used solely as a means of managing self-harming behaviour. Where the patient poses a risk of self-harm as well as harm to others, seclusion should be used only when the professionals involved are satisfied that the need to protect other people outweighs any increased risk to the patient's health or safety and that any such risk can be properly managed.

15.46 Seclusion of an informal patient should be taken as an indication of the need to consider formal detention.

15.47 Hospital policies should include clear written guidelines on the use of seclusion. Guidelines should:

- ensure the safety and wellbeing of the patient;

- ensure that the patient receives the care and support rendered necessary by their seclusion both during and after it has taken place;

- distinguish between seclusion and psychological behaviour therapy interventions (such as "time out");

- specify a suitable environment that takes account of the patient's dignity and physical wellbeing;

- set out the roles and responsibilities of staff; and

- set requirements for recording, monitoring and reviewing the use of seclusion and any follow-up action.

Procedure for seclusion

15.48 Local policies should set out the procedures for starting and reviewing seclusion.

15.49 The decision to use seclusion can be made in the first instance by a doctor, a suitably qualified approved clinician or the professional in charge of the ward. Where the professional in charge of the ward takes the decision, the patient's responsible clinician or the duty doctor (or equivalent) should be notified at once and should attend immediately unless the seclusion is only for a very brief period. It is for hospitals to determine which of their non-medical approved clinicians are suitably qualified to fulfil functions in relation to seclusion.

15.50 An initial multi-disciplinary review of the need for seclusion should be carried out as soon as practicable after the seclusion begins. If it is concluded that seclusion needs to continue, the review should establish the individual care needs of the patient while they are in seclusion and the steps that should be taken in order to bring the need for seclusion to an end as quickly as possible.

15.51 Unless the initial multi-disciplinary review concludes that different arrangements are appropriate, the need to continue seclusion should be reviewed:

- every two hours by two nurses or other suitably skilled professionals (one of whom was not involved directly in the decision to seclude); and

- every four hours by a doctor or a suitably qualified approved clinician.

15.52 However, local policies may allow different review arrangements to be applied during the night when patients in seclusion are asleep.

15.53 If the review concludes that seclusion is no longer necessary, it should be ended.

CHAPTER

15

Safe and
therapeutic
responses
to disturbed
behaviour

15.54 If the patient is secluded for more than:

- 8 hours consecutively; or

- 12 hours over a period of 48 hours,

a multi-disciplinary review should be completed by a senior doctor or suitably qualified approved clinician, and nurses and other professionals who were not involved in the incident which led to the seclusion. Where an independent multi-disciplinary review takes place it is good practice for those involved in the original decision to be consulted in the review.

15.55 A suitably skilled professional should be readily available within sight and sound of the seclusion room at all times throughout the period of the patient's seclusion.

15.56 The aim of this observation is to monitor the condition and behaviour of the patient and to identify the time at which seclusion can be ended. The level of observation should be decided on an individual basis. A documented report must be made at least every 15 minutes.

15.57 For patients who have received sedation a skilled professional will need to be outside the door at all times with adequate call facilities available to them.

15.58 Any professional taking over responsibility for observing a patient in seclusion should have a full handover, including details of the incident that resulted in the need for seclusion and subsequent reviews.

15.59 If the need for seclusion is disputed by any member of the multi-disciplinary team, the local policy should set out arrangements for the matter to be referred to a senior manager or clinician.

Conditions of seclusion

15.60 The room used for seclusion should:

- provide privacy from other patients, but enable staff to observe the patient at all times;

- be safe and secure and should not contain anything which could cause harm to the patient or others;

- be adequately furnished, heated, lit and ventilated; and

- be quiet but not soundproofed and should have some means of calling for attention (operation of which should be explained to the patient).

15.61 Staff may decide what a patient may take into the seclusion room, but the patient should always be clothed.

Record keeping

15.62 Detailed and contemporaneous records should be kept in the patient's case notes of any use of seclusion, the reasons for its use, and subsequent activity. Records should also be kept in a special seclusion recording system which should contain a step-by-step account of the seclusion procedure in every instance. Responsibility for the accuracy and completeness of these records should lie with the professional in charge of the ward. Local policies should require the records of each episode of seclusion to be reviewed by a more senior professional.

Longer-term segregation

15.63 There is a very small number of patients who are not responsive to short-term management of their aggression and violence and who could be described as "long-term dangerous". By this it is meant that they present a risk to others which is a constant feature of their presentation and is not subject to amelioration by a short period of seclusion combined with any other form of treatment. The clinical judgement in these cases is that, if the patient were allowed to mix freely in the general ward environment, other patients or staff would continuously be open to the potential of serious injury or harm.

15.64 It is permissible to manage this small number of patients by ensuring that their contact with the general ward population is strictly limited. When not locked in a room on their own (which can be their own bedroom rather than a seclusion room), they may be accompanied by staff at all times.

CHAPTER

15

Safe and
therapeutic
responses
to disturbed
behaviour

15.65 In these cases, the way that the patient's situation is reviewed needs to reflect the specific nature of their management plan. The purpose of a review is to determine whether the patient has settled sufficiently to return to the ward community and to check on their general health and welfare. The decision to return the patient to the general community will be taken by their multi-disciplinary team, following a thorough risk assessment and observations from staff of the patient's presentation during close monitoring of the patient in the company of others.

15.66 Hospitals proposing to allow longer-term segregation should have a policy in place that sets out when it is to be used and how it is to be kept under review. Policies should provide for the use of long-term segregation to be subject to periodic review by a senior clinician who is not involved with the case. The outcome of each review (whether internal or external) and the reasons for continued segregation should be recorded.

Deprivation of daytime clothing

15.67 Patients should never be deprived of appropriate daytime clothing during the day with the intention of restricting their freedom of movement. They should not be deprived of other aids necessary for their daily living.

Related material

- *Violence: The Short-term Management of Disturbed/Violent Behaviour in Psychiatric In-patient Settings and Emergency Departments,* National Institute for Clinical Excellence clinical guideline 25, 2005

- *Promoting Safer and Therapeutic Services – Implementing the National Syllabus in Mental Health and Learning Disability Services –* The NHS security management service October 2005

This material does not form part of the Code. It is provided for assistance only.

APPLYING THE PRINCIPLES

This scenario is not intended to provide a template for decisions in applying the principles in similar situations. The scenario itself is only illustrative and does not form part of the Code itself.

SAFE AND THERAPEUTIC MANAGEMENT OF PATIENTS

Abby is a 34 year old woman; she has been in hospital for ten days following her admission under section 2. Abby has been very distressed on the ward and has been verbally aggressive and threatening towards other patients and staff. The ward is very busy and staff are aware that Abby finds the environment difficult to cope with; they have tried to engage with Abby about ways in which they can support her on the ward and she has had several meetings with her primary nurse to discuss her care plan. Staff have also met with members of Abby's family including her husband and her mother. Abby's family are very concerned about her and visit every day.

Following an incident on the ward involving another patient, Abby's disturbed behaviour escalates; she becomes involved in a fight with another patient and tries to assault staff as they intervene in the incident. In order to prevent Abby from harming those around her and herself, Abby is restrained for a short period and placed in seclusion.

The ward staff need to decide whether Abby should remain in seclusion and how she should be looked after once out of seclusion. The ward staff apply the guiding principles of this Code, and among the things they might wish to consider in making a decision in these circumstances are the following.

CHAPTER

15

Safe and
therapeutic
responses
to disturbed
behaviour

Purpose principle

- What factors need to be considered in managing Abby's safety and wellbeing?

- To what extent is protecting other people an issue? How can other patients and staff be protected? What might be the best course of action for that?

- Can any risk presented by Abby only be managed by continuing to seclude Abby?

- Have any physical health factors been considered?

Least restriction principle

- What are the possible alternatives to the continued use of seclusion?

  - Increased levels of observation?

  - Giving Abby a chance to talk with someone at length?

  - Getting Abby and the patient with whom she had the fight to have a supervised talk?

Respect principle

- Does Abby have any views about why the incident occurred?

- Is Abby feeling particularly vulnerable, upset or excluded for some reason?

- Has anyone asked her why she is so distressed?

- Are there any cultural or gender matters that are prohibiting Abby from engaging with her team, eg would Abby prefer to discuss her care with a female nurse? Or are there any cultural issues that are prohibiting Abby from engaging with other patients, eg language barriers? Does Abby have the opportunity to attend a prayer room?

- Has Abby expressed any views, either now or previously, on what she would like to happen if she loses her temper or becomes aggressive?

- If a similar incident has occurred in the past, does Abby have any views about what has worked to help manage the situation and what has not and why not?

Participation principle

- Is Abby calm enough now to talk about what might happen next?

- What is the best way of discussing with Abby the need for seclusion, the process for reviewing its use and consideration of what might happen next?

- Can Abby give her interpretation of why she became so distressed?

- Has Abby been given an opportunity to talk to someone about her concerns?

- Have Abby's family expressed any views about what they think may help? What have her family said when they have visited?

Effectiveness, efficiency and equity principle

- Is there some way of reorganising things so that staff can spend more time with Abby without taking staff away from other patients' needs?

CHAPTER 16
Privacy and safety

16.1   This chapter deals with privacy and safety in hospitals
        where patients are detained under the Act, including access
        to telephones and other equipment and the use of searches.

Respect for privacy

16.2   Article 8 of the European Convention on Human Rights
        requires public authorities to respect a person's right to a
        private life. This includes people detained under the Act.
        Privacy and safety are therefore important constituents of
        the therapeutic environment. Hospital staff should make
        conscious efforts to respect the privacy of patients while
        maintaining safety. This encompasses the circumstances in
        which patients may meet or communicate with people of
        their choosing in private and the protection of their
        private property.

Private telephone calls and e-mail and internet access

16.3   Hospitals should make every effort to support the patient
        in making and maintaining contact with family and friends
        by telephone and to enable such calls to be made with
        appropriate privacy. Most wards contain coin-operated
        and card-operated telephones. Hospital managers should
        ensure that patients can use them without being overheard.
        Installing booths or hoods around them may help to
        provide the necessary level of privacy.

16.4   The principle that should underpin hospital or ward
        policies on all telephone use is that detained patients
        are not, of course, free to leave the premises and that
        individual freedom to communicate with family and
        friends should therefore be maintained as far as is
        possible. Any restrictions imposed should be the minimum
        necessary, so as to ensure that this principle is adhered to.

16.5 Hospital managers should have a policy on the possession and use of mobile phones by patients and their visitors.

16.6 When drawing up their policy on the use of mobile phones, hospital managers should bear in mind the following points:

- given that mobile phones provide a readily available means of communication with family and friends and are in widespread use, most detained patients are likely to have one. It is unlikely to be appropriate to impose a blanket ban on their use except in units specifically designed to provide enhanced levels of security in order to protect the public;

- different considerations will apply to different locations within the hospital. There may be valid reasons for banning or limiting the use of mobile phones in some parts of the premises to which detained patients have access, for example because of a perceived risk of interference with medical and other electronic equipment which could adversely affect the health of patients or because of intrusion into the lives of other patients or individuals in the community;

- it is necessary to recognise that each patient has a right to expect a peaceful environment, and that constant interruptions from ringing telephones have a potentially anti-therapeutic effect;

- it may be reasonable to require mobile phones to be switched off except where their use is permitted and to restrict their use to designated areas to which detained patients have access;

- many mobile phones have cameras and give access to the internet. This creates potential for the violation of the privacy and dignity of other patients, staff and visitors to the ward, and may constitute a security risk. It would therefore be appropriate to stipulate the circumstances in which photographs and videos can be taken, for example only with specific permission from hospital staff;

- the difficulty in identifying when camera functions are being used may be an additional reason for restricting the areas in which mobile phones may be used;

- it is important to ensure that the hospital's policy on the use of mobile phones can be enforced effectively. For example, it may be appropriate in certain circumstances to confiscate phones from patients who consistently refuse to comply with the rules;

- any decision to prevent the use of cameras or to confiscate a mobile phone should be fully documented and be subject to periodic review;

- there should be rules on when staff and visitors can bring mobile phones into a secure setting;

- the normal rules governing the use of the hospital's power supply to charge mobile phones or other such electrical devices may need to be varied for detained patients (given the restrictions with which such patients are faced);

- staff need to be fully informed of the hospital's policy, and steps must be taken to communicate it to all patients and visitors; and

- the policy will need to be reviewed regularly and updated, where necessary, in the light of experience.

16.7 Managers should also have guidance on patients' access to e-mail and internet facilities by means of the hospital's IT infrastructure. This guidance should cover the availability of such facilities and rules prohibiting access to illegal or what would otherwise be considered inappropriate material.

Private property

16.8 Hospitals should provide adequate lockable facilities (with staff override) for the storage of the clothing and other personal possessions which patients may keep with them on the ward and for the secure central storage of items of value or which may pose a risk to the patient or to others, eg razors. Information about arrangements for storage should be easily accessible to patients on the ward. Hospitals should compile an inventory of what has been allowed and stored and give a copy to the patient. The inventory should be updated when necessary.

Separate facilities for men and women

16.9 All sleeping areas (bedrooms and bed bays) must be segregated, and members of one sex should not have to walk through an area occupied by the other sex to reach toilets or bathrooms. Separate male- and female-only toilets and bathrooms must be provided, as should separate day rooms. If in an emergency it is necessary to treat a patient in an environment intended for the opposite sex, senior management should be informed, steps should be taken to rectify the situation as soon as possible, and staff should protect the patient's privacy against intrusions – particularly in sleeping accommodation, toilets and bathrooms. Consideration should be given to the particular needs of transgender patients.

Personal and other searches

16.10 Hospital managers should ensure that there is an operational policy on searching patients detained under the Act, their belongings and surroundings and their visitors. When preparing the policy, hospital managers should consider the position of informal patients.

16.11 The policy should be based on the following clear principles:

- the intention is to create and maintain a therapeutic environment in which treatment may take place and to ensure the security of the premises and the safety of patients, staff and the public;

- the authority to conduct a search of a person or their property is controlled by law, and it is important that hospital staff are aware of whether they have legal authority to carry out any such search;

- searching should be proportionate to the identified risk
  and should involve the minimum possible intrusion into
  the person's privacy; and

- all searches will be undertaken with due regard to and
  respect for the person's dignity.

16.12 The policy may extend to the routine and random searching
without cause of detained patients, if necessary without
their consent, but only in exceptional circumstances.
For example, such searches may be necessary if the
patients detained in a particular unit tend to have
dangerous or violent propensities which create a self-
evident pressing need for additional security.

16.13 Patients, staff and visitors should be informed that there is
a policy on searching. Information about searches should
be provided in a variety of formats to meet patients' and
visitors' needs and should be readily available.

Conducting personal and other searches

16.14 The consent of the person should always be sought
before a personal search or a search of their possessions
is attempted. If consent is given, the search should be
carried out with regard to the dignity of the individual
and the need to ensure maximum privacy.

16.15 Consent obtained by means of a threat, intimidation
or inducement is likely to render the search illegal.
Any person who is to be searched personally or whose
possessions are to be searched must be informed that
they do not have to consent.

16.16 A person being searched or whose possessions are the
subject of a search should be kept informed of what is
happening and why. If they do not understand or are not
fluent in English, the services of an interpreter should be
sought, if practicable. The specific needs of people with
impaired hearing or a learning disability, and those of
children and young people, should be considered.

16.17 A personal search should be carried out by a member of the same sex, unless necessity dictates otherwise. The search should be carried out in a way that maintains the person's privacy and dignity and respects issues of gender, culture and faith. It is always advisable to have another member of the hospital staff present during a search if it is not possible to conduct a same-sex search.

16.18 A comprehensive record of every search, including the reasons for it and details of any consequent risk assessment, should be made.

16.19 Staff involved in undertaking searches should receive appropriate instruction and refresher training.

16.20 In certain circumstances, it may be necessary to search a detained patient or their possessions without their consent.

16.21 If a detained patient refuses consent, their responsible clinician (or, failing that, another senior clinician with knowledge of the patient's case) should be contacted without delay, if practicable, so that any clinical objection to searching by force may be raised. The patient should be kept separated and under close observation, while being informed of what is happening and why, in terms appropriate to their understanding. Searches should not be delayed if there is reason to think that the person is in possession of anything that may pose an immediate risk to their own safety or that of anyone else.

16.22 If a search is considered necessary, despite the patient's objections, and there is no clinical objection to one being conducted, the search should be carried out. If force has to be used, it should be the minimum necessary.

16.23 The policy should set out the steps to be taken to resolve any disagreement or dispute where there is a clinical objection to a search.

16.24 Where a patient physically resists being personally searched, physical intervention should normally only proceed on the basis of a multi-disciplinary assessment, unless it is urgently required. A post-incident review should follow every search undertaken where consent has been withheld.

16.25 There should be support for patients and staff who are affected by the process of searching. This may be particularly necessary where a personal search has had to proceed without consent or has involved physical intervention.

16.26 Where a patient's belongings are removed during a search, the patient should be given a receipt for them and told where the items will be stored.

16.27 The exercise of powers of search should be audited regularly and the outcomes reported to the hospital managers.

Hospital accommodation offering conditions of enhanced security

16.28 There are some detained patients who may be liable to present a particular danger to themselves or to others and who therefore need to be accommodated in wards or units specifically designed to offer enhanced levels of physical security. For patients detained under Part 3 of the Act, this may be a requirement of a court or of the Secretary of State for Justice, but in many cases the decision will lie primarily with the patient's responsible clinician.

16.29 When considering whether patients should be placed in, be moved to or remain in such a ward or unit, responsible clinicians should, in consultation with the multi-disciplinary team, ensure that:

• they have carefully weighed the patient's individual circumstances and the degree of risk involved; and

• they have assessed the relative clinical implications of placing the patient in an environment with enhanced physical security, in addition to or as opposed to providing care by way of intensive staffing.

16.30 Treatment in conditions of enhanced security should last for the minimum period necessary. Where responsible clinicians have taken the decision to transfer a patient within a hospital to a ward with enhanced security, they should ensure that arrangements are made to facilitate the patient's prompt return to a less secure ward when that enhanced security is no longer required.

16.31 Where responsible clinicians believe that patients no longer require conditions of enhanced security (or the current level of security), they should take steps to arrange their transfer to more appropriate accommodation. Where necessary, this may involve identifying another hospital that is willing and able to offer the patient suitable accommodation.

16.32 In the case of restricted patients, it will be necessary to seek the consent of the Secretary of State for Justice for a transfer to another hospital or, where the patient's detention is restricted to a particular unit, for a move within the same hospital.

16.33 Managers of hospitals offering accommodation with enhanced levels of security should ensure that:

- accommodation specifically designated for this purpose has adequate staffing levels; and

- they have written guidelines, setting out the categories of patient for whom it is appropriate to use physically secure conditions and those for whom it is not appropriate.

Physical security in other hospital accommodation

16.34 Hospital managers will need to consider what arrangements should be put in place to ensure the safety of patients who are not subject to enhanced security.

16.35 Patients admitted to acute wards, whether or not they are formally detained there, will have complex and specific needs. In such an environment, ward staff must balance competing priorities and interests when determining what safety measures are necessary.

16.36 The intention should be to protect patients, in particular those who are at risk of suicide, self-harm, accidents or inflicting harm on others unless they are prevented from leaving the ward. Arrangements should also aim not to impose any unnecessary or disproportionate restrictions on patients or to make them feel as though they are subject to such restrictions. It may also be necessary to have in place arrangements for protecting patients and others from people whose mere presence on a ward may pose a risk to their health or safety.

16.37 It should be borne in mind that the nature of engagement with patients and of therapeutic interventions, and the structure and quality of life on the ward, are important factors in encouraging patients to remain in the ward and in minimising a culture of containment.

16.38 Locking doors, placing staff on reception to control entry to particular areas, and the use of electronic swipe cards, electronic key fobs and other technological innovations of this sort are all methods that hospitals should consider to manage entry to and exit from clinical areas to ensure the safety of their patients and others.

16.39 If hospitals are to manage entry to and exit from the ward effectively, they will need to have a policy for doing so. A written policy that sets out precisely what the ward arrangements are and how patients can exit from the ward, if they are legally free to leave and made available to all patients on the ward. The policy should be explained to patients on admission and to their visitors. In addition to producing the policy in English, hospitals may need to consider translating it into other languages if these are in common use in the local area.

16.40 If managing entry and exit by means of locked external doors (or other physical barriers) is considered to be an appropriate way to maintain safety, the practice adopted must be reviewed regularly to ensure that there are clear benefits for patients and that it is not being used for the convenience of staff. It should never be necessary to lock patients and others in wards simply because of inadequate staffing levels. In conjunction with clinical staff, managers should regularly review and evaluate the mix of patients (there may, for example, be some patients who ought to be in a more secure environment), staffing levels and the skills mix and training needs of staff.

Related material

- *Using Mobile Phones in NHS Hospitals,* May 2007

- The Safety and Security in Ashworth, Broadmoor and Rampton Hospitals Directions, 2000 (as amended)

This material does not form part of the Code. It is provided for assistance only.

CHAPTER 17
Wishes expressed in advance

17.1   This chapter gives guidance on statements by patients who are subject to compulsory measures under the Act about their preferences for what they would or would not like to happen if particular situations arise in future. This includes legally binding advance decisions to refuse treatment.

Definitions

17.2   This chapter distinguishes between advance decisions to refuse medical treatment and other statements of views, wishes and feelings that patients make in advance.

17.3   An advance decision means a decision to refuse specified medical treatment made in advance by a person who has the mental capacity to do so. Advance decisions are a way in which people can refuse medical treatment for a time in the future when they may lack the capacity to consent to or refuse that treatment.

17.4   Advance decisions are concerned only with refusal of medical treatment. Other advance expressions of views, wishes and feelings may be about medical treatment or about any other aspect of a patient's care, and may be about what the patient wants to happen as much as about what they would prefer not to happen.

Advance decisions under the Mental Capacity Act

17.5   The Mental Capacity Act 2005 (MCA) says that people who have the capacity to do so, and who are at least 18 years old, may make an advance decision to refuse specified treatment which will have effect at a time when they no longer have capacity to refuse or consent to treatment. If a valid and applicable advance decision exists, it has the same effect as if the patient has capacity and makes a contemporaneous decision to refuse treatment.

141

17.6   Sometimes, the fact that a patient has made an advance decision refusing treatment for mental disorder will be one of the reasons why a decision is taken to detain them under the Mental Health Act. That may be the only way to ensure they get the treatment they need.

17.7   In certain circumstances, described in **chapter 24**, the Mental Health Act allows patients to be given medical treatment for their mental disorder without their consent and therefore even though they have made a valid and applicable advance decision to refuse the treatment. This only applies to patients who are detained under the Act and to patients on supervised community treatment (SCT). Furthermore, except in emergencies, it only applies to SCT patients if they have been recalled to hospital by their responsible clinician.

17.8   Even where clinicians may lawfully treat a patient compulsorily under the Mental Health Act, they should, where practicable, try to comply with the patient's wishes as expressed in an advance decision. They should, for example, consider whether it is possible to use a different form of treatment not refused by the advance decision.

17.9   Except where the Mental Health Act means that they need not, clinicians must follow all other advance decisions made by their patients which they are satisfied are valid and applicable, even if the patients concerned are detained under the Act or are on SCT. By definition, this includes all valid and applicable advance decisions made by detained and SCT patients to refuse treatment which is not for mental disorder.

17.10   Clinicians should always start from the assumption that a person had the mental capacity at the time in question to make the advance decision. However, if a clinician is not satisfied that the person had capacity at the time they made the advance decision, or if there are genuine doubts about its validity or applicability, they can treat the person without fear of liability, so long as they comply with the other requirements of the MCA, including the requirement to act in the patient's best interests.

17.11 For more information on what constitutes an advance
decision, the effect they have and when they are valid
and applicable (including specific additional requirements
about the way advance decisions to refuse life-sustaining
treatment must be documented), please refer to the Code
of Practice to the MCA.

Advance statements of wishes and feelings

17.12 There may be times when, because of their mental disorder,
patients who are subject to compulsory measures under
the Mental Health Act are unable or unwilling to express
their views or participate as fully as they otherwise would
in decisions about their care or treatment under the Act.
In such cases, patients' past wishes and feelings – so far
as they are known – take on a greater significance.

17.13 Some patients will deliberately state their wishes in
advance about a variety of issues, including their medical
treatment, the steps that should be taken in emergencies
and what should be done if particular situations occur.
Such wishes should be given the same consideration as
wishes expressed at any other time.

17.14 Encouraging patients to set out their wishes in advance will
often be a helpful therapeutic tool, promoting collaboration
and trust between patients and professionals. It is also a way
in which effective use can be made of patients' expertise
in the management of crises in their own conditions.

17.15 Whenever expressing a preference for their future
treatment and care, patients should be encouraged to
identify as precisely as possible the circumstances they
have in mind. If they are saying that there are certain
things that they do not want to happen – for example,
being given a particular type of treatment, or being
restrained in a particular way – they should be encouraged
also to give their views on what should be done instead.

17.16 Patients should, however, be made aware that expressing
their preference for a particular form of treatment or care
in advance like this does not legally compel professionals
to meet that preference.

17.17 Where patients express views to any of the professionals involved in their care about how they should be treated or about ways they would not wish to be treated in future, the professional should record those views in the patient's notes. If the views are provided in a written form, they should be kept with the patient's notes.

17.18 Whether the patient or the professional records the patient's views, steps should be taken, unless the patient objects, to ensure that the information:

- is drawn to the attention of other professionals who ought to know about it; and

- is included in care plans and other documentation which will help ensure that the patient's views are remembered and considered in situations where they are relevant in future.

17.19 Advance decisions to refuse treatment should also be recorded and documented in the same way.

17.20 If the professional to whom the wish is being expressed forms the opinion that the patient lacks capacity to understand the wish they are expressing, the professional should record their opinion, and their reasons for it, alongside the record of the patient's wish.

17.21 The fact that a patient has expressed their wishes about a particular matter in the past is not a substitute for seeking their views on it when the situation actually arises, even if they are no longer in a position to think about their views as clearly as they did when they expressed their wishes previously. Everyone has the right to change their mind. In particular, where patients have the mental capacity to express a clear wish in the present, that wish should always be assumed to have overtaken their previous wishes, even if it is significantly different.

17.22 Where patients lack the capacity to formulate and express their views on an issue on which they have given their views in advance, the professionals should record whether they make a decision under the Mental Health Act which is contrary to those previously expressed views. They should also record their reasons for the decision, just as they would if they were going against wishes that a patient was expressing in the present.

Related material

- Mental Capacity Act 2005
- *Mental Capacity Act 2005 Code of Practice*, TSO, 2007

  This material does not form part of the Code. It is provided for assistance only.

CHAPTER 18 Confidentiality and information sharing

18.1   This chapter deals with issues about confidentiality and information sharing which arise in connection with the Act.

General points

18.2   Except where the Act itself says otherwise, the law on confidentiality is the same for patients subject to the Act as it is for any other patients. The box below gives a brief summary of the most fundamental points of the general law. There are some additional considerations in relation to children and young people (see **chapter 36**).

Confidentiality – a brief summary

In common law, a duty of confidence arises when one person discloses information to another in circumstances where it is reasonable to expect that the information will be held in confidence. Certain situations, such as discussions with a health professional or social worker, are generally presumed to be confidential.

However, there are circumstances in which it is both justifiable and important to share otherwise confidential patient information with people outside the immediate team treating a patient.

Before considering such disclosure of confidential patient information, the individual's consent should normally be sought.

If a person lacks the capacity to consent to the disclosure, it may nonetheless be acceptable and appropriate to disclose the information in the person's best interests.

Otherwise, confidential patient information should be disclosed outside the team only:

• with the person's consent (where the person has capacity to consent);

- if there is a specific legal obligation or authority to do so; or

- where there is an overriding public interest in disclosing the information.

The "public interest" is not the same as what might be of interest to the public. Where confidential patient information is involved, public interest justifications for overriding confidentiality could include (but are not limited to) protecting other people from serious harm and preventing serious crime.

The common law does not normally permit disclosure of confidential patient information solely in the person's own interests, where they have capacity to consent to the disclosure but refuse to do so.

A person's right to have their privacy respected is also protected by Article 8 of the European Convention on Human Rights. The disclosure of confidential information may be a breach of that right unless it is a necessary and proportionate response to the situation.

18.3   Information sharing between professionals can contribute to the care and treatment of patients and help to protect people from harm. This includes information sharing as part of the Care Programme Approach (or its equivalent).

18.4   A range of public services is involved in the provision of services to patients who are subject to compulsory measures under the Act, including housing and social services. Patients must be consulted about what information it may be helpful to share with these services and when. Professionals should be clear about how the sharing of such information could benefit the patient or help to prevent serious harm to others and whether there are any potential negative consequences. Advocates and advice services can support patients in helping them decide what information should be shared.

18.5   Sharing information with carers and other people with a valid interest in the care and wellbeing of the patient can also contribute to and support their care and treatment. Where patients have capacity to agree and are willing to do so, carers and other people with a valid interest should be given information about the patient's progress to help them offer views about the patient's care. A patient's agreement to such disclosure must be freely given. In the case of patients detained under Part 3 of the Act, people with a valid interest may include victims and the families of victims (see **paragraphs 18.18-18.20**).

Disclosure of confidential patient information for the purposes of the Act

18.6   The Act creates a number of situations where confidential information about patients will need to be disclosed, even if the patient does not consent. These include:

- reports to the Tribunal when a patient's case is to be considered;

- reports to the Commission in relation to patients who have been treated on the basis of a certificate issued by a second opinion appointed doctor (SOAD); and

- reports to the Secretary of State for Justice on restricted patients.

18.7   The Act also gives certain people and bodies – including the Commission, SOADs and (in certain circumstances) independent mental health advocates[1] – the right to access records relating to patients.

18.8   In addition, where the Act allows steps to be taken in relation to patients without their consent, it is implicit that confidential patient information may be disclosed to the extent that it is necessary to take those steps. So, for example, confidential patient information may be shared to the extent that it is necessary for:

[1] Independent mental health advocacy services under the Act are expected to be introduced in April 2009.

- medical treatment which may be given without a patient's consent under the Act;

- safely and securely conveying a patient to hospital (or anywhere else) under the Act;

- finding and returning a patient who has absconded from legal custody or who is absent without leave; or

- transferring responsibility for a patient who is subject to the Act from one set of people to another (eg where a detained patient is to be transferred from one hospital to another, or where responsibility for a patient is to be transferred between England and another jurisdiction).

18.9 Even though information may be disclosed in these cases, it is still necessary for people proposing to disclose the information to assure themselves that it is necessary in the circumstances, that the aim of the disclosure cannot reasonably be achieved without it, and that any breach of the patient's confidentiality is a proportionate response given the purpose for which the disclosure is being considered. Care must also always be taken to ensure that any information disclosed is accurate.

Limitations on sharing information with carers, relatives and friends

18.10 Simply asking for information from carers, relatives, friends or other people about a patient without that patient's consent need not involve any breach of confidentiality, provided the person requesting the information does not reveal any personal confidential information about the patient which the carer, relative, friend or other person being asked would not legitimately know anyway.

18.11 Apart from information which must be given to nearest relatives, the Act does not create any exceptions to the general law about disclosing confidential patient information to carers, relatives or friends.

18.12 Carers, relatives and friends cannot be told a patient's particular diagnosis or be given any other confidential personal information about the patient unless the patient consents or there is another basis on which to disclose it in accordance with the law. But carers should always be offered information which may help them understand the nature of mental disorder generally, the ways it is treated and the operation of the Act.

18.13 Carers, relatives, friends and other people also have a right to expect that any personal information about themselves, or any information about the patient which they pass on to professionals in confidence, will be treated as confidential. Unless there is an overriding reason that makes it necessary and there is legal authority to do so, information they provide about patients should not be repeated to patients in a way that might reveal its source, unless the carer, relative, friend or other person was made aware that that could happen and has not objected to it.

Sharing information to manage risk

18.14 Although information may be disclosed only in line with the law, there is no reason in practice why patient confidentiality should make it impossible for professionals and agencies to share information needed to manage any serious risks which certain patients pose to other people.

18.15 Where the issue is the management of the risk of serious harm, the judgement required is normally a balance between the public interest in disclosure, including the need to prevent harm to others, and both the rights of the individual concerned and the public interest in maintaining trust in a confidential service.

18.16 Whether there is an overriding public interest in disclosing confidential patient information may vary according to the type of information. Even in cases where there is no overriding public interest in disclosing detailed clinical information about a patient's state of health, there may nonetheless be an overriding public interest in sharing

more limited information about the patient's current and
past status under the Act, if that will help ensure properly
informed risk management by the relevant authorities.

Recording disclosure without consent

18.17 Any decision to disclose confidential information about
patients – for any reason – should be fully documented.
The relevant facts should be recorded, along with the
reasons for the decision and the identity of all those
involved in the process of reaching it. Reasons should be
given by reference to the grounds on which the disclosure
is to be justified.

Information for victims of crimes

Sections 35-45
of the Domestic
Violence, Crime
and Victims
Act 2004

18.18 The victims of certain mentally disordered offenders
detained in hospital have rights under the Domestic
Violence, Crime and Victims Act 2004 (DVCV Act) to
make representations and receive information about that
patient's discharge.

18.19 In other circumstances, professionals should encourage
(but cannot require) mentally disordered offender patients
to agree to share information that will enable victims and
victims' families to be informed about their progress.
Among other benefits, disclosure of such information
can sometimes serve to reduce the danger of harmful
confrontations after a discharge of which victims were
unaware.

18.20 Professionals should be ready to discuss with patients the
benefits of enabling some information to be given by
professionals to victims, within the spirit of the Code of
Practice for Victims of Crime issued under the DVCV Act.

Related material

- *Public Sector Data Sharing: Guidance on the Law,* Ministry of Justice, November 2003
- *Confidentiality: NHS Code of Practice,* Department of Health, November 2003
- Domestic Violence, Crime and Victims Act 2004
- *The Code of Practice for Victims of Crime,* Office for Criminal Justice Reform, October 2005
- *Guidance for Clinicians – Duties to Victims under the Domestic Violence, Crime and Victims Act 2004,* Home Office Mental Health Unit, 2005[2]
- Mental Capacity Act 2005
- *Mental Capacity Act 2005 Code of Practice,* TSO, 2007
- Data Protection Act 1998
- Human Rights Act 1998

This material does not form part of the Code. It is provided for assistance only.

CHAPTER 19
Visiting patients in hospital

19.1   This chapter covers visiting patients in hospital and those circumstances where it may be necessary to consider the exclusion of visitors. The chapter also refers to particular considerations for child visitors.

Arrangements for visits to patients

19.2   All patients have the right to maintain contact with and be visited by anyone they wish to see, subject to carefully limited exceptions. The value of visits in maintaining links with family and community networks is recognised as a key element in a patient's care and treatment.

19.3   Visits should be encouraged and made as comfortable and easy as possible for the visitor and the patient. Reasonable and flexible visiting times, access to refreshment and pleasant surroundings will all contribute to a sense of respect for the patient's entitlement to be visited.

19.4   In addition to visits, every effort should be made to assist the patient, where appropriate, to maintain contact with relatives, friends and advocates in other ways. In particular, patients should have readily accessible and appropriate daytime telephone facilities (see **chapter 16**).

People with a right to visit patients

19.5   The Act gives certain people the right to visit patients in private if they wish. This includes second opinion appointed doctors (SOADs), independent doctors or approved clinicians appointed to examine the patient in relation to an application or reference to the Tribunal, people visiting on behalf of the Commission, and independent mental health advocates (IMHAs).[1]

19.6   Hospital managers must ensure that such visits can take place in private, if that is what the person concerned wants.

[1] Independent mental health advocacy services under the Act are expected to be introduced in April 2009.

19.7 If there are particular concerns for the security of the visitor, they should be discussed with the visitor with a view to agreeing suitable security arrangements.

19.8 Hospital managers should also ensure that patients can communicate with their legal representatives in private, and should facilitate visits by those representatives when they request them.

Exclusion or restriction of visitors

19.9 There are circumstances where hospital managers may restrict visitors, refuse them entry or require them to leave. Managers should have a policy on the circumstances in which visits to patients may be restricted, to which both clinical staff and patients may refer.

19.10 There are two principal grounds which could justify the restriction or exclusion of a visitor: clinical grounds and security grounds.

19.11 The decision to prohibit a visit by any person whom the patient has requested to visit or has agreed to see should be regarded as a serious interference with the rights of the patient. There may be circumstances when a visitor has to be excluded, but these instances should be exceptional and any decision should be taken only after other means to deal with the problem have been considered and (where appropriate) tried. Any such decision should be fully documented and include the reasons for the exclusion, and it should be made available for independent scrutiny by the Commission.

Restriction or exclusion on clinical grounds

19.12 From time to time, the patient's responsible clinician may decide, after assessment and discussion with the multi-disciplinary team, that some visits could be detrimental to the safety or wellbeing of the patient, the visitor, other patients, or staff on the ward. In these circumstances, the responsible clinician may make special arrangements for the visit, impose reasonable conditions or if necessary exclude the visitor. In any of these cases, the reasons for the restriction should be recorded and explained to the patient and the visitor, both orally and in writing (subject to the normal considerations of patient confidentiality).

Exclusion on security grounds

19.13 The behaviour of a particular visitor may be disruptive, or may have been disruptive in the past, to the degree that exclusion from the hospital is necessary as a last resort. Examples of such behaviour include:

- incitement to abscond;

- smuggling of illicit drugs or alcohol into the hospital or unit;

- transfer of potential weapons;

- unacceptable aggression; and

- attempts by members of the media to gain unauthorised access.

19.14 A decision to exclude a visitor on the grounds of their behaviour should be fully documented and explained to the patient orally and in writing. Where possible and appropriate, the reason for the decision should be communicated to the person being excluded (subject to the normal considerations of patient confidentiality and any overriding security concerns).

Monitoring by hospital managers

19.15 Hospital managers should regularly monitor the exclusion from the hospital of visitors to detained patients.

19.16 Restricting visitors to informal patients who lack capacity to decide whether to remain in hospital could amount to or contribute to a deprivation of liberty and may indicate that an authorisation under the deprivation of liberty safeguards[2] of the Mental Capacity Act 2005 may need to be sought.

[2] The deprivation of liberty safeguards are expected to be in force from April 2009.

Children and young people

19.17 All hospitals should have written policies and procedures regarding the arrangements for children and young people who visit patients in hospital and for visits to patients who are children or young people. Policies should be drawn up in consultation with local social services authorities and local safeguarding children boards.[3]

19.18 Local policies should ensure that the best interests and safety of the children and young people concerned are always considered and that visits by or to children and young people are not allowed if they are not in their best interests. However, within that overarching framework, hospitals should do all they can to facilitate the maintenance of children's and young people's contact with friends and family and offer privacy within which that can happen.

19.19 Information about visiting should be explained to children and young people in a way that they are able to understand. Environments that are friendly to children and young people should be provided where necessary.

19.20 Where a child or young person is being detained, it should not be assumed simply because of their age that they would welcome all visitors, and like adults their views should be sought.

[3]The Secretary of State for Health has issued directions which set out more detailed restrictions on visits by children to patients in high security psychiatric hospitals.

CHAPTER 20 Independent mental health advocates

20.1 This chapter explains the role of independent mental health advocates (IMHAs) under the Act.

Reference Guide chapter 34

Purpose of independent mental health advocacy services

20.2 Independent mental health advocacy services provide an additional safeguard for patients who are subject to the Act. IMHAs are specialist advocates who are trained specifically to work within the framework of the Act to meet the needs of patients.[1]

20.3 Independent mental health advocacy services do not replace any other advocacy and support services that are available to patients, but are intended to operate in conjunction with those services.

Patients who are eligible for independent mental health advocacy services (qualifying patients)

Section 130C

20.4 Patients are eligible for support from an IMHA if they are:

- detained under the Act (even if they are currently on leave of absence from hospital);

- conditionally discharged restricted patients;

- subject to guardianship; or

- supervised community treatment (SCT) patients.

20.5 For these purposes, detention does not include being detained:

- on the basis of an emergency application (section 4) until the second medical recommendation is received (see **chapter 5**);

---

[1] Independent mental health advocacy services under the Act are expected to be introduced in April 2009.

- under the holding powers in section 5; or

- in a place of safety under section 135 or 136.

20.6   Other patients ("informal patients") are eligible if they are:

- being considered for a treatment to which section 57 applies ("a section 57 treatment"); or

- under 18 and being considered for electro-convulsive therapy or any other treatment to which section 58A applies ("a section 58A treatment").

20.7   The Act calls patients who are eligible for the support of an IMHA "qualifying patients".

Section 130B(1) and (2) The role of independent mental health advocates

20.8   The Act says that the support which IMHAs provide must include helping patients to obtain information about and understand the following:

- their rights under the Act;

- the rights which other people (eg nearest relatives) have in relation to them under the Act;

- the particular parts of the Act which apply to them (eg the basis on which they are detained) and which therefore make them eligible for advocacy;

- any conditions or restrictions to which they are subject (eg as a condition of leave of absence from hospital, as a condition of a community treatment order, or as a condition of conditional discharge);

- any medical treatment that they are receiving or might be given;

- the reasons for that treatment (or proposed treatment); and

- the legal authority for providing that treatment, and the safeguards and other requirements of the Act which would apply to that treatment.

20.9 It also includes helping patients to exercise their rights, which can include representing them and speaking on their behalf.

20.10 IMHAs may also support patients in a range of other ways to ensure they can participate in the decisions that are made about their care and treatment.

20.11 The involvement of an IMHA does not affect a patient's right (nor the right of their nearest relative) to seek advice from a lawyer. Nor does it affect any entitlement to legal aid.

Duty to inform patients about the availability of independent mental health advocacy services

Section 130D

20.12 Certain people have a duty to take whatever steps are practicable to ensure that patients understand that help is available to them from IMHA services and how they can obtain that help, as set out in the following table. This must include giving the relevant information both orally and in writing.

Duty to provide patients with information about advocacy services

Type of patient	Steps to be taken by	As soon as practicable after
Detained patient	The managers of the hospital in which the patient is liable to be detained	The patient becomes liable to be detained
Guardianship patient	The responsible local social services authority	The patient becomes subject to guardianship
SCT patient	The managers of the responsible hospital	The patient becomes an SCT patient
Conditionally discharged patient	The patient's responsible clinician	The patient is conditionally discharged
Informal patient	The doctor or approved clinician who first discusses with the patient the possibility of them being given the section 57 or 58A treatment in question	That discussion (or during it)

20.13 The relevant person must also take whatever steps are practicable to give a copy of the written information to the patient's nearest relative, unless the patient requests otherwise (and subject to the normal considerations about involving nearest relatives – see **paragraphs 2.27-2.33**).

20.14 However, any information about independent mental health advocacy services should make clear that the services are for patients and are not advocacy services for nearest relatives themselves.

20.15 The duty to give information to nearest relatives does not apply to informal patients, nor to patients detained in hospital under Part 3 of the Act (although it does apply to those patients if they subsequently become SCT patients).

Seeking help from an independent mental health advocate

20.16 A qualifying patient may request the support of an IMHA at any time after they become a qualifying patient. Patients have the right to access the independent mental health advocacy service itself, rather than the services of a particular IMHA, though where possible it would normally be good practice for the same IMHA to remain involved while the person's case stays open.

20.17 A patient may choose to end the support they are receiving from an IMHA at any time.

20.18 IMHAs must also comply with any reasonable request to visit and interview a qualifying patient, if the request is made by the patient's nearest relative, an approved mental health professional (AMHP) or the patient's responsible clinician (if they have one). But patients may refuse to be interviewed and do not have to accept help from an IMHA if they do not want it.

Section 130B(5)

20.19 AMHPs and responsible clinicians should consider requesting an IMHA to visit a qualifying patient if they think that the patient might benefit from an IMHA's visit but is unable or unlikely for whatever reason to request an IMHA's help themselves.

20.20 Before requesting an IMHA to visit a patient, they should, wherever practicable, first discuss the idea with the patient, and give the patient the opportunity to decide for themselves whether to request an IMHA's help. AMHPs and responsible clinicians should not request an IMHA to visit where they know, or strongly suspect, that the patient does not want an IMHA's help, or the help of the particular IMHA in question.

Independent mental health advocates' access to patients and professionals

20.21 Patients should have access to a telephone on which they can contact the independent mental health advocacy service and talk to them in private.

20.22 IMHAs should:

- have access to wards and units on which patients are resident;

- be able to meet with the patients they are helping in private, where they think it appropriate; and

- be able to attend meetings between patients and the professionals involved in their care and treatment when asked to do so by patients.

Section 130B(3) 20.23 When instructed by a patient, the nearest relative, an AMHP or the responsible clinician, an IMHA has the right to meet the patient in private. IMHAs also have a right to visit and speak to any person who is currently professionally concerned with a patient's medical treatment, provided it is for the purpose of supporting that patient in their capacity as an IMHA.

20.24 Professionals should remember that the normal rules on patient confidentiality apply to conversations with IMHAs, even when the conversation is at the patient's request. IMHAs have a right of access to patients' records in certain cases (described below), but otherwise professionals should be careful not to share confidential information with IMHAs, unless the patient has consented to the disclosure or the disclosure is justified on the normal grounds (see **chapter 18**).

Independent mental health advocates' access to patients' records

Section 130B(3) and (4)

20.25 Where the patient consents, IMHAs have a right to see any clinical or other records relating to the patient's detention or treatment in any hospital, or relating to any after-care services provided to the patient. IMHAs have a similar right to see any records relating to the patient held by a local social services authority.

20.26 Where the patient does not have the capacity (or in the case of a child, the competence) to consent to an IMHA having access to their records, the holder of the records must allow the IMHA access if they think that it is appropriate and that the records in question are relevant to the help to be provided by the IMHA.

20.27 When an IMHA seeks access to the records of a patient who does not have the capacity or the competence to consent, the person who holds the records should ask the IMHA to explain what information they think is relevant to the help they are providing to the patient and why they think it is appropriate for them to be able to see that information.

20.28 The Act does not define any further what it means by access being appropriate, so the record holder needs to consider all the facts of the case. But the starting point should always be what is best for the patient and not (for example) what would be most convenient for the organisation which holds the records.

20.29 In deciding whether it is appropriate to allow the IMHA access, the holder of the records needs to consider whether disclosure of the confidential patient information contained in the records is justified.

20.30 The key consideration will therefore be whether the disclosure is in the patient's best interests. That decision should be taken in accordance with the Mental Capacity Act 2005 (MCA) (or, for children under 16, the common law), like any other decision in connection with the care or treatment of patients who cannot make the decision for themselves.

20.31 Record holders should start from a general presumption that it is likely to be in-patients' interests to be represented by an IMHA who is knowledgeable about their case. But each decision must still be taken on its merits, and the record holder must, in particular, take into account what they know about the patient's wishes and feelings, including any written statements made in advance. (For further information on taking decisions in the best interests of people who lack capacity to make the decision themselves, please see the Code of Practice to the MCA.)

20.32 Records must not be disclosed if that would conflict with a decision made on the patient's behalf by the patient's attorney or deputy, or by the Court of Protection.

20.33 If the record holder thinks that disclosing the confidential patient information in the records to the IMHA would be in the patient's best interests, it is likely to be appropriate to allow the IMHA access to those records in all but the most exceptional cases.

Related material

- Mental Capacity Act 2005
- Mental Capacity Act 2005 Code of Practice, TSO, 2007

This material does not form part of the Code. It is provided for assistance only.

CHAPTER 21
Leave of absence

21.1   This chapter provides guidance on leave of absence for detained patients under section 17 of the Act. Reference Guide 12.39-12.56

General points

21.2   In general, while patients are detained in a hospital they can leave lawfully – even for a very short period – only if they are given leave of absence by their responsible clinician under section 17 of the Act.[1]

21.3   Responsible clinicians cannot grant leave of absence from hospital to patients who have been remanded to hospital under sections 35 or 36 of the Act or who are subject to interim hospital orders under section 38.

21.4   Except for certain restricted patients (see **paragraph 21.14**), no formal procedure is required to allow patients to move within a hospital or its grounds. Such "ground leave" within a hospital may be encouraged or, where necessary, restricted, as part of each patient's care plan.

21.5   What constitutes a particular hospital for the purpose of leave is a matter of fact which can be determined only in the light of the particular case. Where one building, or set of buildings, includes accommodation under the management of different bodies (eg two different NHS trusts), the accommodation used by each body should be treated as forming separate hospitals. Facilities and grounds shared by both can be regarded as part of both hospitals.

---

[1] Patients will also lawfully be absent from hospital if they are being transferred or taken to another place under the Act, or under another piece of legislation. This would include, for example, patients being transferred to another hospital under section 19 of the Act, or patients who are required to attend court.

Power to grant leave

21.6   Only the patient's responsible clinician can grant leave of absence to a patient detained under the Act. Responsible clinicians cannot delegate the decision to grant leave of absence to anyone else. In the absence of the usual responsible clinician (eg if they are on leave), permission can be granted only by the approved clinician who is for the time being acting as the patient's responsible clinician.

21.7   Responsible clinicians may grant leave for specific occasions or for specific or indefinite periods of time. They may make leave subject to any conditions which they consider necessary in the interests of the patient or for the protection of other people.

21.8   Leave of absence can be an important part of a detained patient's care plan, but can also be a time of risk. When considering and planning leave of absence, responsible clinicians should:

- consider the potential benefits and any risks to the patient's health and safety of granting or refusing leave;

- consider the potential benefits of granting leave for facilitating the patient's recovery;

- balance these benefits against any risks that the leave may pose in terms of the protection of other people (either generally or particular people);

- consider any conditions which should be attached to the leave, eg requiring the patient not to visit particular places or persons;

- be aware of any child protection and child welfare issues in granting leave;

- take account of the patient's wishes, and those of carers, friends and others who may be involved in any planned leave of absence;

- consider what support the patient would require during their leave of absence and whether it can be provided;

- ensure that any community services which will need to provide support for the patient during the leave are involved in the planning of the leave, and that they know the leave dates and times and any conditions placed on the patient during their leave;

- ensure that the patient is aware of any contingency plans put in place for their support, including what they should do if they think they need to return to hospital early; and

- (in the case of mentally disordered offender patients) consider whether there are any issues relating to victims which impact on whether leave should be granted and the conditions to which it should be subject.

21.9   When considering whether to grant leave of absence for more than seven consecutive days, or extending leave so that the total period is more than seven consecutive days, responsible clinicians must first consider whether the patient should go onto supervised community treatment (SCT) instead. This does not apply to restricted patients, nor, in practice, to patients detained for assessment under section 2 of the Act, as they are not eligible for SCT.

Section 17(2A)

21.10 The requirement to consider SCT does not mean that the responsible clinician cannot use longer-term leave if that is the more suitable option, but the responsible clinician will need to be able to show that both options have been duly considered. The decision, and the reasons for it, should be recorded in the patient's notes.

21.11 One use of leave for more than seven days may be to assess a patient's suitability for discharge from detention. Guidance on factors to be considered when deciding between leave of absence and SCT is given in **chapter 28**.

21.12 Hospital managers cannot overrule a responsible clinician's decision to grant leave. However, the fact that a responsible clinician grants leave subject to certain conditions, eg residence at a hostel, does not oblige the hospital managers or anyone else to arrange or fund the particular placement or services the clinician has in mind. Responsible clinicians should not grant leave on such a basis without first taking steps to establish that the necessary services or accommodation (or both) are available.

Restricted patients

Section 41(3) 21.13 Any proposal to grant leave to a restricted patient has to be approved by the Secretary of State for Justice, who should be given as much notice as possible and full details of the proposed leave.

21.14 Where the courts or the Secretary of State have decided that restricted patients are to be detained in a particular unit of a hospital, those patients require leave of absence to go to any other part of that hospital as well as outside the hospital.

21.15 Restricted patients are not eligible for SCT. The Secretary of State would normally consider any request for section 17 leave for a restricted patient to be in the community for more than a few consecutive nights as an application for conditional discharge.

Short-term leave

21.16 Subject to the agreement of the Secretary of State for Justice in the case of restricted patients, responsible clinicians may decide to authorise short-term local leave, which may be managed by other staff. For example, patients may be given leave for a shopping trip of two hours every week to a specific destination, with the decision on which particular two hours to be left to the discretion of the responsible nursing staff.

21.17 The parameters within which this discretion may be exercised must be clearly set out by the responsible clinician, eg the particular places to be visited, any restrictions on the time of day the leave can take place, and any circumstances in which the leave should not go ahead.

21.18 Responsible clinicians should regularly review any short-term leave they authorise on this basis and amend it as necessary.

Longer periods of leave

21.19 Longer-term leave should be planned properly and, where possible, well in advance. Patients should be fully involved in the decision and responsible clinicians should be satisfied that patients are likely to be able to manage outside the hospital. Subject to the normal considerations of patient confidentiality, carers and other relevant people should be consulted before leave is granted (especially where the patient is to reside with them). Relevant community services should also be consulted.

21.20 If patients do not consent to carers or other people who would normally be involved in their care being consulted about their leave, responsible clinicians should reconsider whether or not it is safe and appropriate to grant leave.

Recording leave

21.21 Hospital managers should establish a standardised system by which responsible clinicians can record the leave they authorise and specify the conditions attached to it. Copies of the authorisation should be given to the patient and to any carers, professionals and other people in the community who need to know. A copy should also be kept in the patient's notes. In case they fail to return from leave, an up-to-date description of the patient should be available in their notes.

21.22 The outcome of leave – whether or not it went well, particular problems encountered, concerns raised or benefits achieved – should also be recorded in patients' notes to inform future decision-making. Patients should be encouraged to contribute by giving their own views on their leave; some hospitals provide leave records specifically for this purpose.

Care and treatment while on leave

21.23 Responsible clinicians' responsibilities for their patients remain the same while the patients are on leave.

21.24 A patient who is granted leave under section 17 remains liable to be detained, and the rules in Part 4 of the Act about their medical treatment continue to apply (see **chapter 23**). If it becomes necessary to administer treatment without the patient's consent, consideration should be given to whether it would be more appropriate to recall the patient to hospital (see **paragraphs 21.31-21.34**), although recall is not a legal requirement.

21.25 The duty on local social services authorities and primary care trusts to provide after-care under section 117 of the Act for certain patients who have been discharged from detention also applies to those patients while they are on leave of absence (see **chapter 27**).

Section 17(3) ## Escorted leave

21.26 A responsible clinician may direct that their patient remains in custody while on leave of absence, either in the patient's own interests or for the protection of other people. Patients may be kept in the custody of any officer on the staff of the hospital or any person authorised in writing by the hospital managers. Such an arrangement is often useful, for example, to enable patients to participate in escorted trips or to have compassionate home leave.

21.27 While it may often be appropriate to authorise leave subject to the condition that a patient is accompanied by a friend or relative (eg on a pre-arranged day out from the hospital), responsible clinicians should specify that the patient is to be in the legal custody of a friend or relative only if it is appropriate for that person to be legally responsible for the patient, and if that person understands and accepts the consequent responsibility.

21.28 Escorted leave to Scotland, Northern Ireland or any of the Channel Islands can only be granted if the local legislation allows patients to be kept in custody while in that jurisdiction.[2]

[2]When this edition of the Code comes into force, it is expected that escorted leave to Scotland will be possible – but that is subject to the Scottish Parliament.

Leave to reside in other hospitals

21.29 Responsible clinicians may also require patients, as a condition of leave, to reside at another hospital in England or Wales, and they may then be kept in the custody of staff of that hospital. However, before authorising leave on this basis, responsible clinicians should consider whether it would be more appropriate to transfer the patient to the other hospital instead (see **chapter 30**).

21.30 Where a patient is granted leave of absence to another hospital, the responsible clinician at the first hospital should remain in overall charge of the patient's case. If it is thought that a clinician at the other hospital should become the responsible clinician, the patient should instead be transferred to that hospital. An approved clinician in charge of any particular aspect of the patient's treatment may be from either hospital. (For further guidance on allocating responsible clinicians see **chapter 14**.)

Recall from leave

21.31 A responsible clinician may revoke their patient's leave at any time if they consider it necessary in the interests of the patient's health or safety or for the protection of other people. Responsible clinicians must be satisfied that these criteria are met and should consider what effect being recalled may have on the patient. A refusal to take medication would not on its own be a reason for revocation, although it would almost always be a reason to consider revocation.

21.32 The responsible clinician must arrange for a notice in writing revoking the leave to be served on the patient or on the person who is for the time being in charge of the patient. Hospitals should always know the address of patients who are on leave of absence.

21.33 The reasons for recall should be fully explained to the patient and a record of the explanation included in the patient's notes. A restricted patient's leave may be revoked either by the responsible clinician or by the Secretary of State for Justice.

21.34 It is essential that carers (especially where the patient is residing with them while on leave) and professionals who support the patient while on leave should have easy access to the patient's responsible clinician if they feel consideration should be given to return of the patient before their leave is due to end.

Renewal of authority to detain

21.35 It is possible to renew a patient's detention while they are on leave if the criteria in section 20 of the Act are met (see **chapter 29**). But leave should not be used as an alternative to discharging the patient either completely or onto SCT where that is appropriate. **Chapter 28** gives further guidance on factors to consider when deciding between leave of absence and SCT.

Patients who are in hospital but not detained

21.36 Patients who are not legally detained in hospital have the right to leave at any time. They cannot be required to ask permission to do so, but may be asked to inform staff when they wish to leave the ward.

Related material

- *Guidance for Responsible Medical Officers – Leave of Absence for Patients Subject to Restrictions,* Ministry of Justice Mental Health Unit

This material does not form part of the Code. It is provided for assistance only.

CHAPTER 22
Absence without leave

22.1   This chapter gives guidance about action to be taken
        when patients are absent without leave (AWOL) or have
        otherwise absconded from legal custody under the Act.

General points

22.2   Under section 18 of the Act, patients are considered to be
        AWOL in various circumstances, in particular when they:

  • have left the hospital in which they are detained
    without their absence being agreed (under section 17
    of the Act) by their responsible clinician;

  • have failed to return to the hospital at the time
    required to do so by the conditions of leave under
    section 17;

  • are absent without permission from a place where they
    are required to reside as a condition of leave under
    section 17;

  • have failed to return to the hospital when their leave
    under section 17 has been revoked;

  • are supervised community treatment (SCT) patients
    who have failed to attend hospital when recalled;

  • are SCT patients who have absconded from hospital
    after being recalled there;

  • are conditionally discharged restricted patients whom
    the Secretary of State for Justice has recalled to
    hospital; or

  • are guardianship patients who are absent without
    permission from the place where they are required to
    live by their guardian.

Reference Guide
12.57-12.64

Detained patients

22.3   Detained patients who are AWOL may be taken into custody and returned by an approved mental health professional (AMHP), any member of the hospital staff, any police officer, or anyone authorised in writing by the hospital managers.

22.4   A patient who has been required to reside in another hospital as a condition of leave of absence can also be taken into custody by any member of that hospital's staff or by any person authorised by that hospital's managers.

22.5   Otherwise, responsibility for the safe return of patients rests with the detaining hospital. If the absconding patient is initially taken to another hospital, that hospital may, with the written authorisation of the managers of the detaining hospital, detain the patient while arrangements are made for their return. In these (and similar) cases people may take a faxed or scanned copy of a written authorisation as evidence that they have the necessary authority without waiting for the original.

Reference Guide
19.86-19.91

Guardianship patients

22.6   Guardianship patients who are AWOL from the place where they are required to live may be taken into custody by any member of the staff of the responsible local social services authority (LSSA) or by any person authorised in writing by the LSSA or by the private guardian (if there is one).

Reference Guide
15.66-15.70

SCT patients

22.7   SCT patients who are AWOL may be taken into custody and returned to the hospital to which they have been recalled by an AMHP, a police officer, a member of staff of the hospital to which they have been recalled, or anyone authorised in writing by the managers of that hospital or by the responsible clinician.

Other situations in which patients are in legal custody

Reference Guide
chapter 31

22.8   In addition, there are various situations in which patients
        are considered to be in legal custody under the Act.
        These include, for example:

   • the detention of patients in places of safety under
     section 135 or 136;

   • the conveyance of patients to hospital (or elsewhere)
     under the Act, including where patients are being
     returned to hospital when they have gone AWOL; and

   • where patients' leave of absence is conditional on their
     being kept in custody by an escort.

   (See **chapters 10, 11** and **21** respectively.)

22.9   If patients who are in legal custody for such other reasons
        abscond, they may also be taken into custody and
        returned to the place they ought to be, in accordance
        with the Act.

Sections 137
and 138

Local policies

22.10 Hospital managers should ensure that there is a clear
       written policy about the action to be taken when a
       detained patient, or a patient on SCT, goes missing. All
       relevant staff should be familiar with this policy. Hospital
       managers should agree their policy with other agencies –
       such as the police and ambulance services – as necessary.

22.11 Policies in relation to detained and SCT patients should
       include guidance about:

   • the immediate action to be taken by any member of
     staff who becomes aware that a patient has gone
     missing, including a requirement that they immediately
     inform the professional in charge of the patient's ward
     (where applicable), who should in turn ensure that the
     patient's responsible clinician is informed;

- the circumstances in which a search of a hospital and its grounds should be made;

- the circumstances in which other local agencies with an interest, including the LSSA, should be notified;

- the circumstances in which the police should be informed, who is responsible for informing the police and the information they should be given (this should be in line with local arrangements agreed with the police);

- how and when other people, including the patient's nearest relative, should be informed (this should include guidance on informing people if there is good reason to think that they might be at risk as a result of the patient's absence);

- when and how an application should be made for a warrant under section 135(2) of the Act to allow the police to enter premises in order to remove a patient who is missing; and

- how and by whom patients are to be returned to the place where they ought to be, and who is responsible for organising any necessary transport (see **chapter 11**).

22.12   LSSAs should have equivalent policies for the action to be taken when they (or a private guardian) become aware that a guardianship patient is AWOL from the place where they are required to live.

22.13   The police should be asked to assist in returning a patient to hospital only if necessary. If the patient's location is known, the role of the police should, wherever possible, be only to assist a suitably qualified and experienced mental health professional in returning the patient to hospital.

22.14 The police should always be informed immediately if a patient is missing who is:

- considered to be particularly vulnerable;

- considered to be dangerous; or

- subject to restrictions under Part 3 of the Act.

There may also be other cases where, although the help of the police is not needed, a patient's history makes it desirable to inform the police that they are AWOL in the area.

22.15 Whenever the police are asked for help in returning a patient, they must be informed of the time limit for taking them into custody.

22.16 Where the police have been informed about a missing patient, they should be told immediately if the patient is found or returns.

22.17 Although every case must be considered on its merits, patient confidentiality will not usually be a barrier to providing basic information about a patient's absence to people – such as those the patient normally lives with or is likely to contact – who may be able to help with finding the patient.

22.18 Where a patient is missing for more than a few hours, their nearest relative should normally be informed (if they have not been already), subject to the normal considerations about involving nearest relatives (see **paragraphs 2.32-2.33**).

22.19 It is good practice when a detained or SCT patient returns after a substantial period of absence without leave always to re-examine the patient to establish whether they still meet the criteria for detention or SCT. Where patients (other than restricted patients) have been AWOL for more than 28 days, section 21B of the Act requires such an examination to take place within a week of the patient's return (or else the patient's detention or SCT will end automatically).

22.20 Incidents in which patients go AWOL or abscond should be reviewed and analysed so that lessons for the future can be learned, including lessons about ways of identifying patients most at risk of going missing.

22.21 All instances of absence without leave should be recorded in the individual patient's notes. Where a patient has gone AWOL previously, it may be useful for the patient's care plan to include specific actions which experience suggests should be taken if that patient were to go missing again.

CHAPTER 23 Medical treatment under the Act

23.1 This chapter gives guidance on medical treatment for mental disorder under the Act, especially treatment given without patients' consent. A summary of when treatment may be given under the Act is presented at the end of the chapter.

Reference Guide chapters 16 and 17

Definitions

23.2 In the Act, "medical treatment" also includes nursing, psychological intervention and specialist mental health habilitation, rehabilitation and care.

Section 145(1)

23.3 The Act defines medical treatment for mental disorder as medical treatment which is for the purpose of alleviating or preventing a worsening of a mental disorder or one or more of its symptoms or manifestations.

Section 145(4)

23.4 This includes treatment of physical health problems only to the extent that such treatment is part of, or ancillary to, treatment for mental disorder (eg treating wounds self-inflicted as a result of mental disorder). Otherwise, the Act does not regulate medical treatment for physical health problems.

Treatments to which special rules and procedures apply

23.5 Sections 57, 58 and 58A of the Act set out types of medical treatment for mental disorder to which special rules and procedures apply, including, in many cases, the need for a certificate from a second opinion appointed doctor (SOAD) approving the treatment.

23.6   Guidance on sections 57, 58 and 58A is given in **chapter 24**, but in summary the treatments involved are as in the table below.

Summary of treatments covered by sections 57, 58 and 58A

Section	Forms of treatment covered
Section 57	Neurosurgery for mental disorder

Surgical implantation of hormones to reduce male sex drive |
| Section 58 | Medication (after an initial three-month period) – except medication administered as part of electro-convulsive therapy (ECT) |
| Section 58A | ECT and medication administered as part of ECT |

Note: it is possible that other forms of treatment may be added to any of these sections by regulations.

Sections 56-64
Reference Guide
chapter 16

Treatment of detained patients and supervised community treatment patients recalled to hospital (Part 4 of the Act)

23.7   Part 4 of the Act deals mainly with the treatment of people who have been detained in hospital, including supervised community treatment (SCT) patients who have been recalled to hospital. They are referred to in this chapter as "detained patients".

23.8   Some patients detained in hospital are not covered by these rules, as set out in the table opposite. When this chapter talks about detained patients, these patients are not included. There are no special rules about treatment for these patients – they are in the same position as patients who are not subject to the Act at all, and they have exactly the same rights to consent to and refuse treatment.

Meaning of detained patients in this chapter

In this chapter "detained patients" means	Exceptions
Patients who are liable to be detained in hospital under any section of the Act (including those on leave of absence or absent without leave)	Patients detained on the basis of an emergency application under section 4 unless or until the second medical recommendation is received

Patients held in hospital under the holding powers in section 5

Patients remanded to hospital for a report on their mental condition under section 35

Patients detained in hospital as a place of safety under section 135 or 136

Patients temporarily detained in hospital as a place of safety under section 37 or 45A, pending admission to the hospital named in their hospital order or hospital direction

Restricted patients who have been conditionally discharged (unless or until they are recalled to hospital) |
| SCT patients who have been recalled to hospital | – |

23.9 Unless sections 57, 58 or 58A apply, section 63 of the Act means that detained patients may be given medical treatment for any kind for mental disorder, if they:

- consent to it; or

- have not consented to it, but the treatment is given by or under the direction of the approved clinician in charge of the treatment in question.

23.10 If sections 57, 58 or 58A apply, detained patients may be given the treatment only if the rules in those sections are followed (see **chapter 24**).

Sections 64A-64K
Reference Guide
chapter 17

Treatment of SCT patients not recalled to hospital (Part 4A of the Act)

23.11 Part 4A of the Act sets out different rules for treatment of SCT patients who have not been recalled to hospital by their responsible clinician. This includes SCT patients who are in hospital without having been recalled (eg if they have been admitted to hospital voluntarily).

23.12 For convenience, this chapter refers to SCT patients who have not been recalled to hospital as "Part 4A patients".

23.13 The rules for Part 4A patients differ depending on whether or not they have the capacity to consent to the treatment in question. For patients aged under 16, capacity means the competence to consent (see **paragraph 23.30** and **chapter 36**).

23.14 Part 4A patients who have the capacity to consent to a treatment may not be given that treatment unless they consent. There are no exceptions to this rule, even in emergencies. The effect is that treatment can be given without their consent only if they are recalled to hospital.

23.15 Part 4A patients who lack the capacity to consent to a treatment may be given it if their attorney or deputy, or the Court of Protection, consents to the treatment on their behalf.

23.16 Part 4A patients who lack capacity to consent to treatment may also be given it, without anyone's consent, by or under the direction of the approved clinician in charge of the treatment, unless:

- (in the case of a patient aged 18 or over) the treatment would be contrary to a valid and applicable advance decision made by the patient (see **chapter 17**);

- (in the case of a patient aged 16 or over) the treatment would be against the decision of someone with the authority under the Mental Capacity Act 2005 (MCA) to refuse it on the patient's behalf (an attorney, a deputy or the Court of Protection); or

- (in the case of a patient of any age) force needs to be used in order to administer the treatment and the patient objects to the treatment.

23.17 In this last case, force means the actual use of physical force on the patient. Where force needs to be used, it is up to the person proposing to give the treatment to decide whether a patient objects to the treatment. The question is simply whether the patient objects – the reasonableness (or unreasonableness) of the objection is irrelevant.

23.18 In deciding whether patients object to treatment, all the relevant evidence should be taken into account, so far as it reasonably can be. In many cases, patients will be perfectly able to state their objection, either verbally or by their dissenting behaviour. But in other cases, especially where patients are unable to communicate (or only able to communicate to a limited extent), clinicians will need to consider the patient's behaviour, wishes, feelings, views, beliefs and values, both present and past, so far as they can be ascertained.

Section 64J

23.19 If there is reason to think that a patient would object, if able to do so, then the patient should be taken to be objecting. Occasionally, it may be that the patient's behaviour initially suggests an objection to being treated, but is in fact not directed at the treatment at all. In that case the patient would not be taken to be objecting.

23.20 Whether or not Part 4A patients consent to treatment, there are certain treatments they can only be given if they have been approved by a SOAD on a "Part 4A certificate". The Mental Health Act refers to this as the "certificate requirement", which is above and beyond the requirements described in **paragraphs 23.14-23.19** (the Act calls these the "authority" to give treatment). Broadly speaking, the certificate requirement applies to any treatment for which a certificate would be necessary under section 58 or 58A of the Act were the patient detained instead (see **chapter 24**).

Emergency treatment under section 64G

23.21 In an emergency, treatment can also be given to Part 4A patients who lack capacity (and who have not been recalled to hospital) by anyone, whether or not they are acting under the direction of an approved clinician.

23.22 It is an emergency only if the treatment is immediately necessary to:

- save the patient's life;

- prevent a serious deterioration of the patient's condition, and the treatment does not have unfavourable physical or psychological consequences which cannot be reversed;

- alleviate serious suffering by the patient and the treatment does not have unfavourable physical or psychological consequences which cannot be reversed and does not entail significant physical hazard; or

- prevent the patient behaving violently or being a danger to themselves or others, and the treatment represents the minimum interference necessary for that purpose, does not have unfavourable physical or psychological consequences which cannot be reversed and does not entail significant physical hazard.

If the treatment is ECT (or medication administered as part of ECT), only the first two categories above apply.

23.23 Where treatment is immediately necessary in these terms, it can be given even though it conflicts with an advance decision or the decision of someone who has the authority under the MCA to refuse it on the patient's behalf.

23.24 In addition, force may be used (whether or not the patient objects), provided that:

- the treatment is necessary to prevent harm to the patient; and

- the force used is proportionate to the likelihood of the patient suffering harm and to the seriousness of that harm.

23.25 These are the only circumstances in which force may be used to treat SCT patients who object, without recalling them to hospital. This exception is for situations where the patient's interests would be better served by being given urgently needed treatment by force outside hospital rather than being recalled to hospital. This might, for example, be where the situation is so urgent that recall is not realistic, or where taking the patient to hospital would exacerbate their condition, damage their recovery or cause them unnecessary anxiety or suffering. Situations like this should be exceptional.

Treatment of other patients

23.26 The Act does not regulate treatment of any other patients, except that:

- the special rules and procedures in section 57 apply to all patients; and   Section 56(1)

- the special rules and procedures in section 58A apply to all patients under the age of 18.   Section 56(5)

(See **chapter 24**.)

Capacity and consent

23.27 The Act frequently requires healthcare professionals to determine:

- whether a patient has the capacity to consent to or refuse a particular form of medical treatment; and

- if so, whether the patient does in fact consent.

The rules for answering these questions are the same as for any other patients.

Capacity to consent: people aged 16 or over

23.28 For people aged 16 or over, capacity to consent is defined by the MCA (see box opposite). The principles of the MCA state (among other things) that:

- people must be assumed to have capacity unless it is established that they lack capacity;

- people are not be to be treated as unable to make a decision unless all practicable steps to help them do so have been taken without success; and

- people are not be to be treated as unable to make a decision merely because they make an unwise decision.

What does the Mental Capacity Act 2005 mean by "lack of capacity"?

Section 2(1) of the MCA states:

> For the purposes of this Act, a person lacks capacity in relation to a matter if at the material time he is unable to make a decision for himself in relation to the matter because of an impairment of, or a disturbance in the functioning of, the mind or brain.

This means that a person lacks capacity if:

- they have an impairment or disturbance (eg a disability, condition or trauma) that affects the way their mind or brain works; and
- the impairment or disturbance means that they are unable to make a specific decision at the time it needs to be made.

Section 2(2) states that the impairment or disturbance does not have to be permanent. A person can lack capacity to make a decision at the time it needs to be made even if:

- the loss of capacity is partial;
- the loss of capacity is temporary; or
- their capacity changes over time.

A person may also lack capacity to make a decision about one issue but not about others.

Section 3(1) says that a person is unable to make a decision if they cannot:

- understand information about the decision to be made (the Act calls this "relevant information");
- retain that information in their mind;
- use or weigh that information as part of the decision-making process; or
- communicate their decision (by talking, using sign language or any other means).

The first three should be applied together. If a person cannot do any of these three things, they will be treated as unable to make the decision. The fourth only applies in situations where people cannot communicate their decision in any way.

For further information see the Code of Practice to the MCA.

23.29 When taking decisions about patients under the Mental Health Act, it should be remembered that:

- mental disorder does not necessarily mean that a patient lacks capacity to give or refuse consent, or to take any other decision;

- any assessment of an individual's capacity has to be made in relation to the particular decision being made – a person may, for example, have the capacity to consent to one form of treatment but not to another;

- capacity in an individual with a mental disorder can vary over time and should be assessed at the time the decision in question needs to be taken;

- where a patient's capacity fluctuates in this way, consideration should be given, if a decision is not urgently required, to delaying the decision until the patient has capacity again to make it for themselves;

- not everyone is equally capable of understanding the same explanation – explanations should be appropriate to the level of the patient's assessed ability; and

- all assessments of a patient's capacity should be fully recorded in their notes.

Competence to consent: children under 16

23.30 The MCA does not apply to medical treatment for children under 16. Children who have sufficient understanding and intelligence to enable them fully to understand what is involved in a proposed treatment are considered to be competent (or "Gillick competent") to consent to it. The common law deals with cases where children are not capable of consenting. See **chapter 36**.

Consent

23.31 Consent is the voluntary and continuing permission of a patient to be given a particular treatment, based on a sufficient knowledge of the purpose, nature, likely effects and risks of that treatment, including the likelihood of its

success and any alternatives to it. Permission given under
any unfair or undue pressure is not consent.

23.32 By definition, a person who lacks capacity to consent does
not consent to treatment, even if they co-operate with
the treatment or actively seek it.

23.33 It is the duty of everyone seeking consent to use
reasonable care and skill, not only in giving information
prior to seeking consent, but also in meeting the
continuing obligation to provide the patient with sufficient
information about the proposed treatment and
alternatives to it.

23.34 The information which must be given should be related
to the particular patient, the particular treatment and
relevant clinical knowledge and practice. In every case,
sufficient information must be given to the patient to
ensure that they understand in broad terms the nature,
likely effects and all significant possible adverse outcomes
of that treatment, including the likelihood of its success
and any alternatives to it. A record should be kept of
information provided to patients.

23.35 Patients should be invited to ask questions and
professionals should answer fully, frankly and truthfully.
There may sometimes be a compelling reason, in the
patient's interests, for not disclosing certain information.
A professional who chooses not to disclose information
must be prepared to justify the decision. A professional
who chooses not to answer a patient's question should
make this clear to the patient so that the patient knows
where they stand.

23.36 Patients should be told that their consent to treatment
can be withdrawn at any time. Where patients withdraw
their consent (or are considering withdrawing it), they
should be given a clear explanation of the likely
consequences of not receiving the treatment and (where
relevant) the circumstances in which the treatment may
be given without their consent under the Mental Health
Act. A record should be kept of the information provided
to patients.

Treatment without consent – general points

23.37 Although the Mental Health Act permits some medical treatment for mental disorder to be given without consent, the patient's consent should still be sought before treatment is given, wherever practicable. The patient's consent or refusal should be recorded in their notes, as should the treating clinician's assessment of the patient's capacity to consent.

23.38 If a patient initially consents, but then withdraws that consent (or loses the capacity to consent), the treatment should be reviewed. The clinician in charge of the treatment must consider whether to proceed in the absence of consent, to provide alternative treatment instead or to give no further treatment.

23.39 Clinicians authorising or administering treatment without consent under the Mental Health Act are performing a function of a public nature and are therefore subject to the provisions of the Human Rights Act 1998. It is unlawful for them to act in a way which is incompatible with a patient's rights as set out in the European Convention on Human Rights ("the Convention").

23.40 In particular, the following should be noted:

- compulsory administration of treatment which would otherwise require consent is invariably an infringement of Article 8 of the Convention (respect for family and private life). However, it may be justified where it is in accordance with law (in this case the procedures in the Mental Health Act) and where it is proportionate to a legitimate aim (in this case, the reduction of the risk posed by a person's mental disorder and the improvement of their health);

- compulsory treatment is capable of being inhuman treatment (or in extreme cases even torture) contrary to Article 3 of the Convention, if its effect on the person concerned reaches a sufficient level of severity. But the European Court of Human Rights has said that a measure which is convincingly shown to be of therapeutic necessity from the point of view of established principles of medicine cannot in principle be regarded as inhuman and degrading.

23.41 Scrupulous adherence to the requirements of the legislation and good clinical practice should ensure that there is no such incompatibility. But if clinicians have concerns about a potential breach of a person's human rights they should seek senior clinical and, if necessary, legal advice.

Treatment plans

23.42 Treatment plans are essential for patients being treated for mental disorder under the Mental Health Act. A patient's responsible clinician is responsible for ensuring that a treatment plan is in place for that patient.

23.43 A treatment plan should include a description of the immediate and long-term goals for the patient and should give a clear indication of the treatments proposed and the methods of treatment.

23.44 The treatment plan should form part of a coherent care plan under the Care Programme Approach (or its equivalent), and be recorded in the patient's notes.

23.45 Psychological therapies form an important part of modern mental healthcare and are part of a holistic approach to an individual's care, which looks at the individual in the round.

23.46 Psychological therapies should be considered as a routine treatment option at all stages, including the initial formulation of a treatment plan and each subsequent review of that plan. Any programme of psychological intervention should form part of the agreed treatment plan and be recorded in the patient's notes as such. At no time should it be used as an isolated and spontaneous reaction to particular behaviour.

23.47 Wherever possible, the whole treatment plan should be discussed with the patient. Patients should be encouraged and assisted to make use of advocacy support available to them, if they want it. This includes, but need not be restricted to, independent mental health advocacy services under the Act.[1] Where patients cannot (or do not wish to) participate in discussion about their treatment plan, any views they have expressed previously should be taken into consideration (see **chapter 17**).

23.48 Subject to the normal considerations of patient confidentiality, the treatment plan should also be discussed with their carers, with a view to enabling them to contribute to it and express agreement or disagreement.

23.49 Discussion with carers is particularly important where carers will themselves be providing care to the patient while the plan is in force. However, carers still have an important role to play even if the patient is to be detained in hospital. Plans should not be based on any assumptions about the willingness or ability of carers to support patients, unless those assumptions have been discussed and agreed with the carers in question.

23.50 For patients aged under 16 (and in some cases those aged 16 or 17), the plan should similarly be discussed with the people who have parental responsibility for them. Again, this is subject to the normal considerations of patient confidentiality for children and young people.

23.51 Treatment plans should be regularly reviewed and the results of reviews recorded in the patient's notes.

Interface between Parts 4 and 4A of the Mental Health Act and section 28 of the Mental Capacity Act 2005

23.52 Insofar as it deals with decisions about medical treatment for people aged 16 or over who lack capacity to consent to such treatment, the MCA applies to patients subject to the Mental Health Act in the same way as to anyone else, with exceptions set out in the following table. These exceptions apply only to medical treatment for mental disorder.

[1] Independent mental health advocacy services under the Act are expected to be introduced in April 2009.

**Medical treatment of patients subject to the Mental Health Act
– exceptions to the normal rules on treatment and consent in
the Mental Capacity Act 2005**

Situation	Exceptions to the normal rules in the MCA
Section 57 treatment (neurosurgery for mental disorder etc)	The MCA may not be used to give anyone treatment to which section 57 applies (see **chapter 24** for guidance on section 57).
Section 58A treatment (ECT and related medication)	The MCA may not be used to give detained patients (as defined in **paragraphs 23.7-23.8**) ECT or any other treatment to which section 58A applies.
Treatment for detained patients	The MCA may not be used to give detained patients (as defined in this chapter) any other medical treatment for mental disorder. Treatment must be given in accordance with Part 4 of the Mental Health Act instead (see **paragraphs 23.7-23.10**).
Treatment for SCT patients who have not been recalled to hospital (Part 4A patients)	The MCA may not generally be used to give these SCT patients any medical treatment for mental disorder, but attorneys, deputies and the Court of Protection may consent to such treatment on behalf of these SCT patients.

Situation	Exceptions to the normal rules in the MCA
Advance decisions to refuse treatment (as defined in the MCA)	Where the Mental Health Act allows treatment to be given against the wishes of a patient who has capacity to consent, it also allows treatment to be given despite the existence of a valid and applicable advance decision made under the MCA (see **chapter 17**). But note that, except in emergencies: • treatment to which section 58A applies cannot be given contrary to a valid and applicable advance decision; and • treatment cannot be given to SCT patients who have not been recalled to hospital (Part 4A patients) contrary to a valid and applicable advance decision.
Patients who have attorneys or court-appointed deputies under the MCA with authority to take decisions on their behalf about their medical treatment	Attorneys and deputies (acting within the scope of their authority under the MCA) may not: • consent to treatment to which section 57 applies on behalf of any patient; • consent to treatment to which section 58A applies – but note that (except in emergencies) they may refuse it on a patient's behalf; or • consent to or refuse any other treatment on behalf of detained patients (as defined in **paragraphs 23.7-23.8**). But note that attorneys and deputies may: • consent to treatment on behalf of SCT patients who have not been recalled to hospital (Part 4A patients), even if treatment is to be given forcibly; and • except in emergencies, also refuse treatment on behalf of those patients.

23.53 See **chapter 4** for guidance on the interface between detention under the Mental Health Act and the deprivation of liberty safeguards under the MCA. See **chapter 26** for the interface between the powers of guardians under the Mental Health Act and the MCA.

The Court of Protection and other courts

23.54 Although the Mental Health Act refers only to decisions of the Court of Protection, other courts may, in certain circumstances, have the power to order that treatment must not be given. Should such an order be made, legal advice should be sought on the legal authority for continuing or starting any such treatment.

Summary of when medical treatment for mental disorder may be given under the Mental Health Act

Type of patient (and relevant part of the Act)	When treatment can be given	Notes (for further detail see chapter 24)
Detained patient – see definition in **paragraphs 23.7-23.8**	If sections 57, 58 or 58A apply, treatment may be given only in accordance with those sections. Otherwise, treatment may be given: • with the patient's consent; or • without the patient's consent under section 63, if the treatment is by or under the direction of the approved clinician in charge.	Neurosurgery for mental disorder and other treatments to which section 57 applies cannot be given without the patient's consent and must always be approved by a SOAD. ECT and other treatments to which section 58A applies cannot be given to a patient who has capacity to consent but refuses to do so. They can be given to patients who lack capacity (or who are under 18) only if approved by a SOAD. Medication to which section 58 applies can be given without the patient's consent, but only with the approval of a SOAD. Sections 57, 58 and 58A do not apply in emergencies, where treatment is defined in section 62 as immediately necessary.

Type of patient (and relevant part of the Act)	When treatment can be given	Notes (for further detail see chapter 24)
SCT patient who has not been recalled to hospital (Part 4A patient)	If section 57 applies, treatment can be given only with the patient's consent and if the other rules in section 57 are followed. Otherwise, if the patient has capacity to consent, treatment may be given only with the patient's consent. Or, if the patient lacks capacity to consent, treatment may be given: • with the consent of an attorney, deputy or the Court of Protection; • without anyone's consent, provided that (i) the treatment is given by or under the direction of the approved clinician in charge; (ii) it is not inconsistent with a valid and applicable advance decision, or a decision of an attorney, deputy or the Court of Protection; and either (iii) no force needs to be used, or (iv) force does need to be used but the patient does not object; • in an emergency only, if (i) the treatment is immediately necessary; and (ii) if force is to be used, the treatment is needed to protect the patient from harm and any force used is proportionate to the risk of harm.	Unless it is an emergency, if the treatment is one to which section 58 or 58A applies, it normally has to be approved by a SOAD on a Part 4A certificate as well.

Type of patient (and relevant part of the Act)	When treatment can be given	Notes (for further detail see chapter 24)
Other patients	Treatment is not regulated by the Act, except that: • where section 57 applies, patients can be given treatment only if they consent and the other rules in section 57 are followed; and • patients under 18 cannot be given ECT or other treatments to which section 58A applies, unless it is approved by a SOAD. (Sections 57 and 58A do not apply in emergencies.)	

Related material

- Mental Capacity Act 2005
- *Mental Capacity Act 2005 Code of Practice*, TSO, 2007

  This material does not form part of the Code. It is provided for assistance only.

CHAPTER 24 Treatments subject to special rules and procedures

24.1 This chapter gives guidance on the special rules and procedures in the Act for certain types of medical treatment for mental disorder.

Reference Guide chapters 16 and 17

Definitions

24.2 In this chapter:

- "detained patients" means the same as in the previous chapter (see **paragraphs 23.7-23.8**);

- "SOAD" means a second opinion doctor appointed by the Commission to approve certain forms of treatment;

- "SOAD certificate" means a certificate issued by a SOAD approving treatment for a particular patient;

- "Part 4A patient" means a supervised community treatment (SCT) patient who has not been recalled to hospital; and

- "Part 4A certificate" means a SOAD certificate issued under Part 4A of the Act in respect of the treatment of an SCT patient.

Clinician in charge of treatment

24.3 This chapter frequently refers to the "clinician in charge of treatment". This means the clinician in charge of the particular treatment in question for a patient, who need not be the same as the responsible clinician in charge of a patient's case overall.

24.4 In many cases, for detained and SCT patients the clinician in charge of treatment must be an approved clinician, as set out in the following table.

Summary of when the clinician in charge of treatment under the Act must be an approved clinician

Type of patient	When the clinician in charge of treatment must be an approved clinician
Detained patient	When the treatment is being: • given without the patient's consent; • given with the patient's consent, on the basis of a certificate issued under section 58 or 58A by an approved clinician (rather than a SOAD) – see **paragraphs 24.13** and **24.20**; or • continued with the consent of an SCT patient who has been recalled to hospital (including one whose community treatment order has then been revoked) to avoid serious suffering to the patient, pending compliance with section 58 – see **paragraph 24.28**.
Part 4A patient	When the treatment is being given to a patient who lacks capacity to consent to it and without the consent of an attorney, deputy or the Court of Protection (unless it is immediately necessary and being given under section 64G – see **paragraphs 23.21-23.22**).

24.5 Hospital managers should keep a record of approved clinicians who are available to treat patients for whom they are responsible and should ensure that approved clinicians are in charge of treatment where the Act requires it.

CHAPTER

24

Treatments
subject
to special
rules and
procedures

Treatments requiring consent and a second opinion under section 57

24.6   Section 57 applies to neurosurgery for mental disorder and to surgical implantation of hormones to reduce male sex drive. It applies to all patients, whether or not they are otherwise subject to the Act.

24.7   Where section 57 applies, these treatments can be given only if all three of the following requirements are met:

- the patient consents to the treatment;

- a SOAD (and two other people by the Commission) certify that the patient has the capacity to consent[1] and has done so; and

- the SOAD also certifies that it is appropriate for the treatment to be given to the patient.

24.8   A decision to administer treatments to which section 57 applies requires particularly careful consideration, given their significance and sensitivity. Hospitals proposing to offer such treatments are strongly encouraged to agree with the Commission the procedures which will be followed to implement the requirements of section 57.

24.9   Before asking the Commission to put in hand the process of issuing a certificate, referring professionals should personally satisfy themselves that the patient is capable of giving valid consent and is willing to consent. The restrictions and procedures imposed by section 57 should be explained to the patient, and it should be made clear to the patient that their willingness to receive treatment does not necessarily mean that the treatment will be given.

---

[1]In fact, here and in sections 58 and 58A, the Act refers to the patient being "capable of understanding the nature, purpose and likely effects" of the treatment. However, for all practical purposes this can be understood to mean the same as the test of whether the patient has the capacity to consent (or, if under 16, the competence to do so).

Treatments requiring consent or a second opinion under section 58

24.10 Section 58 applies to the administration of medication for mental disorder. But it only applies once three months have passed from the day on which any form of medication for mental disorder was first administered to the patient during the patient's current period of detention under the Act ("the three-month period").

24.11 For these purposes, the patient's current period of detention continues even if the section under which the patient is detained changes. It also includes any time the patient has spent on SCT.

24.12 Section 58 does not apply to medication administered as part of electro-convulsive therapy (ECT). That is covered by section 58A instead (see **paragraphs 24.18-24.24**).

24.13 Section 58 applies only to detained patients. They cannot be given medication to which section 58 applies unless:

- the approved clinician in charge of the treatment, or a SOAD, certifies that the patient has the capacity to consent and has done so; or

- a SOAD certifies that the treatment is appropriate and either that:

  - the patient does not have the capacity to consent; or

  - the patient has the capacity to consent but has refused to do so.

24.14 Hospital managers should ensure that systems are in place to remind both the clinician in charge of the medication and the patient at least four weeks before the expiry of the three-month period.

24.15 Warning systems must be capable of dealing with the possibility that a patient may become an SCT patient, and may also have their community treatment order revoked, during the three-month period. A patient's move between

CHAPTER

24

Treatments
subject
to special
rules and
procedures

detention and SCT does not change the date on which
the three-month period expires.

24.16 Where approved clinicians certify the treatment of a
patient who consents, they should not rely on the
certificate as the only record of their reasons for believing
that the patient has consented to the treatment. A record
of their discussion with the patient, and of the steps taken
to confirm that the patient has the capacity to consent,
should be made in the patient's notes as normal.

24.17 Certificates under this section must clearly set out the
specific forms of treatment to which they apply. All the
relevant drugs should be listed, including medication to
be given "as required" (prn), either by name or by the
classes described in the British National Formulary (BNF).
If drugs are specified by class, the certificate should state
clearly the number of drugs authorised in each class, and
whether any drugs within the class are excluded. The
maximum dosage and route of administration should
be clearly indicated for each drug or category of drugs
proposed. This can exceed the dosages listed in the BNF,
but particular care is required in these cases.

Electro-convulsive therapy under section 58A

24.18 Section 58A applies to ECT and to medication
administered as part of ECT. It applies to detained patients
and to all patients aged under 18 (whether or not they
are detained).

24.19 The key differences from section 58 are that:

- patients who have the capacity to consent may not be
  given treatment under section 58A unless they do in
  fact consent;

- no patient aged under 18 can be given treatment
  under section 58A unless a SOAD has certified that the
  treatment is appropriate; and

- there is no initial three-month period during which a certificate is not needed (even for the medication administered as part of the ECT).

24.20 A patient who has capacity to consent may not be given treatment under section 58A unless the clinician in charge, or a SOAD, has certified that the patient has the capacity to consent and has done so. If the patient is under 18, only a SOAD may give the certificate, and the SOAD must also certify that the treatment is appropriate.

24.21 A patient who lacks the capacity to consent may not be given treatment under section 58A unless a SOAD certifies that the patient lacks capacity to consent and that:

- the treatment is appropriate;

- no valid and applicable advance decision has been made by the patient under the Mental Capacity Act 2005 (MCA) refusing the treatment;

- no suitably authorised attorney or deputy objects to the treatment on the patient's behalf; and

- the treatment would not conflict with a decision of the Court of Protection which prevents the treatment being given.

24.22 In all cases, SOADs should indicate on the certificate the maximum number of administrations of ECT which it approves.

24.23 For children and young people under 18, a SOAD certificate by itself is not sufficient to authorise the treatment, unless they are detained. Clinicians must also have the patient's own consent or some other legal authority, just as they would if section 58A did not exist (see **chapter 36**).

CHAPTER

24

Treatments
subject
to special
rules and
procedures

24.24 Whether or not section 58A applies, patients of all ages to be treated with ECT should be given written information before their treatment starts which helps them to understand and remember, both during and after the course of ECT, the advice given about its nature, purpose and likely effects.

Part 4A certificates

24.25 Part 4A patients may be given certain treatments for mental disorder only if a SOAD has certified that the treatment is appropriate, using a Part 4A certificate. The requirement to have a certificate is in addition to the other rules governing treatment of SCT patients, described in **chapter 23**.

Sections 64B,
64C, 64E
and 64H

24.26 A Part 4A certificate is needed for:

- treatments which would require a certificate under section 58 if the patient were detained – ie medication after an initial three-month period ("section 58 type treatment"); and

- ECT and any other types of treatment to which section 58A applies ("section 58A type treatment").

However, a certificate is not required for section 58 type treatment during the first month following a patient's discharge from detention onto SCT (even if the three-month period in section 58 has already expired or expires during that first month).

24.27 When giving Part 4A certificates, SOADs do not have to certify whether a patient has, or lacks, capacity to consent to the treatments in question, nor whether a patient with capacity is consenting or refusing. But they may make it a condition of their approval that particular treatments are given only in certain circumstances. For example, they might specify that a particular treatment is to be given only with the patient's consent. Similarly, they might specify that a medication may be given up to a certain dosage if the patient lacks capacity to consent, but that a higher dosage may be given with the patient's consent.

Section 62A
Reference Guide
17.33-17.44

SCT patients recalled to hospital – exceptions to the need for certificates under section 58 or 58A

24.28 In general, SCT patients recalled to hospital are subject to sections 58 and 58A in the same way as other detained patients. But there are three exceptions, as follows:

- a certificate under section 58 is not needed for medication if less than one month has passed since the patient was discharged from hospital and became an SCT patient;

- a certificate is not needed under either section 58 or 58A if the treatment in question is already explicitly authorised for administration on recall on the patient's Part 4A certificate; and

- treatment that was already being given on the basis of a Part 4A certificate may be continued, even though it is not authorised for administration on recall, if the approved clinician in charge of the treatment considers that discontinuing it would cause the patient serious suffering. But it may only be continued pending compliance with section 58 or 58A (as applicable) – in other words while steps are taken to obtain a new certificate.

24.29 As a result, SOADs giving Part 4A certificates need to consider what (if any) treatments to approve should the patient be recalled to hospital. They must also decide whether to impose any conditions on that approval. Unless they specify otherwise, the certificate will authorise the treatment even if the patient has capacity to refuse it (unless it is a section 58A type treatment).

24.30 The potential advantage of authorising treatments to be given on recall to hospital is that it will enable such treatments to be given quickly without the need to obtain a new certificate. However, SOADs should do so only where they believe they have sufficient information on which properly to make such a judgement.

CHAPTER

24

Treatments
subject
to special
rules and
procedures

24.31 The exceptions to the requirement to have a certificate under section 58 or 58A set out in **paragraph 24.28** continue to apply if the patient's community treatment order (CTO) is revoked, but only while steps are taken to comply with section 58 (where relevant). Responsible clinicians should ensure that steps are put in hand to obtain a new SOAD certificate under section 58 or 58A, if one is needed, as soon as they revoke a CTO.

Urgent cases where certificates are not required (sections 62, 64B, 64C and 64E)

24.32 Sections 57, 58 and 58A do not apply in urgent cases where treatment is immediately necessary (section 62). Similarly, a Part 4A certificate is not required in urgent cases where the treatment is immediately necessary (sections 64B, 64C and 64E).

24.33 This applies only if the treatment in question is immediately necessary to:

- save the patient's life;

- prevent a serious deterioration of the patient's condition, and the treatment does not have unfavourable physical or psychological consequences which cannot be reversed;

- alleviate serious suffering by the patient, and the treatment does not have unfavourable physical or psychological consequences which cannot be reversed and does not entail significant physical hazard; or

- prevent patients behaving violently or being a danger to themselves or others, and the treatment represents the minimum interference necessary for that purpose, does not have unfavourable physical or psychological consequences which cannot be reversed and does not entail significant physical hazard.

If the treatment is ECT (or medication administered as part of ECT) only the first two categories above apply.

24.34 These are strict tests. It is not enough for there to be an urgent need for treatment or for the clinicians involved to believe the treatment is necessary or beneficial.

24.35 Urgent treatment under these sections can continue only for as long as it remains immediately necessary. If it is no longer immediately necessary, the normal requirements for certificates apply.

24.36 Although certificates are not required where treatment is immediately necessary, the other requirements of Parts 4 and 4A of the Act still apply. The treatment is not necessarily allowed just because no certificate is required.

24.37 Hospital managers should monitor the use of these exceptions to the certificate requirements to ensure that they are not used inappropriately or excessively. They are advised to provide a form (or other method) by which the clinician in charge of the treatment in question can record details of:

- the proposed treatment;

- why it is immediately necessary to give the treatment; and

- the length of time for which the treatment is given.

Requesting a SOAD visit

24.38 If a SOAD certificate is required, the clinician in charge of the treatment in question has the personal responsibility of ensuring that a request is made to the Commission for a SOAD to visit.

24.39 Clinicians should not normally request a visit from a SOAD in order to obtain a certificate which they could issue themselves confirming that a patient has consented to treatment. They should request a visit for that purpose only if they are genuinely unable to determine for themselves whether the patient has the capacity to consent or whether the patient is in fact consenting.

CHAPTER

24

Treatments
subject
to special
rules and
procedures

Arranging and preparing for SOAD visits

24.40 SOADs will visit detained patients in hospital. For SCT patients, hospital managers should ensure that arrangements are made for the SOAD to see the patient at a mutually agreed place, eg at an out-patient clinic or somewhere that the patient might visit regularly.

24.41 Attending hospital for examination by a SOAD is a condition of all CTOs. If SCT patients fail to attend when asked to do so, they may be recalled to hospital for the examination, if necessary. But that should only ever be a last resort. (See **paragraph 25.49**.)

24.42 The treatment proposal for the patient, together with notes of any relevant multi-disciplinary discussion on which it was based, must be given to the SOAD before or at the time of the visit. If a Part 4A certificate is being requested, the proposal should clearly indicate which (if any) treatments it is proposed should be authorised in the case of the patient's recall to hospital.

24.43 During a visit, SOADs should:

- satisfy themselves that the patient's detention or SCT papers are in order (where applicable); and

- interview the patient in private if possible. Others may attend if the patient and the SOAD wish, or if it is thought that the SOAD would be at significant risk of physical harm from the patient (and the SOAD agrees).

24.44 Hospital managers are responsible for ensuring that people whom the SOAD wishes to meet (including the clinician in charge of the treatment) are available in person at the time the SOAD visits.

24.45 The managers are also responsible for ensuring that all relevant documentation, including the patient's full clinical notes, are available for the SOAD's inspection.

24.46 SOADs have a right to access records without the patient's consent, if necessary, but only those records relating to the treatment of the patient in the hospital or other establishment in which they are examining the patient. If an SCT patient with capacity to do so refuses the SOAD access to records which the SOAD thinks are relevant, the examination should be arranged in a hospital where the relevant records would be available.

24.47 Where the proposed treatment includes medication, the SOAD's attention should be drawn specifically to any recent review of the patient's medication. Clinicians should consider seeking a review by a specialist mental health pharmacist before seeking a SOAD certificate, particularly if the patient's medication regimen is complex or unusual.

24.48 Approved clinicians should ensure that SOADs are informed if the hospital knows that the patient has an attorney or deputy who is authorised under the MCA to make decisions about medical treatment on the patient's behalf. Details of any relevant advance decisions, or advance statements of views, wishes or feelings, should already be recorded in the patient's notes. But if they are not, they should be drawn to the SOAD's attention.

Statutory consultees

Sections 57(3), 58(4), 58A(6) and 64H(3)

24.49 SOADs are required to consult two people ("statutory consultees") before issuing certificates approving treatment. One of the statutory consultees must be a nurse; the other must not be either a nurse or a doctor. Both must have been professionally concerned with the patient's medical treatment, and neither may be the clinician in charge of the proposed treatment or the responsible clinician (if the patient has one).

24.50 The Act does not specify who the statutory consultees should be, but they should be people whose knowledge of the patient and the patient's treatment can help the SOAD decide whether the proposed treatment is

CHAPTER

24

Treatments
subject
to special
rules and
procedures

appropriate. People who may be particularly well placed to act as statutory consultees include the patient's care co-ordinator (if they have one) and, where medication is concerned, a mental health pharmacist who has been involved in any recent review of the patient's medication.

24.51   The statutory consultees whom the SOAD proposes to consult should consider whether they are sufficiently concerned professionally with the patient's care to fulfil the function. If not, or if a consultee feels that someone else is better placed to fulfil the function, they should make this known to the clinician in charge of the treatment and to the SOAD in good time.

24.52   Statutory consultees may expect to have a private discussion with the SOAD and to be listened to with consideration. Among the issues that the consultees should consider commenting on are:

- the proposed treatment and the patient's ability to consent to it;

- their understanding of the past and present views and wishes of the patient;

- other treatment options and the way in which the decision on the treatment proposal was arrived at;

- the patient's progress and the views of the patient's carers; and

- where relevant, the implications of imposing treatment on a patient who does not want it and the reasons why the patient is refusing treatment.

24.53   If the SOAD wishes to speak to the statutory consultees face to face, the hospital managers should ensure that the SOAD is able to do so.

24.54   Consultees should ensure that they make a record of their consultation with the SOAD, which is then placed in the patient's notes.

24.55 SOADs should also be prepared, where appropriate, to consult a wider range of people who are concerned with the patient's care than those required by the Act. That might include the patient's GP and, unless the patient objects, the patient's nearest relative, parents (where relevant), other family and carers, and any independent mental health advocate[2] (or other advocate) representing the patient.

The SOAD's decision and reasons

24.56 The SOAD's role is to provide an additional safeguard to protect the patient's rights, primarily by deciding whether certain treatments are appropriate and issuing certificates accordingly. Although appointed by the Commission, SOADs act as independent professionals and must reach their own judgement about whether the proposed treatment is appropriate.

24.57 When deciding whether it is appropriate for treatment to be given to a patient, SOADs are required to consider both the clinical appropriateness of the treatment to the patient's mental disorder and its appropriateness in the light of all the other circumstances of the patient's case.

24.58 SOADs should, in particular:

- consider the appropriateness of alternative forms of treatment, not just that proposed;

- balance the potential therapeutic efficacy of the proposed treatment against the side effects and any other potential disadvantages to the patient;

- seek to understand the patient's views on the proposed treatment, and the reasons for them;

- give due weight to the patient's views, including any objection to the proposed treatment and any preference for an alternative;

- take into account any previous experience of comparable treatment for a similar episode of disorder; and

[2] Independent mental health advocacy services under the Act are expected to be introduced in April 2009.

CHAPTER
24

Treatments
subject
to special
rules and
procedures

• give due weight to the opinions, knowledge, experience and skills of those consulted.

24.59 SOADs must provide written reasons in support of their decisions to approve specific treatments for patients. SOADs do not have to give an exhaustive explanation, but should provide their reasons for what they consider to be the substantive points on which they made their clinical judgement. These reasons can be recorded on the certificate itself when it is given, or can be provided to the clinician in charge of the treatment separately as soon as possible afterwards.

24.60 A certificate may be acted on even though the SOAD's reasons have yet to be received. But if there is no pressing need for treatment to begin immediately, it is preferable to wait until the reasons are received, especially if the patient is likely to be unhappy with the decision.

24.61 When giving reasons, SOADs will need to indicate whether, in their view, disclosure of the reasons to the patient would be likely to cause serious harm to the patient's physical or mental health or to that of any other person.

24.62 It is the personal responsibility of the clinician in charge of the treatment to communicate the results of the SOAD visit to the patient. This need not wait until any separate statement of reasons has been received from the SOAD. But when a separate statement is received from the SOAD, the patient should be given the opportunity to see it as soon as possible, unless the clinician in charge of the treatment (or the SOAD) thinks that it would be likely to cause serious harm to the physical or mental health of the patient or any other person.

24.63 Documents provided by SOADs are a part of – and should be kept in – the patient's notes. The clinician in charge of the treatment should record their actions in providing patients with (or withholding) the reasons supplied by a SOAD.

24.64 Every attempt should be made by the clinician in charge of the treatment and the SOAD to reach agreement. A generally sound plan need not be rejected as a whole because of a minor disagreement about one aspect of it.

24.65 If SOADs are unable to agree with the clinician in charge of the treatment, they should inform the clinician personally as soon as possible. It is good practice for SOADs to give reasons for their disagreement.

24.66 Neither the SOAD nor the approved clinician should allow a disagreement in any way to prejudice the interests of the patient. If agreement cannot be reached, the position should be recorded in the patient's notes by the clinician in charge of the treatment in question, and the patient's responsible clinician (if different) should be informed.

24.67 The opinion given by the SOAD is the SOAD's personal responsibility. There can be no appeal to the Commission against the opinion.

Status of certificates under Part 4 and Part 4A

24.68 A certificate issued by an approved clinician or by a SOAD is not an instruction to administer treatment.

24.69 The fact that the SOAD has authorised a particular treatment does not mean that it will always be appropriate to administer it on any given occasion, or even at all. People administering the treatment (or directing its administration) must still satisfy themselves that it is an appropriate treatment in the circumstances.

24.70 They also need to take reasonable steps to assure themselves that the treatment is, in fact, authorised by the certificate, given what is said in the certificate about the patient's capacity and willingness to consent (see **paragraph 24.79**).

24.71 Original signed certificates should be kept with the documents which authorise the patient's detention or SCT, and copies should be kept in the patient's notes. As a matter of good practice, a copy of the certificate relating

CHAPTER

24

Treatments
subject
to special
rules and
procedures

to medication should also be kept with the patient's medicine chart (if there is one) to minimise the risk of the patient being given treatment in contravention of the provisions of the Act.

Review of treatment and withdrawal of approval (sections 61 and 64H)

24.72 Although the Act does not require the validity of certificates to be reviewed after any particular period, it is good practice for the clinician in charge of the treatment to review them (in consultation with the responsible clinician, if different) at regular intervals.

24.73 The clinician in charge of any treatment given in accordance with a SOAD certificate must provide a written report on that treatment and the relevant patient's condition at any time if requested to do so by the Commission under section 61 or 64H of the Act. This is in addition to the reports they are automatically required to provide periodically under those sections.[3] Copies of reports should be given to patients.

24.74 Under sections 61 and 64H, the Commission may also, at any time, direct that a certificate is no longer to approve either some or all of the treatments specified in it from a particular date.

24.75 However, where the Commission revokes approval in that way, treatment (or a course of treatment) which is already in progress may continue, pending a new certificate, if the clinician in charge of it considers that discontinuing it would cause the patient serious suffering.

24.76 This exception only applies pending compliance with the relevant requirement to have a certificate – in other words, while steps are taken to obtain a new certificate. It cannot be used to continue treatment under section 57 or section 58A against the wishes of a patient who has the capacity to refuse the treatment, because in those cases there is no prospect of obtaining a new certificate.

---

[3]At the time of publication, the Mental Health Act Commission expects these reports to be submitted on form MHAC1 which it provides for the purpose.

Action where treatment is continued pending a new certificate

24.77 Where treatment is continued to avoid serious suffering pending compliance with a certificate requirement, the clinician in charge of the treatment should immediately take steps to ask for a SOAD visit. This applies both to cases where certificates have been withdrawn by the Commission and to cases where the treatment of SCT patients is being continued pending a new certificate following their recall to hospital (see **paragraphs 24.28** and **24.31**). If the SOAD visits and decides not to give a certificate for treatment which requires one, the treatment must end immediately.

24.78 As with immediately necessary treatment given without a certificate, hospital managers should monitor the use of these exceptions. They should require clinicians to record details of why it was necessary to continue treatment without a certificate and how long it took to obtain a new certificate.

Other circumstances when certificates cease to be effective

24.79 There are a number of other circumstances in which a certificate will cease to authorise treatment (or a particular treatment). These are summarised in the following table. People administering treatment on the basis of a certificate should always take reasonable steps to satisfy themselves that the certificate remains applicable to the circumstances.

CHAPTER

24

Treatments
subject
to special
rules and
procedures

Circumstances in which certificates cease to authorise treatment, even though they have not been withdrawn

Type of certificate	Circumstances in which the certificate ceases to authorise treatment
Certificate issued by approved clinician under section 58 or 58A	The clinician concerned stops being the approved clinician in charge of the treatment.
SOAD certificate under section 57	The patient no longer consents to the treatment. The patient no longer has capacity to consent to the treatment.
SOAD certificate under section 58 or 58A	The patient stops (even if only temporarily) being either a detained patient or an SCT patient – except in the case of section 58A certificates for patients aged under 18. The SOAD specified a time limit on the approval of a course of treatment, and the time limit expires. The certificate was given on the basis that the patient consented, but the patient no longer consents or has lost the capacity to consent. The certificate was given on the basis that the patient lacked capacity to consent, but the patient now has that capacity. (Section 58 only.) The certificate was given on the basis that the patient had capacity to consent but was refusing, and either the patient is now consenting or the patient has lost the capacity to consent.

Type of certificate	Circumstances in which the certificate ceases to authorise treatment
SOAD certificate under section 58 or 58A (continued)	(Section 58A only.) The certificate was given on the understanding that the treatment would not conflict with an advance decision to refuse treatment, but the person giving the treatment becomes aware that there is such a conflict. (Section 58A only.) The certificate was given on the understanding that the treatment would not conflict with a decision of an attorney, a deputy or the Court of Protection, but the person giving the treatment becomes aware that there is such a conflict; or an attorney, deputy or the Court of Protection makes a new decision that the treatment should not be given.
Part 4A certificate	The patient stops (even if only temporarily) being either a detained patient or an SCT patient. (But note that a Part 4A certificate authorises section 58 type treatment for a patient whose CTO has been revoked only pending compliance with section 58 itself.) The SOAD specified a time limit on the approval of a course of treatment, and the time limit has expired.

CHAPTER

24

Treatments
subject
to special
rules and
procedures

24.80 In all the circumstances listed in the table, treatment cannot be continued while a new certificate is obtained, unless no certificate is needed because the treatment is immediately necessary (see **paragraphs 24.32-24.35**).

24.81 It is not good practice to use a certificate that was issued to a patient when detained and who has since been discharged onto SCT to authorise treatment if the patient is then recalled to hospital, even if the certificate remains technically valid. A new certificate should be obtained as necessary.

24.82 Hospital managers should make sure that arrangements are in place so that certificates which no longer authorise treatment (or particular treatments) are clearly marked as such, as are all copies of those certificates kept with the patient's notes and medication chart.

Related material

- British National Formulary, British Medical Association and Royal Pharmaceutical Society of Great Britain

  This material does not form part of the Code. It is provided for assistance only.

CHAPTER 25 **Supervised community treatment**

Reference Guide chapter 15 25.1 This chapter gives guidance on supervised community treatment (SCT).

Purpose of SCT

25.2 The purpose of SCT is to allow suitable patients to be safely treated in the community rather than under detention in hospital, and to provide a way to help prevent relapse and any harm – to the patient or to others – that this might cause. It is intended to help patients to maintain stable mental health outside hospital and to promote recovery.

25.3 SCT provides a framework for the management of patient care in the community and gives the responsible clinician the power to recall the patient to hospital for treatment if necessary.

Section 17A ## Who can be discharged onto SCT?

25.4 Only patients who are detained in hospital for treatment under section 3 of the Act, or are unrestricted Part 3 patients, can be considered for SCT. Patients detained in hospital for assessment under section 2 of the Act are not eligible. (See also **paragraphs 36.64-36.65** on children and young people.)

25.5 SCT is an option only for patients who meet the criteria set out in the Act, which are that:

- the patient is suffering from a mental disorder of a nature or degree which makes it appropriate for them to receive medical treatment;

- it is necessary for the patient's health or safety or for the protection of others that the patient should receive such treatment;

- subject to the patient being liable to be recalled as mentioned below, such treatment can be provided without the patient continuing to be detained in a hospital;

- it is necessary that the responsible clinician should be able to exercise the power under section 17E(1) of the Act to recall the patient to hospital; and

- appropriate medical treatment is available for the patient.

Assessment for SCT

25.6 The decision as to whether SCT is the right option for any patient is taken by the responsible clinician and requires the agreement of an approved mental health professional (AMHP). SCT may be used only if it would not be possible to achieve the desired objectives for the patient's care and treatment without it. Consultation at an early stage with the patient and those involved in the patient's care will be important.

25.7 In assessing the patient's suitability for SCT, the responsible clinician must be satisfied that the patient requires medical treatment for mental disorder for their own health or safety or for the protection of others, and that appropriate treatment is, or would be, available for the patient in the community. The key factor in the decision is whether the patient can safely be treated for mental disorder in the community only if the responsible clinician can exercise the power to recall the patient to hospital for treatment if that becomes necessary (see **paragraphs 25.47-25.53**).

25.8 In making that decision the responsible clinician must assess what risk there would be of the patient's condition deteriorating after discharge, for example as a result of refusing or neglecting to receive treatment.

25.9   In assessing that risk the responsible clinician must take into consideration:

- the patient's history of mental disorder; and

- any other relevant factors.

25.10 Whether or not a patient has previously had repeated admissions, the patient's history may be relevant to the decision. For example, a tendency to fail to follow a treatment plan or to discontinue medication in the community, making relapse more likely, may suggest a risk justifying use of SCT.

25.11 Other relevant factors will vary but are likely to include the patient's current mental state, the patient's insight and attitude to treatment, and the circumstances into which the patient would be discharged.

25.12 Taken together, all these factors should help the responsible clinician to assess the risk of the patient's condition deteriorating after discharge, and inform the decision as to whether continued detention, SCT or discharge would be the right option for the patient at that particular time.

25.13 A risk that the patient's condition will deteriorate is a significant consideration, but does not necessarily mean that the patient should be discharged onto SCT. The responsible clinician must be satisfied that the risk of harm arising from the patient's disorder is sufficiently serious to justify the power to recall the patient to hospital for treatment.

25.14 Patients do not have to consent formally to SCT. But in practice, patients will need to be involved in decisions about the treatment to be provided in the community and how and where it is to be given, and be prepared to co-operate with the proposed treatment.

Action upon Tribunal recommendation

25.15 When a detained patient makes an application to the Tribunal for discharge, the Tribunal may decide not to order discharge, but to recommend that the responsible clinician should consider whether the patient should go onto SCT. In that event, the responsible clinician should carry out the assessment of the patient's suitability for SCT in the usual way. It will be for the responsible clinician to decide whether or not SCT is appropriate for that patient.

Care planning, treatment and support in the community

25.16 Good care planning, in line with the Care Programme Approach (CPA) (or its equivalent) will be essential to the success of SCT. A care co-ordinator will need to be identified. This is likely to be a different person from the responsible clinician, but need not be.

25.17 The care plan should be prepared in the light of consultation with the patient and (subject to the normal considerations of patient confidentiality):

- the nearest relative;

- any carers;

- anyone with authority under the Mental Capacity Act 2005 (MCA) to act on the patient's behalf;

- the multi-disciplinary team involved in the patient's care; and

- the patient's GP (if there is one). It is important that the patient's GP should be aware that the patient is to go onto SCT. A patient who does not have a GP should be encouraged and helped to register with a practice.

25.18 If a different responsible clinician is to take over responsibility for the patient, it will be essential to liaise with that clinician, and the community team, at an early stage. Where needed, arrangements should be made for a second opinion appointed doctor (SOAD) to provide the Part 4A certificate to enable treatment to be given (see **paragraphs 24.25-24.27**).

25.19 The care plan should set out the practicalities of how the patient will receive treatment, care and support from day to day, and should not place undue reliance on carers or members of the patient's family. If the patient so wishes, help should be given to access independent advocacy[1] or other support where this is available (see also **chapter 20**).

25.20 The care plan should take account of the patient's age. Where the patient is under the age of 18 the responsible clinician and the AMHP should bear in mind that the most age-appropriate treatment will normally be that provided by child and adolescent mental health services (CAMHS). It may also be necessary to involve the patient's parent, or whoever will be responsible for looking after the patient, to ensure that they will be ready and able to provide the assistance and support which the patient may need.

25.21 Similarly, specialist services for older people may have a role in the delivery of services for older SCT patients.

25.22 Patients on SCT are entitled to after-care services under section 117 of the Act. The after-care arrangements should be drawn up as part of the normal care planning arrangements. The Primary Care Trust and local social services authority (LSSA) must continue to provide after-care services under section 117 for as long as the patient remains on SCT. (See also **chapter 27**.)

25.23 The care plan should be reviewed regularly, and the services required may vary should the patient's needs change.

[1] Independent mental health advocacy services under the Act are expected to be introduced in April 2009.

Role of the AMHP

25.24 The AMHP must decide whether to agree with the patient's responsible clinician that the patient meets the criteria for SCT, and (if so) whether SCT is appropriate. Even if the criteria for SCT are met, it does not mean that the patient must be discharged onto SCT. In making that decision, the AMHP should consider the wider social context for the patient. Relevant factors may include any support networks the patient may have, the potential impact on the rest of the patient's family, and employment issues.

25.25 The AMHP should consider how the patient's social and cultural background may influence the family environment in which they will be living and the support structures potentially available. But no assumptions should be made simply on the basis of the patient's ethnicity or social or cultural background.

25.26 The Act does not specify who this AMHP should be. It may (but need not) be an AMHP who is already involved in the patient's care and treatment as part of the multi-disciplinary team. It can be an AMHP acting on behalf of any willing LSSA, and LSSAs may agree with each other and with hospital managers the arrangements that are likely to be most convenient and best for patients. But if no other LSSA is willing, responsibility for ensuring that an AMHP considers the case should lie with the LSSA which would become responsible under section 117 for the patient's after-care if the patient were discharged.

25.27 If the AMHP does not agree with the responsible clinician that the patient should go onto SCT, then SCT cannot go ahead. A record of the AMHP's decision and the full reasons for it should be kept in the patient's notes. It would not be appropriate for the responsible clinician to approach another AMHP for an alternative view.

Making the community treatment order

25.28 If the responsible clinician and AMHP agree that the patient should be discharged onto SCT, they should complete the relevant statutory form and send it to the hospital managers. The responsible clinician must specify on the form the date that the community treatment order (CTO) is to be made. This date is the authority for SCT to begin, and may be a short while after the date on which the form is signed, to allow time for arrangements to be put in place for the patient's discharge.

Section 17B

Conditions to be attached to the community treatment order

25.29 The CTO must include the conditions with which the patient is required to comply while on SCT. There are two conditions which must be included in all cases. Patients are required to make themselves available for medical examination:

- when needed for consideration of extension of the CTO; and

- if necessary, to allow a SOAD to provide a Part 4A certificate authorising treatment.

25.30 Responsible clinicians may also, with the AMHP's agreement, set other conditions which they think are necessary or appropriate to:

- ensure that the patient receives medical treatment for mental disorder;

- prevent a risk of harm to the patient's health or safety;

- protect other people.

25.31 Conditions may be set for any or all of these purposes, but not for any other reason. The AMHP's agreement to the proposed conditions must be obtained before the CTO can be made.

25.32 In considering what conditions might be necessary or appropriate, the responsible clinician should always keep in view the patient's specific cultural needs and background. The patient, and (subject to the normal considerations of patient confidentiality) any others with an interest such as a parent or carer, should be consulted.

25.33 The conditions should:

- be kept to a minimum number consistent with achieving their purpose;

- restrict the patient's liberty as little as possible while being consistent with achieving their purpose;

- have a clear rationale, linked to one or more of the purposes in **paragraph 25.30**; and

- be clearly and precisely expressed, so that the patient can readily understand what is expected.

25.34 The nature of the conditions will depend on the patient's individual circumstances. Subject to **paragraph 25.33**, they might cover matters such as where and when the patient is to receive treatment in the community; where the patient is to live; and avoidance of known risk factors or high-risk situations relevant to the patient's mental disorder.

25.35 The reasons for any conditions should be explained to the patient and others, as appropriate, and recorded in the patient's notes. It will be important, if SCT is to be successful, that the patient agrees to keep to the conditions, or to try to do so, and that patients have access to the help they need to be able to comply.

Information for SCT patients and others

25.36 As soon as the decision is made to discharge a patient onto SCT, the responsible clinician should inform the patient and others consulted of the decision, the conditions to be applied to the CTO, and the services which will be available for the patient in the community.

25.37 There is a duty on hospital managers to take steps to ensure that patients understand what SCT means for them and their rights to apply for discharge. This includes giving patients information both orally and in writing and must be done as soon as practicable after the patient goes onto SCT. Hospital managers' information policies should set out whether this information is to be provided by the responsible clinician, by another member of the professional team or by someone else. A copy of this information must also be provided to the nearest relative (subject to the normal considerations about involving nearest relatives – see **paragraphs 2.27-2.33**). (See also **paragraphs 18.18-18.20** and **30.29** on information to be given to the victims of certain Part 3 patients.)

Monitoring SCT patients

25.38 It will be important to maintain close contact with a patient on SCT and to monitor their mental health and wellbeing after they leave hospital. The type and scope of the arrangements will vary depending on the patient's needs and individual circumstances and the way in which local services are organised. All those involved will need to agree to the arrangements. Respective responsibilities should be clearly set out in the patient's care plan. The care co-ordinator will normally be responsible for co-ordinating the care plan, working with the responsible clinician (if they are different people), the team responsible for the patient's care and any others with an interest.

25.39 Appropriate action will need to be taken if the patient becomes unwell, engages in high-risk behaviour as a result of mental disorder or withdraws consent to treatment (or begins to object to it). The responsible clinician should consider, with the patient (and others where appropriate), the reasons for this and what the next steps should be. If the patient refuses crucial treatment, an urgent review of the situation will be needed, and recalling the patient to hospital will be an option if the risk justifies it. If suitable alternative treatment is available which would allow SCT to continue safely and which the patient would accept, the responsible clinician should consider such treatment if this can be offered. If so, the treatment plan, and if necessary the conditions of the CTO, should be varied accordingly (note that a revised Part 4A certificate may be required).

25.40 If the patient is not complying with any condition of the CTO the reasons for this will need to be properly investigated. Recall to hospital may need to be considered if it is no longer safe and appropriate for the patient to remain in the community. The conditions may need to be reviewed – for example, if the patient's health has improved a particular condition may no longer be relevant or necessary. The responsible clinician may vary conditions as appropriate (see **paragraphs 25.41-25.45**). Changes may also be needed to the patient's care or treatment plan.

Varying and suspending conditions

25.41 The responsible clinician has the power to vary the conditions of the patient's CTO, or to suspend any of them. The responsible clinician does not need to agree any variation or suspension with the AMHP. However, it would not be good practice to vary conditions which had recently been agreed with an AMHP without discussion with that AMHP.

25.42 Suspension of one or more of the conditions may be appropriate to allow for a temporary change in circumstances, for example, the patient's temporary absence or a change in treatment regime. The responsible clinician should record any decision to suspend conditions in the patient's notes, with reasons.

25.43 A variation of the conditions might be appropriate where the patient's treatment needs or living circumstances have changed. Any condition no longer required should be removed.

25.44 It will be important to discuss any proposed changes to the conditions with the patient and to ensure that the patient, and anyone else affected by the changes (subject to the patient's right to confidentiality), knows that they are being considered, and why. As when the conditions were first set, the patient will need to agree to try to keep to any new or varied conditions if SCT is to work successfully, and any help the patient needs to comply with them should be made available. (See also **paragraphs 18.10-18.13**.)

25.45 Any variation in the conditions must be recorded on the relevant statutory form, which should be sent to the hospital managers.

Responding to concerns raised by the patient's carer or relatives

25.46 Particular attention should be paid to carers and relatives when they raise a concern that the patient is not complying with the conditions or that the patient's mental health appears to be deteriorating. The team responsible for the patient needs to give due weight to those concerns and any requests made by the carers or relatives in deciding what action to take. Carers and relatives are typically in much more frequent contact with the patient than professionals, even under well-run care plans. Their concerns may prompt a review of how SCT is working for that patient and whether the criteria for recall to hospital might be met. The managers of responsible hospitals should ensure that local protocols are in place to cover how concerns raised should be addressed and taken forward. (See also **paragraphs 18.2-18.5**.)

Section 17E ## Recall to hospital

25.47 The recall power is intended to provide a means to respond to evidence of relapse or high-risk behaviour relating to mental disorder before the situation becomes critical and leads to the patient or other people being harmed. The need for recall might arise as a result of relapse, or through a change in the patient's circumstances giving rise to increased risk.

25.48 The responsible clinician may recall a patient on SCT to hospital for treatment if:

- the patient needs to receive treatment for mental disorder in hospital (either as an in-patient or as an out-patient); and

- there would be a risk of harm to the health or safety of the patient or to other people if the patient were not recalled.

25.49 A patient may also be recalled to hospital if they break either of the two mandatory conditions which must be included in all CTOs – that is, by failing to make themselves available for medical examination to allow consideration of extension of the CTO or to enable a SOAD to complete a Part 4A certificate. The patient must always be given the opportunity to comply with the condition before recall is considered. Before exercising the recall power for this reason, the responsible clinician should consider whether the patient has a valid reason for failing to comply, and should take any further action accordingly.

25.50 The responsible clinician must be satisfied that the criteria are met before using the recall power. Any action should be proportionate to the level of risk. For some patients, the risk arising from a failure to comply with treatment could indicate an immediate need for recall. In other cases, negotiation with the patient – and with the nearest relative and any carer (unless the patient objects or it is not reasonably practicable) – may resolve the problem and so avert the need for recall.

25.51 The responsible clinician should consider in each case whether recalling the patient to hospital is justified in all the circumstances. For example, it might be sufficient to monitor a patient who has failed to comply with a condition to attend for treatment, before deciding whether the lack of treatment means that recall is necessary. A patient may also agree to admission to hospital on a voluntary basis. Failure to comply with a condition (apart from those relating to availability for medical examination, as above) does not in itself trigger recall. Only if the breach of a condition results in an increased risk of harm to the patient or to anyone else will recall be justified.

25.52 However, it may be necessary to recall a patient whose condition is deteriorating despite compliance with treatment, if the risk cannot be managed otherwise.

25.53 Recall to hospital for treatment should not become a regular or normal event for any patient on SCT. If recall is being used frequently, the responsible clinician should review the patient's treatment plan to consider whether it could be made more acceptable to the patient, or whether, in the individual circumstances of the case, SCT continues to be appropriate.

Procedure for recall to hospital

25.54 The responsible clinician has responsibility for co-ordinating the recall process, unless it has been agreed locally that someone else will do this. It will be important to ensure that the practical impact of recalling the patient on the patient's domestic circumstances is considered and managed.

25.55 The responsible clinician must complete a written notice of recall to hospital, which is effective only when served on the patient. It is important that, wherever possible, the notice should be handed to the patient personally. Otherwise, the notice is served by delivery to the patient's usual or last known address. (See **paragraphs 25.57-25.58**.)

25.56 Once the recall notice has been served, the patient can, if necessary, be treated as absent without leave, and taken and conveyed to hospital (and a patient who leaves the hospital without permission can be returned there). The time at which the notice is deemed to be served will vary according to the method of delivery.

25.57 It will not usually be appropriate to post a notice of recall
to the patient. This may, however, be an option if the
patient has failed to attend for medical examination as
required by the conditions of the CTO, despite having
been requested to do so, when the need for the
examination is not urgent (see **paragraph 25.49**).
First class post should be used. The notice is deemed to
be served on the second working day after posting, and
it will be important to allow sufficient time for the patient
to receive the notice before any action is taken to
ensure compliance.

25.58 Where the need for recall is urgent, as will usually be the
case, it will be important that there is certainty as to the
timing of delivery of the notice. A notice handed to the
patient is effective immediately. However, it may not be
possible to achieve this if the patient's whereabouts are
unknown, or if the patient is unavailable or simply refuses
to accept the notice. In that event the notice should be
delivered by hand to the patient's usual or last known
address. The notice is then deemed to be served (even
though it may not actually be received by the patient) on
the day after it is delivered – that is, the day (which does
not have to be a working day) beginning immediately
after midnight following delivery.

25.59 If the patient's whereabouts are known but access to the
patient cannot be obtained, it may be necessary to
consider whether a warrant issued under section 135(2)
is needed (see **chapter 10**).

25.60 The patient should be conveyed to hospital in the least
restrictive manner possible. If appropriate, the patient
may be accompanied by a family member, carer or friend.
(See also **chapter 11**.)

25.61 The responsible clinician should ensure that the hospital to
which the patient is recalled is ready to receive the patient
and to provide treatment. While recall must be to a
hospital, the required treatment may then be given on an
out-patient basis, if appropriate.

25.62 The hospital need not be the patient's responsible hospital (that is, the hospital where the patient was detained immediately before going onto SCT) or under the same management as that hospital. A copy of the notice of recall, which provides the authority to detain the patient, should be sent to the managers of the hospital to which the patient is being recalled.

25.63 When the patient arrives at hospital after recall, the clinical team will need to assess the patient's condition, provide the necessary treatment and determine the next steps. The patient may be well enough to return to the community once treatment has been given, or may need a longer period of assessment or treatment in hospital. The patient may be detained in hospital for a maximum of 72 hours after recall to allow the responsible clinician to determine what should happen next. During this period the patient remains an SCT patient, even if they remain in hospital for one or more nights. The responsible clinician may allow the patient to leave the hospital at any time within the 72-hour period. Once 72 hours from the time of admission have elapsed, the patient must be allowed to leave if the responsible clinician has not revoked the CTO (see **paragraphs 25.65-25.70**). On leaving hospital the patient will remain on SCT as before.

25.64 In considering the options, the responsible clinician and the clinical team will need to consider the reasons why it was necessary to exercise the recall power and whether SCT remains the right option for that patient. They will also need to consider, with the patient, the nearest relative (subject to the normal considerations about involving nearest relatives), and any carers, what changes might be needed to help to prevent the circumstances that led to recall from recurring. It may be that a variation in the conditions is required, or a change in the care plan (or both).

Revoking the CTO

25.65 If the patient requires in-patient treatment for longer than 72 hours after arrival at the hospital, the responsible clinician should consider revoking the CTO. The effect of revoking the CTO is that the patient will again be detained under the powers of the Act.

25.66 The CTO may be revoked if:

- the responsible clinician considers that the patient again needs to be admitted to hospital for medical treatment under the Act; and

- an AMHP agrees with that assessment, and also believes that it is appropriate to revoke the CTO.

25.67 In making the decision as to whether it is appropriate to revoke a CTO, the AMHP should consider the wider social context for the patient, in the same way as when making decisions about applications for admissions under the Act (see **chapter 4**).

25.68 As before, the AMHP carrying out this role may (but need not) be already involved in the patient's care and treatment, or can be an AMHP acting on behalf of any willing LSSA. If no other LSSA is willing, responsibility for ensuring that an AMHP considers the case should lie with the LSSA which has been responsible for the patient's after-care.

25.69 If the AMHP does not agree that the CTO should be revoked, then the patient cannot be detained in hospital after the end of the maximum recall period of 72 hours. The patient will therefore remain on SCT. A record of the AMHP's decision and the full reasons for it should be kept in the patient's notes. It would not be appropriate for the responsible clinician to approach another AMHP for an alternative view.

25.70 If the responsible clinician and the AMHP agree that the CTO should be revoked, they must complete the relevant statutory form for the revocation to take legal effect, and send it to the hospital managers. The patient is then detained again under the powers of the Act exactly as before going onto SCT, except that a new detention period of six months begins for the purposes of review and applications to the Tribunal (see also **paragraph 24.31**).

Hospital managers' responsibilities

25.71 It is the responsibility of the hospital managers to ensure that no patient is detained following recall for longer than 72 hours unless the CTO is revoked. The relevant statutory form must be completed on the patient's arrival at hospital. Hospital managers should ensure that arrangements are in place to monitor the patient's length of stay following the time of detention after recall, as recorded on the form, so that the maximum period of detention is not exceeded. (See also **paragraphs 2.8-2.15** on information for patients.)

25.72 The hospital managers should also ensure that arrangements are in place to cover any necessary transfers of responsibility between responsible clinicians in the community and in hospital.

25.73 If a patient's CTO is revoked and the patient is detained in a hospital other than the one which was the responsible hospital at the time of recall, the hospital managers of the new hospital must send a copy of the revocation form to the managers of the original hospital.

25.74 The hospital managers have a duty to ensure that a patient whose CTO is revoked is referred to the Tribunal without delay.

Review of SCT

25.75 In addition to the statutory requirements in the Act for review of SCT, it is good practice to review the patient's progress on SCT as part of all reviews of the CPA care plan or its equivalent.

25.76 Reviews should cover whether SCT is meeting the patient's treatment needs and, if not, what action is necessary to address this. A patient who no longer satisfies all the criteria for SCT must be discharged without delay.

Discharge from SCT

Sections 23 and 72

25.77 SCT patients may be discharged in the same way as detained patients, by the Tribunal, the hospital managers, or (for Part 2 patients) the nearest relative. The responsible clinician may also discharge an SCT patient at any time and must do so if the patient no longer meets the criteria for SCT. A patient's CTO should not simply be allowed to lapse.

25.78 The reasons for discharge should be explained to the patient, and any concerns on the part of the patient, the nearest relative or any carer should be considered and dealt with as far as possible. On discharge from SCT, the team should ensure that any after-care services the patient continues to need under section 117 of the Act will be available.

25.79 If guardianship is considered the better option for a patient on SCT, an application may be made in the usual way.

Related material

- *Refocusing the Care Programme Approach,* Care Programme Approach guidance, March 2008

  This material does not form part of the Code. It is provided for assistance only.

APPLYING THE PRINCIPLES

This scenario is not intended to provide a template for decisions in applying the principles in similar situations. The scenario itself is only illustrative and does not form part of the Code itself.

RECALL OF A SUPERVISED COMMUNITY TREATMENT PATIENT TO HOSPITAL

Mary has a long-standing bipolar disorder. She has been on SCT for the past 12 months following an initial two months' detention in hospital.

Mary's condition has been managed successfully by a care plan which includes oral medication. However, it has transpired that Mary has missed taking a significant amount of her medication over the past couple of weeks.

One of the conditions of Mary's CTO is that she regularly attends a named clinic to review her treatment and progress. For the first time since her discharge from hospital, she fails to attend.

The responsible clinician meets with members of the multi-disciplinary team to decide whether Mary needs to be recalled to hospital for treatment.

When the multi-disciplinary team members meet, they are required to consider the principles. Among the questions they might wish to consider in making a decision in these circumstances are the following.

Purpose principle
- What are the risks to Mary and others if she does not receive her medication? How soon might those risks arise and in what circumstances?

- What will be best for Mary's wellbeing overall?

Least restriction principle

- What are the possible alternatives for managing Mary's care? For example, the multi-disciplinary team contacting Mary, or arranging a home visit to see her.

- Would varying the conditions of the CTO assist Mary to comply with her treatment programme?

- Might Mary be prepared to accept another treatment regime if there is an alternative which would be as clinically effective?

- Have alternative options been explored with Mary before?

Respect principle

- What is Mary's view of why she has stopped taking her medication?

- Is Mary's failure to attend clinic anything to do with a conscious decision to refuse medication, or is there some other reason? Have all possible reasons been considered?

- Are there any social, cultural or family-related factors, which may have led Mary to miss her appointment?

- Taking into account Mary's history and known past and present wishes, are there any particular reasons why Mary may not have presented at the clinic?

- Has Mary expressed any views about what she would like to happen if she stopped taking her medication?

Participation principle

- Is Mary willing to discuss what is going on?

- What might be the best way of approaching Mary to discuss the current situation?

- Are Mary's family or carers involved in her day-to-day care aware that she is on SCT, and if so should their views be sought on the best way to help Mary to re-establish contact with services?

- What is Mary's view about her family being contacted?

- Have Mary's family or carers expressed any views about what they think may help Mary?

- Does Mary's GP have any ideas about engaging Mary?

Effectiveness, efficiency and equity principle

- Mary has said in the past that she enjoys her contact with the team's community psychiatric nurse (CPN) – would giving her more time with the CPN be an effective way of tackling the current situation? Could it be done without other patients with the same or greater clinical needs being disadvantaged?

CHAPTER 26
Guardianship

26.1   This chapter gives guidance on guardianship under the Act.

Reference Guide chapter 19

Purpose of guardianship

26.2   The purpose of guardianship is to enable patients to receive care outside hospital when it cannot be provided without the use of compulsory powers. Such care may or may not include specialist medical treatment for mental disorder.

26.3   A guardian may be a local social services authority (LSSA) or someone else approved by an LSSA (a "private guardian"). Guardians have three specific powers as follows:

Section 8

- they have the exclusive right to decide where a patient should live, taking precedence even over an attorney or deputy appointed under the Mental Capacity Act 2005 (MCA);

- they can require the patient to attend for treatment, work, training or education at specific times and places (but they cannot use force to take the patient there);

- they can demand that a doctor, approved mental health professional (AMHP) or another relevant person has access to the patient at the place where the patient lives.

26.4   Guardianship therefore provides an authoritative framework for working with a patient, with a minimum of constraint, to achieve as independent a life as possible within the community. Where it is used, it should be part of the patient's overall care plan.

26.5 Guardianship does not give anyone the right to treat the patient without their permission or to consent to treatment on their behalf.

26.6 While the reception of a patient into guardianship does not affect the continued authority of an attorney or deputy appointed under the MCA, such attorneys and deputies will not be able to take decisions about where a guardianship patient is to reside, or take any other decisions which conflict with those of the guardian.

Assessment for guardianship

26.7 An application for guardianship may be made on the grounds that:

- the patient is suffering from mental disorder of a nature or degree which warrants their reception into guardianship; and

- it is necessary, in the interests of the welfare of the patient or for the protection of other persons, that the patient should be so received.

26.8 Guardianship is most likely to be appropriate where:

- the patient is thought to be likely to respond well to the authority and attention of a guardian and so be more willing to comply with necessary treatment and care for their mental disorder; or

- there is a particular need for someone to have the authority to decide where the patient should live or to insist that doctors, AMHPs or other people be given access to the patient.

26.9 As with applications for detention in hospital, AMHPs and doctors making recommendations should consider whether the objectives of the proposed application could be achieved in another, less restrictive, way, without the use of guardianship.

26.10 Where patients lack capacity to make some or all important decisions concerning their own welfare, one potential alternative to guardianship will be to rely solely on the MCA – especially the protection from liability for actions taken in connection with care or treatment provided by section 5 of the MCA. While this is a factor to be taken into account, it will not by itself determine whether guardianship is necessary or unnecessary. AMHPs and doctors need to consider all the circumstances of the particular case.

26.11 Where an adult is assessed as requiring residential care but lacks the capacity to make a decision about whether they wish to be placed there, guardianship is unlikely to be necessary where the move can properly, quickly and efficiently be carried out on the basis of:

- section 5 of the MCA or the decision of an attorney or deputy; or

- (where relevant) the MCA's deprivation of liberty safeguards.[1]

26.12 But guardianship may still be appropriate in such cases if:

- there are other reasons – unconnected to the move to residential care – to think that the patient might benefit from the attention and authority of a guardian;

- there is a particular need to have explicit statutory authority for the patient to be returned to the place where the patient is to live should they go absent; or

- it is thought to be important that decisions about where the patient is to live are placed in the hands of a single person or authority – for example, where there have been long-running or particularly difficult disputes about where the person should live.

26.13 However, it will not always be best to use guardianship as the way of deciding where patients who lack capacity to decide for themselves must live. In cases which raise unusual issues, or where guardianship is being considered

[1] The deprivation of liberty safeguards are expected to be in force from April 2009.

243

in the interests of the patient's welfare and there are finely balanced arguments about where the patient should live, it may be preferable instead to seek a best interests decision from the Court of Protection under the MCA.

26.14 Where the relevant criteria are met, guardianship may be considered in respect of a patient who is to be discharged from detention under the Mental Health Act. However, if it is thought that the patient needs to remain liable to be recalled to hospital (and the patient is eligible), supervised community treatment is likely to be more appropriate (see **chapter 28**).

Responsibilities of local social services authorities

26.15 Each LSSA should have a policy setting out the arrangements for:

- receiving, scrutinising and accepting or refusing applications for guardianship. Such arrangements should ensure that applications are properly but quickly dealt with;

- monitoring the progress of each patient's guardianship, including steps to be taken to fulfil the authority's statutory obligations in relation to private guardians and to arrange visits to the patient;

- ensuring the suitability of any proposed private guardian, and that they are able to understand and carry out their duties under the Act;

- ensuring that patients under guardianship receive, both orally and in writing, information in accordance with regulations under the Act;

- ensuring that patients are aware of their right to apply to the Tribunal and that they are given the name of someone who will give them the necessary assistance, on behalf of the LSSA, in making such an application;

- authorising an approved clinician to be the patient's responsible clinician;

- maintaining detailed records relating to guardianship patients;

- ensuring that the need to continue guardianship is reviewed in the last two months of each period of guardianship in accordance with the Act; and

- discharging patients from guardianship as soon as it is no longer required.

26.16 Patients may be discharged from guardianship at any time by the LSSA, the responsible clinician authorised by the LSSA, or (in most cases) the patient's nearest relative. Section 23

26.17 Discharge decisions by LSSAs may be taken only by the LSSA itself, or by three or more members of the LSSA or of a committee or sub-committee of the LSSA authorised for that purpose. Where decisions are taken by three or more members of the LSSA (or a committee or sub-committee), all three people (or at least three of them, if there are more) must agree.

26.18 LSSAs may consider discharging patients from guardianship at any time, but must consider doing so when they receive a report from the patient's nominated medical attendant or responsible clinician renewing their guardianship under section 20 of the Act.

Components of effective guardianship

Care planning

26.19 An application for guardianship should be accompanied by a comprehensive care plan established on the basis of multi-disciplinary discussions in accordance with the Care Programme Approach (or its equivalent).

26.20 The plan should identify the services needed by the patient and who will provide them. It should also indicate which of the powers that guardians have under the Act are necessary to achieve the plan. If none of the powers are required, guardianship should not be used.

26.21 Key elements of the plan are likely to be:

- suitable accommodation to help meet the patient's needs;

- access to day care, education and training facilities, as appropriate;

- effective co-operation and communication between all those concerned in implementing the plan; and

- (if there is to be a private guardian) support from the LSSA for the guardian.

26.22 A private guardian should be prepared to advocate on behalf of the patient in relation to those agencies whose services are needed to carry out the care plan. So should an LSSA which is itself the guardian.

26.23 A private guardian should be a person who can appreciate any special disabilities and needs of a mentally disordered person and who will look after the patient in an appropriate and sympathetic way. The guardian should display an interest in promoting the patient's physical and mental health and in providing for their occupation, training, employment, recreation and general welfare in a suitable way. The LSSA must satisfy itself that a proposed private guardian is capable of carrying out their functions and it should assist them with advice and other forms of support.

26.24 Regulations require private guardians to appoint a doctor as the patient's nominated medical attendant. It is the nominated medical attendant who must examine the patient during the last two months of each period of guardianship and decide whether to make a report extending the patient's guardianship. (Where the patient's guardian is the LSSA itself, this is done by the responsible clinician authorised by the LSSA.)

26.25 It is for private guardians themselves to decide whom to appoint as the nominated medical attendant, but they should first consult the LSSA. The nominated medical attendant may be the patient's GP, if the GP agrees.

Power to require a patient to live in a particular place

26.26 Guardians have the power to decide where patients should live. If patients leave the place where they are required to live without the guardian's permission, they can be taken into legal custody and brought back there (see **chapter 22**). Section 18(3)

26.27 This power can also be used to take patients for the first time to the place they are required to live, if patients do not (or, in practice, cannot) go there by themselves. Section 18(7)

26.28 Patients should always be consulted first about where they are to be required to live, unless their mental state makes that impossible. Guardians should not use this power to make a patient move without warning.

26.29 The power to take or return patients to the place they are required to live may be used, for example, to discourage them from:

- living somewhere the guardian considers unsuitable;

- breaking off contact with services;

- leaving the area before proper arrangements can be made; or

- sleeping rough.

But it may not be used to restrict their freedom to come and go so much that they are effectively being detained.

26.30 The power to require patients to reside in a particular place may not be used to require them to live in a situation in which they are deprived of liberty, unless that is authorised separately under the MCA. That authorisation will only be possible if the patient lacks capacity to decide where to live. If deprivation of liberty is authorised under the MCA, the LSSA should consider whether guardianship remains necessary, bearing in mind the guidance earlier in this chapter.

Guardianship and hospital care

26.31 Guardianship does not restrict patients' access to hospital services on an informal basis. Patients who require treatment but do not need to be detained may be admitted informally in the same way as any other patient. This applies to both physical and mental healthcare.

26.32 Nor does guardianship prevent an authorisation being granted under the deprivation of liberty safeguards[2] in the MCA, if the person needs to be detained in a hospital in their best interests in order to receive care and treatment, so long as it would not be inconsistent with the guardian's decision about where the patient should live.

26.33 Otherwise, guardianship should not be used to require a patient to reside in a hospital except where it is necessary for a very short time in order to provide shelter while accommodation in the community is being arranged.

Section 6

26.34 Guardianship can remain in force if the patient is detained in hospital under section 2 or 4 of the Mental Health Act for assessment, but it ends automatically if a patient is detained for treatment as a result of an application under section 3. Regulations also allow a patient to be transferred from guardianship to detention in hospital under section 3. The normal requirements for an application and medical recommendations must be met, and the transfer must be agreed by the LSSA.

Patients who resist the authority of the guardian

26.35 If a patient consistently resists exercise by the guardian of any of their powers, it can normally be concluded that guardianship is not the most appropriate form of care for that person, and the guardianship should be discharged. However, the LSSA should first consider whether a change of guardian – or change in the person who, in practice, exercises the LSSA's powers as guardian – might be appropriate instead.

[2] The deprivation of liberty safeguards are expected to be in force from April 2009.

Guardianship orders under section 37

Reference Guide
19.60-19.66

26.36 Guardianship may be used by courts as an alternative to hospital orders for offenders with mental disorders where the criteria set out in the Act are met. The court must first be satisfied that the LSSA or named person is willing to act as guardian. In considering the appropriateness of the patient being received into their guardianship, LSSAs should be guided by the same considerations as apply to applications for guardianship under Part 2 of the Act.

26.37 The guidance in this chapter on components of effective guardianship applies to guardianship order patients in the same way as it applies to other guardianship patients. The main difference between applications for guardianship under Part 2 of the Act and guardianship orders is that nearest relatives may not discharge patients from guardianship orders. Nearest relatives have rights to apply to the Tribunal instead.

Related material

- Mental Capacity Act 2005

- *Mental Capacity Act 2005 Code of Practice*, TSO, 2007

- *Deprivation of Liberty Safeguards*, Addendum to the *Mental Capacity Act 2005 Code of Practice*[3]

  This material does not form part of the Code. It is provided for assistance only.

---

[3]To be published later in 2008.

CHAPTER 27
After-care

Reference Guide
chapter 24 27.1 This chapter gives guidance on the duty to provide after-care for patients under section 117 of the Act.

Section 117 after-care

27.2 Section 117 of the Act requires primary care trusts (PCTs) and local social services authorities (LSSAs), in co-operation with voluntary agencies, to provide after-care to patients detained in hospital for treatment under section 3, 37, 45A, 47 or 48 of the Act who then cease to be detained. This includes patients granted leave of absence under section 17 and patients going onto supervised community treatment (SCT).

27.3 The duty to provide after-care services continues as long as the patient is in need of such services. In the case of a patient on SCT, after-care must be provided for the entire period they are on SCT, but this does not mean that the patient's need for after-care will necessarily cease as soon as they are no longer on SCT.

27.4 Services provided under section 117 can include services provided directly by PCTs or LSSAs as well as services they commission from other providers.

27.5 After-care is a vital component in patients' overall treatment and care. As well as meeting their immediate needs for health and social care, after-care should aim to support them in regaining or enhancing their skills, or learning new skills, in order to cope with life outside hospital.

27.6 Where eligible patients have remained in hospital informally after ceasing to be detained under the Act, they are still entitled to after-care under section 117 once they leave hospital. This also applies when patients are released from prison, having spent part of their sentence detained in hospital under a relevant section of the Act.

After-care planning

27.7 When considering relevant patients' cases, the Tribunal and hospital managers will expect to be provided with information from the professionals concerned on what after-care arrangements might be made for them under section 117 if they were to be discharged. Some discussion of after-care needs, involving LSSAs and other relevant agencies, should take place in advance of the hearing.

27.8 Although the duty to provide after-care begins when the patient leaves hospital, the planning of after-care needs to start as soon as the patient is admitted to hospital. PCTs and LSSAs should take reasonable steps to identify appropriate after-care services for patients before their actual discharge from hospital.

27.9 Where a Tribunal or hospital managers' hearing has been arranged for a patient who might be entitled to after-care under section 117 of the Act, the hospital managers should ensure that the relevant PCT and LSSA have been informed. The PCT and LSSA should consider putting practical preparations in hand for after-care in every case, but should in particular consider doing so where there is a strong possibility that the patient will be discharged if appropriate after-care can be arranged. Where the Tribunal has provisionally decided to give a restricted patient a conditional discharge, the PCT and LSSA must do their best to put after-care in place which would allow that discharge to take place.

27.10 Before deciding to discharge, or grant more than very short-term leave of absence to, a patient, or to place a patient onto SCT, the responsible clinician should ensure that the patient's needs for after-care have been fully assessed, discussed with the patient and addressed in their care plan. If the patient is being given leave for only a short period, a less comprehensive review may be sufficient, but the arrangements for the patient's care should still be properly recorded.

27.11 After-care for all patients admitted to hospital for treatment for mental disorder should be planned within the framework of the Care Programme Approach (or its equivalent), whether or not they are detained or will be entitled to receive after-care under section 117 of the Act. But because of the specific statutory obligation it is important that all patients who are entitled to after-care under section 117 are identified and that records are kept of what after-care is provided to them under that section.

27.12 In order to ensure that the after-care plan reflects the needs of each patient, it is important to consider who needs to be involved, in addition to patients themselves. This may include:

- the patient's responsible clinician;

- nurses and other professionals involved in caring for the patient in hospital;

- a clinical psychologist, community mental health nurse and other members of the community team;

- the patient's GP and primary care team;

- subject to the patient's views, any carer who will be involved in looking after them outside hospital, the patient's nearest relative or other family members;

- a representative of any relevant voluntary organisations;

- in the case of a restricted patient, the probation service;

- a representative of housing authorities, if accommodation is an issue;

- an employment expert, if employment is an issue;

- an independent mental health advocate,[1] if the patient has one;

- an independent mental capacity advocate, if the patient has one;

- the patient's attorney or deputy, if the patient has one; and

- any other representative nominated by the patient.

[1] Independent mental health advocacy services under the Act are expected to be introduced in April 2009.

27.13 A thorough assessment is likely to involve consideration of:

- continuing mental healthcare, whether in the community or on an out-patient basis;

- the psychological needs of the patient and, where appropriate, of their family and carers;

- physical healthcare;

- daytime activities or employment;

- appropriate accommodation;

- identified risks and safety issues;

- any specific needs arising from, for example, co-existing physical disability, sensory impairment, learning disability or autistic spectrum disorder;

- any specific needs arising from drug, alcohol or substance misuse (if relevant);

- any parenting or caring needs;

- social, cultural or spiritual needs;

- counselling and personal support;

- assistance in welfare rights and managing finances;

- the involvement of authorities and agencies in a different area, if the patient is not going to live locally;

- the involvement of other agencies, for example the probation service or voluntary organisations;

- for a restricted patient, the conditions which the Secretary of State for Justice or the Tribunal has imposed or is likely to impose on their conditional discharge; and

- contingency plans (should the patient's mental health deteriorate) and crisis contact details.

27.14 The professionals concerned should, in discussion with the patient, establish an agreed outline of the patient's needs and agree a timescale for the implementation of the various aspects of the after-care plan. All key people with specific responsibilities with regard to the patient should be properly identified.

27.15 It is important that those who are involved are able to take decisions regarding their own involvement and, as far as possible, that of their agency. If approval for plans needs to be obtained from more senior levels, it is important that this causes no delay to the implementation of the after-care plan.

27.16 If accommodation is to be offered as part of the after-care plan to patients who are offenders, the circumstances of any victims of the patient's offence(s) and their families should be taken into account when deciding where the accommodation should be offered. Where the patient is to live may be one of the conditions imposed by the Secretary of State for Justice or the Tribunal when conditionally discharging a restricted patient.

27.17 The after-care plan should be recorded in writing. Once the plan is agreed, it is essential that any changes are discussed with the patient as well as others involved with the patient before being implemented.

27.18 The after-care plan should be regularly reviewed. It will be the responsibility of the care co-ordinator (or other officer responsible for its review) to arrange reviews of the plan until it is agreed that it is no longer necessary.

Ending section 117 after-care services

27.19 The duty to provide after-care services exists until both the PCT and the LSSA are satisfied that the patient no longer requires them. The circumstances in which it is appropriate to end section 117 after-care will vary from person to person and according to the nature of the services being provided. The most clear-cut circumstance in which after-care will end is where the person's mental health has improved to a point where they no longer need services because of their mental disorder. But if these services include, for example, care in a specialist residential setting, the arrangements for their move to more appropriate accommodation will need to be in place before support under section 117 is finally withdrawn. Fully involving the patient in the decision-making process will play an important part in the successful ending of after-care.

27.20 After-care services under section 117 should not be withdrawn solely on the grounds that:

- the patient has been discharged from the care of specialist mental health services;

- an arbitrary period has passed since the care was first provided;

- the patient is deprived of their liberty under the Mental Capacity Act 2005;

- the patient may return to hospital informally or under section 2; or

- the patient is no longer on SCT or section 17 leave.

27.21 Even when the provision of after-care has been successful in that the patient is now well settled in the community, the patient may still continue to need after-care services, for example to prevent a relapse or further deterioration in their condition.

27.22 Patients are under no obligation to accept the after-care services they are offered, but any decisions they may make to decline them should be fully informed. An unwillingness to accept services does not mean that patients have no need to receive services, nor should it preclude them from receiving them under section 117 should they change their minds.

Related material

- *Refocusing the Care Programme Approach: Policy and Positive Practice Guidance*, March 2008

This material does not form part of the Code. It is provided for assistance only.

CHAPTER 28 Guardianship, leave of absence or SCT?

28.1 This chapter gives advice on deciding between guardianship, leave of absence and supervised community treatment (SCT) as ways of supporting patients once it is safe for them to leave hospital.

Deciding between guardianship, leave of absence and SCT

28.2 There are three ways in which an unrestricted patient may be subject to the powers of the Act while living in the community: guardianship, leave of absence and SCT.

28.3 **Guardianship** (section 7 of the Act) is social care-led and is primarily focused on patients with welfare needs. Its purpose is to enable patients to receive care in the community where it cannot be provided without the use of compulsory powers. (See **chapter 26**.)

Section 17(2A)

28.4 **Leave of absence** (section 17) is primarily intended to allow a patient detained under the Act to be temporarily absent from hospital where further in-patient treatment as a detained patient is still thought to be necessary. It is clearly suitable for short-term absences, to allow visits to family and so on. It may also be useful in the longer term, where the clinical team wish to see how the patient manages outside hospital before making the decision to discharge. However, for a number of patients, SCT may be a better option than longer-term leave for the ongoing management of their care. Reflecting this, whenever considering longer-term leave for a patient (that is, for more than seven consecutive days), the responsible clinician must first consider whether the patient should be discharged onto SCT instead. (See **chapter 21**.)

28.5 **SCT** (section 17A) is principally aimed at preventing the "revolving door" scenario and the prevention of harm which could arise from relapse. It is a more structured system than leave of absence and has more safeguards for patients. A key feature of SCT is that it is suitable only where there is no reason to think that the patient will need further treatment as a detained in-patient for the time being, but the responsible clinician needs to be able to recall the patient to hospital. (See **chapter 25**.)

28.6 Some pointers to the use of the three options are given in the following boxes.

SCT or longer-term leave of absence: relevant factors to consider

Factors suggesting longer-term leave	Factors suggesting SCT
• Discharge from hospital is for a specific purpose or a fixed period. • The patient's discharge from hospital is deliberately on a "trial" basis. • The patient is likely to need further in-patient treatment without their consent or compliance. • There is a serious risk of arrangements in the community breaking down or being unsatisfactory – more so than for SCT.	• There is confidence that the patient is ready for discharge from hospital on an indefinite basis. • There are good reasons to expect that the patient will not need to be detained for the treatment they need to be given. • The patient appears prepared to consent or comply with the treatment they need – but risks as below mean that recall may be necessary. • The risk of arrangements in the community breaking down, or of the patient needing to be recalled to hospital for treatment, is sufficiently serious to justify SCT, but not to the extent that it is very likely to happen.

SCT or guardianship: relevant factors to consider

Factors suggesting guardianship	Factors suggesting SCT
• The focus is on the patient's general welfare, rather than specifically on medical treatment. • There is little risk of the patient needing to be admitted compulsorily and quickly to hospital. • There is a need for enforceable power to require the patient to reside at a particular place.	• The main focus is on ensuring that the patient continues to receive necessary medical treatment for mental disorder, without having to be detained again. • Compulsory recall may well be necessary, and speed is likely to be important.

Deprivation of liberty[1] while on SCT, on leave or subject to guardianship

28.7   Patients who are on SCT or on leave, and who lack capacity to consent to the arrangements required for their care or treatment, may occasionally need to be detained in a care home for further care or treatment for their mental disorder in circumstances in which recall to hospital for this purpose is not considered necessary. The same might apply to admission to a care home or hospital because of physical health problems.

28.8   If so, the procedures for the deprivation of liberty safeguards in the Mental Capacity Act 2005 (MCA) should be followed. Deprivation of liberty under the MCA can exist alongside SCT or leave of absence, provided that there is no conflict with the conditions of SCT or leave of absence set by the patient's responsible clinician.

[1] The deprivation of liberty safeguards are expected to be in force from April 2009.

28.9   Where patients on SCT or on leave who lack capacity to
        consent to the arrangements required for their care or
        treatment need to be detained in hospital for further
        treatment for mental disorder, they should be recalled
        under the Mental Health Act itself. The MCA deprivation
        of liberty safeguards cannot be used instead.

28.10   For guidance on the interface between guardianship and
        the deprivation of liberty safeguards, see **chapter 26**
        on guardianship.

CHAPTER 29
Detention and SCT: renewal, extension and discharge

29.1 This chapter gives guidance on how the procedures in the Act for renewing detention and extending supervised community treatment (SCT) should be applied, and on responsible clinicians' and nearest relatives' power to discharge patients.

Reference Guide
12.65-12.95

Renewal of detention

29.2 Before it expires, responsible clinicians must decide whether patients' current period of detention should be renewed. Responsible clinicians must examine the patient and decide within the two months leading up to the expiry of the patient's detention whether the criteria for renewing detention under section 20 of the Act are met. They must also consult one or more other people who have been professionally concerned with the patient's medical treatment.

29.3 Where responsible clinicians are satisfied that the criteria for renewing the patient's detention are met, they must submit a report to that effect to the hospital managers.

29.4 But before responsible clinicians can submit that report, they are required to obtain the written agreement of another professional ("the second professional") that the criteria are met. This second professional must be professionally concerned with the patient's treatment and must not belong to the same profession as the responsible clinician.

29.5 Apart from that, the Act does not say who the second professional should be. Hospital managers should determine their own local policies on the selection of the second professional. Policies should be based on the principle that the involvement of a second professional is intended to provide an additional safeguard for patients by ensuring that:

CHAPTER

29

Detention
and SCT:
renewal,
extension
and
discharge

- renewal is formally agreed by at least two suitably qualified and competent professionals who are familiar with the patient's case;

- those two professionals are from different disciplines, and so bring different, but complementary, professional perspectives to bear; and

- the two professionals are able to reach their own decisions independently of one another.

29.6 Accordingly, second professionals should:

- have sufficient experience and expertise to decide whether the patient's continued detention is necessary and lawful, but need not be approved clinicians (nor be qualified to be one);

- have been actively involved in the planning, management or delivery of the patient's treatment; and

- have had sufficient recent contact with the patient to be able to make an informed judgement about the patient's case.

29.7 Second professionals should satisfy themselves, in line with the local policies, that they have sufficient information on which to make the decision. Whether that requires a separate clinical interview or examination of the patient will depend on the nature of the contact that the second professional already has with the patient and on the other circumstances of the case.

29.8 Before examining patients to decide whether to make a renewal report, responsible clinicians should identify and record who the second professional is to be. Hospital managers' policies may, if the hospital managers wish, say that the identity of the second professional is to be decided or agreed by a third party – such as a senior clinician or manager – but the Act does not require that.

29.9 Unless there are exceptional circumstances, the decision of the identified second professional should be accepted, even if the responsible clinician does not agree with it. If, in exceptional circumstances, it is decided that the agreement

261

of a different second professional should be sought, that decision should be drawn to the attention of the hospital managers if, as a result, a renewal report is made.

Reference Guide
15.71-15.103 ## Extending supervised community treatment

29.10 Only responsible clinicians may extend the period of a patient's SCT by extending the period of the community treatment order (CTO). To do so, responsible clinicians must examine the patient and decide, during the two months leading up to the day on which the patient's CTO is due to expire, whether the criteria for extending SCT under section 20A of the Act are met. They must also consult one or more other people who have been professionally concerned with the patient's medical treatment.

29.11 Where responsible clinicians are satisfied that the criteria for extending the patient's SCT are met, they must submit a report to that effect to the managers of the responsible hospital.

29.12 But before responsible clinicians can submit that report, they must obtain the written agreement of an approved mental health professional (AMHP).

29.13 This does not have to be the same AMHP who originally agreed that the patient should become an SCT patient. It may (but need not) be an AMHP who is already involved in the patient's care and treatment. It can be an AMHP acting on behalf of any willing local social services authority (LSSA). But if no other LSSA is willing, responsibility for ensuring that an AMHP considers the case should lie with the LSSA which is responsible under section 117 for the patient's after-care.

29.14 The role of the AMHP is to consider whether or not the criteria for extending SCT are met and, if so, whether an extension is appropriate.

Reference Guide
12.113-12.116 ## The responsible clinician's power of discharge

29.15 Section 23 of the Act allows responsible clinicians to discharge most detained patients and all SCT patients by giving an order in writing.

CHAPTER

29

Detention
and SCT:
renewal,
extension
and
discharge

29.16 Because responsible clinicians have the power to discharge patients, they must keep under review the appropriateness of using that power. If, at any time, responsible clinicians conclude that the criteria which would justify renewing a patient's detention or extending the patient's SCT (as the case may be) are not met, they should exercise their power of discharge. They should not wait until the patient's detention or SCT is due to expire.

29.17 A decision by a second professional not to agree to the renewal of detention does not bring a patient's current period of detention to an end before it is otherwise due to expire. Similarly, a decision by an AMHP not to agree to the extension of a patient's SCT does not end the existing period of SCT. But in both cases, it would normally be a reason for responsible clinicians to review whether they should use their power to discharge the patient.

The nearest relative's power of discharge

Reference Guide
12.101-12.112
(detention) and
15.104-15.112
(SCT)

29.18 Patients detained for assessment or treatment under Part 2 of the Act may also be discharged by their nearest relatives.

29.19 Before giving a discharge order, nearest relatives must give the hospital managers at least 72 hours' notice in writing of their intention to discharge the patient.

29.20 During that period, the patient's responsible clinician can block the discharge by issuing a "barring report" stating that, if discharged, the patient is likely to act in a manner dangerous to themselves or others.

Section 25(1)

29.21 This question focuses on the probability of dangerous acts, such as causing serious physical injury or lasting psychological harm, not merely on the patient's general need for safety and others' general need for protection.

29.22 The nearest relative's notice and discharge order must both be given in writing, but do not have to be in any specific form. In practice, hospital managers should treat a discharge order given without prior notice as being both notice of intention to discharge the patient after 72 hours and the actual order to do so.

263

29.23 Hospital managers should offer nearest relatives any help they require, such as providing them with a standard letter to complete. The following box illustrates what a standard letter might look like.

Illustrative standard letter for nearest relatives to use to discharge patients

---

To the managers of [INSERT NAME AND ADDRESS OF HOSPITAL IN WHICH THE PATIENT IS DETAINED, OR (FOR A SUPERVISED COMMUNITY TREATMENT PATIENT) THE RESPONSIBLE HOSPITAL.]

Order for discharge under section 23 of the Mental Health Act 1983

My name is [GIVE YOUR NAME] and my address is [GIVE YOUR ADDRESS]

[Complete A, B or C below]

A. To the best of my knowledge and belief, I am the nearest relative (within the meaning of the Mental Health Act 1983) of [NAME OF PATIENT].

OR

B. I have been authorised to exercise the functions of the nearest relative of [NAME OF PATIENT] by the county court.

OR

C. I have been authorised to exercise the functions of the nearest relative of [NAME OF PATIENT] by that person's nearest relative.

I give you notice of my intention to discharge the person named above, and I order their discharge from [SAY WHEN YOU WANT THE PATIENT DISCHARGED FROM DETENTION OR SUPERVISED COMMUNITY TREATMENT].

[Please note: you must leave at least 72 hours between when the hospital managers get this letter and when you want the patient discharged.]

Signed _____

Date _____

Discharge by the hospital managers and the Tribunal

29.24 Patients may also be discharged by the hospital managers and by the Tribunal. See **chapter 31** and **chapter 32** respectively.

CHAPTER

29

Detention
and SCT:
renewal,
extension
and
discharge

APPLYING THE PRINCIPLES

This scenario is not intended to provide a template for decisions in applying the principles in similar situations. The scenario itself is only illustrative and does not form part of the Code itself.

CONSIDERING RENEWAL OF DETENTION

Adele is a middle-aged woman who has been detained in hospital for five months. Adele has a long-term history of mental disorder and has been in hospital for periods totalling five of the past 30 years. In the past, she has been readmitted to hospital on more than one occasion after her condition relapsed following her discharge.

Adele is being examined so that a decision can be taken about whether to renew her detention, which is due to expire in six weeks. This involves considering the alternatives to renewing detention. The responsible clinician and the second professional apply the guiding principles of this Code, and accordingly consider the following.

Purpose principle

- Why is Adele being detained? What is the risk posed by her mental disorder and to whom? Can any risk only be managed by continuing to detain Adele?
- What effect does being detained in hospital have on Adele's wellbeing generally?
- What are the risks to Adele if she stays detained?

Least restriction principle

- What are the possible alternatives to renewal, eg specific community-based care and treatment (with or without SCT or guardianship)?
- If detention does need to be renewed, could Adele nonetheless safely be given more freedom – such as more frequent or longer leave of absence?

Respect principle

- What are Adele's views on her current condition and treatment plan? Does she think treatment in hospital should continue and, if so, does she think she still needs to be detained?

- Does Adele have a view on the risk to herself or others, were she not detained in hospital? Has she any ideas on how those risks could best be managed?

- Has Adele expressed any views, either now or previously, on similar circumstances in the past and how they were managed? Does Adele have any views on what worked and what did not and why?

- What are Adele's individual characteristics, her needs, aspirations and values, and how could these be supported?

- If Adele were a young man rather than a middle-aged woman, would the decision be approached differently? Is any difference justified?

Participation principle

- What is the best way of informing Adele of the purpose and process for undertaking the examination and of communicating the outcome? What might be the best way of explaining the reasoning for any decision that is contrary to what Adele wants?

- Does Adele want someone present to support her during the examination? Are there any valid reasons for not following her wishes?

- Are there any paid or unpaid carers, family members and friends, or anyone else, whose views ought to be sought? What does Adele think about the idea of involving these people?

- Does Adele, or do any of the other people to be consulted, have any particular communication needs which need to be taken into account and addressed?

- Has Adele been reminded of her right to an independent mental health advocate (IMHA) to enable support through this process?[1]

[1] Independent mental health advocacy services under the Act are expected to be introduced in April 2009.

CHAPTER

29

Detention
and SCT:
renewal,
extension
and
discharge

- Has the responsible clinician considered requesting an IMHA to contact Adele directly?

Effectiveness, efficiency and equity principle

- Are there resources in the community to safely help Adele manage her mental health?
- Based on the available evidence, how likely is a community treatment programme to work? Would there be a benefit for Adele's condition and her general wellbeing and that of her family?

CHAPTER 30 **Functions of hospital managers**

30.1 This chapter gives general guidance on the responsibilities of hospital managers under the Act, and on specific powers and duties not addressed in other chapters, including those in relation to transfers between hospitals, victims of crime, patients' correspondence and references to the Tribunal.

Reference Guide 1.32-1.35 ## Identification of hospital managers

30.2 In England, NHS hospitals are managed by NHS trusts, NHS foundation trusts and primary care trusts (PCTs). For these hospitals, the trusts themselves are defined as the hospital managers for the purposes of the Act. In an independent hospital, the person or persons in whose name the hospital is registered are the hospital managers.

30.3 It is the hospital managers who have the authority to detain patients under the Act. They have the primary responsibility for seeing that the requirements of the Act are followed. In particular, they must ensure that patients are detained only as the Act allows, that their treatment and care accord fully with its provisions, and that they are fully informed of, and are supported in exercising, their statutory rights.

30.4 As managers of what the Act terms "responsible hospitals", hospital managers have equivalent responsibilities towards patients on supervised community treatment (SCT), even if those patients are not actually being treated at one of their hospitals.

30.5 In practice, most of the decisions of the hospital managers are actually taken by individuals (or groups of individuals) on their behalf. In particular, decisions about discharge from detention and SCT are taken by panels of people ("managers' panels") specifically selected for the role.

30.6 In this chapter, unless otherwise stated, "hospital managers" includes anyone authorised to take decisions on their behalf, except managers' panels.

Exercise of hospital managers' functions

Reference Guide 12.5-12.13 (detention) and 15.7-15.8 (SCT)

30.7 Special rules apply to the exercise of the hospital managers' power to discharge patients from detention or SCT. In broad terms, this power can be delegated only to managers' panels made up of people (sometimes called "associate hospital managers") appointed specifically for the purpose who are not officers or employees of the organisation concerned. For guidance on this power see **chapter 31**.

30.8 Otherwise, hospital managers (meaning the organisation, or individual, in charge of the hospital) may arrange for their functions to be carried out, day to day, by particular people on their behalf. In some cases, regulations say they must do so.

30.9 The arrangements for who is authorised to take which decisions should be set out in a scheme of delegation. If the hospital managers are an organisation, that scheme of delegation should be approved by a resolution of the body itself. Unless the Act or the regulations say otherwise, organisations may delegate their functions under the Act to any one and in any way which their constitution or (in the case of NHS bodies) NHS legislation allows them to delegate their other functions.

30.10 Organisations (or individuals) in charge of hospitals retain responsibility for the performance of all hospital managers' functions exercised on their behalf and must ensure that the people acting on their behalf are competent to do so. It is for the organisation (or individual) concerned to decide what arrangements to put in place to monitor and review the way that functions under the Act are exercised on its behalf – but many organisations establish a Mental Health Act steering or scrutiny group especially for that task.

Specific powers and duties of hospital managers

Admission

30.11 It is the hospital managers' responsibility to ensure that the authority for detaining patients is valid and that any relevant admission documents are in order. For guidance on the receipt, scrutiny and rectification of documents see **chapter 13**.

Reference Guide 12.34-12.35 30.12 Where a patient is admitted under the Act on the basis of an application by their nearest relative, the hospital managers must request the relevant local social services authority (LSSA) to provide them with the social circumstances report required by section 14.

Reference Guide chapter 13 ### Transfer between hospitals

30.13 The Act allows hospital managers to authorise the transfer of most detained patients from one hospital to another in accordance with regulations. (For restricted patients, the consent of the Secretary of State for Justice is also required.) Decisions on transfers may be delegated to an officer, who could (but need not be) the patient's responsible clinician.

30.14 The managers do not have the power to insist that another hospital accepts a patient, nor to insist that a proposed new placement is funded by a PCT or anyone else. Decisions about funding should be taken in the same way as for any other patient.

30.15 People authorising transfers on the hospital managers' behalf should ensure that there are good reasons for the transfer and that the needs and interests of the patient have been considered. Transfers are potentially an interference with a patient's right to respect for privacy and family life under Article 8 of the European Convention on Human Rights, and care should be taken to act compatibly with the Convention when deciding whether to authorise a transfer.

30.16 Valid reasons for transfer might be clinical – the need, for example, for the patient to be in a more suitable environment or in a specialist facility. They could also be to move the patient closer to home. In some cases, a transfer may be unavoidable, because the hospital is no longer able to offer the care that the patient needs.

30.17 Wherever practicable, patients should be involved in the process leading to any decision to transfer them to another hospital. It is important to explain the reasons for a proposed transfer to the patient and, where appropriate, their nearest relative and other family or friends, and to record them. Only in exceptional circumstances should patients be transferred to another hospital without warning.

30.18 Among the factors that need to be considered when deciding whether to transfer a patient are:

- whether the transfer would give the patient greater access to family or friends, or have the opposite effect;

- what effect a transfer is likely to have on the course of the patient's disorder or their recovery;

- the availability of appropriate beds at the potential receiving hospital; and

- whether a transfer would be appropriate to enable the patient to be in a more culturally suitable or compatible environment, or whether it would have the opposite effect.

30.19 Detained patients may themselves want a transfer to another hospital – in order to be nearer their family or friends, for example. Or they may have a reasonable wish to be treated by a different clinical team, which could only be met by a transfer.

30.20 The professionals involved in their care should always be prepared to discuss the possibility of a transfer, and should raise the issue themselves with the patient if they think the patient might be interested in, or benefit from, a transfer.

30.21 Requests made by, or on behalf of, patients should be recorded and given careful consideration. Every effort should be made to meet the patient's wishes. If that cannot be done, the patient (or the person who made the request on the patient's behalf) should be given a written statement of the decision and the reasons for it.

30.22 Nearest relatives' consent to transfers is not a statutory requirement. But unless the patient objects, the patient's nearest relative should normally be consulted before a patient is transferred to another hospital, and, in accordance with the regulations, they must normally be notified of the transfer.

30.23 When a patient is transferred, the documents authorising detention, including the authority for transfer, should be sent to the hospital to which the patient is transferred. The transferring hospital should retain copies of these documents.

Transfers to guardianship

Reference Guide 13.35-13.39 and 19.137-19.139

30.24 Regulations allow hospital managers to authorise the transfer of most detained patients into guardianship instead, with the agreement of the relevant LSSA. This is a procedural alternative to discharging the patient from detention and then making an application for guardianship. Again, this decision may be delegated to officers, including the patient's responsible clinician.

30.25 As with transfers between hospitals, people taking decisions on behalf of hospital managers and LSSAs should ensure that there are good reasons for any transfer and that the needs and interests of the patient have been considered.

Transfer and assignment of responsibility for SCT patients

Reference Guide 15.45-15.54

30.26 The managers of a hospital to which an SCT patient has been recalled may authorise the patient's transfer to another hospital during the 72-hour maximum period of recall. These decisions may be delegated in the same way as other transfer decisions described above. The people

exercising this power on the managers' behalf must
ensure that the needs and interests of the patient are
considered before a transfer is authorised, in the same
way as when considering the transfer of a detained patient.

30.27 Hospital managers may also reassign responsibility for SCT
patients so that a different hospital will become the
patient's responsible hospital. The same considerations apply.

Reference Guide
15.128-15.134

Information for patients and relatives

30.28 Sections 132, 132A and 133 of the Act and regulations
require hospital managers to arrange for detained
patients, SCT patients and (where relevant) their nearest
relatives to be given important information about the way
the Act works and about their rights. For further guidance
on the exercise of these duties see **chapter 2**.

Duties in respect of victims of crime

Sections 35-45
of the Domestic
Violence, Crime
and Victims
Act 2004

30.29 The Domestic Violence, Crime and Victims Act 2004
places a number of duties on hospital managers in
relation to certain unrestricted Part 3 patients who have
committed sexual or violent crimes. This includes liaising
with victims in order to:

- advise victims if the patient's discharge is being
  considered or if the patient is about to be discharged;

- forward representations made by victims to people
  responsible for making decisions on discharge or SCT
  and for passing information received from those people
  to the victim;

- informing victims who have asked to be told, if the
  patient is to go onto SCT and of any conditions on the
  community treatment order (CTO) relating to contact
  with them or their family, any variation of the
  conditions, and the date on which the order will cease;
  and

- informing responsible clinicians of any representations
  made by the victim about the conditions attached to
  the CTO.

30.30 These duties complement similar arrangements for restricted Part 3 patients, which are managed by the probation service rather than hospital managers.

30.31 Separate guidance on hospital managers' duties under the Domestic Violence, Crime and Victims Act 2004 is issued by the Ministry of Justice.

Reference Guide chapter 14

Patients' correspondence

30.32 Section 134 allows hospital managers to withhold outgoing post from detained patients if the person to whom it is addressed has made a written request to the hospital managers, the approved clinician with overall responsibility for the patient's case, or the Secretary of State that post from the patient in question should be withheld. The fact that post has been withheld must be recorded in writing by an officer authorised by the hospital managers, and the patient must be informed in accordance with the regulations.

30.33 The managers of high-security psychiatric hospitals have wider powers under section 134 to withhold both incoming and outgoing post from patients in certain circumstances.[1] Their decisions are subject to review by the Commission. The hospital managers of high-security psychiatric hospitals should have a written policy for the exercise of these powers.

Reference Guide 23.1-23.15

Duty to refer cases to Tribunals

30.34 Hospital managers are under a duty to refer a patient's case to the Tribunal in the circumstances set out in section 68 of the Act, summarised in the following table.

---

[1] The Secretary of State for Health has also issued directions requiring the managers of these hospitals to take similar action in respect of correspondence between patients within the hospital, phone calls and items brought in for patients from outside.

Hospital managers' duties to refer cases to the Tribunal

Hospital managers must refer the following patients	When
Patients who are detained under Part 2 of the Act, and patients who were detained under Part 2 but are now SCT patients	Six months have passed since they were first detained, unless: • the patient applied to the Tribunal themselves after they became a section 3 patient; • the patient's nearest relative applied to the Tribunal after the patient became a section 3 patient; • the patient's case was referred to the Tribunal by the Secretary of State after the patient became a section 3 patient; or • the managers have already referred the patient's case to the Tribunal because their CTO was revoked (see below). (If the patient is still a section 2 patient pending the outcome of an application to the county court for a change in their nearest relative, there are no exceptions.)
Patients who are detained under Part 2 of the Act, or were detained under Part 2 but are now SCT patients	Three years have passed since their case was last considered by the Tribunal (one year if they are under 18).
Patients detained under hospital orders, hospital directions or transfer directions under Part 3 of the Act without being subject to special restrictions, or who were detained under Part 3 of the Act but are now SCT patients	Three years have passed without their case being considered by the Tribunal (one year if they are under 18).

Hospital managers must refer the following patients	When
People who were SCT patients but whose CTOs have been revoked	As soon as practicable after the responsible clinician revokes the CTO.

Note: for these purposes:

- detention under Part 2 of the Act does not include any time spent detained under the holding powers in section 5 (see **chapter 12**); and

- applications to the Tribunal do not count if they are withdrawn before they are determined.

30.35 Hospitals will be able to comply properly with these duties only if they maintain full and accurate records about:

- the detention and discharge of the patients for whom they are responsible;

- applications made by those patients to the Tribunal; and

- applications and references to the Tribunal made by other people in respect of those patients.

30.36 Hospital managers should ensure that they have systems in place to alert them (or the officers to whom the function is delegated) in good time to the need to make a reference. Officers exercising this function for the managers should be familiar with the relevant requirements of the Tribunal itself and the procedural rules by which it operates.

30.37 When hospital managers are required to refer the case of an SCT patient whose CTO is revoked to the Tribunal, this must be done as soon as practicable after the CTO is revoked.

30.38 Hospital managers should from time to time audit the timeliness with which they comply with their duties to refer patients to the Tribunal.

References by the Secretary of State for Health

Reference Guide 23.16-23.22

30.39 The Secretary of State for Health may at any time refer the case of most detained patients, and all SCT patients, to the Tribunal. Anyone may request such a reference, and the Secretary of State will consider all such requests on their merits.

30.40 Hospital managers should consider asking the Secretary of State to make a reference in respect of any patients whose rights under Article 5(4) of the European Convention on Human Rights might otherwise be at risk of being violated because they are unable (for whatever reason) to have their cases considered by the Tribunal speedily following their initial detention or at reasonable intervals afterwards.

30.41 In particular, they should normally seek such a reference in any case where:

- a patient's detention under section 2 has been extended under section 29 of the Act pending the outcome of an application to the county court for the displacement of their nearest relative;

- the patient lacks the capacity to request a reference; and

- either the patient's case has never been considered by the Tribunal, or a significant period has passed since it was last considered.

Reference Guide
12.30-12.33

Hospital accommodation for children and young people

30.42 Section 131A of the Act puts a duty on hospital managers to ensure that any children or young people aged under 18 receiving in-patient care for mental disorder in their hospitals are accommodated in an environment which is suitable for their age (subject to their needs).[2] For guidance on this see **chapter 36**. The duty applies to children and young people admitted informally to hospitals, as well as those detained under the Act.

Related material

- *The Code of Practice for Victims of Crime*, Office for Criminal Justice Reform, October 2005

- *Guidance for Clinicians – Duties to Victims under the Domestic Violence, Crime and Victims Act 2004*, Home Office Mental Health Unit, 2005

This material does not form part of the Code. It is provided for assistance only.

---

[2] This duty is expected to be in force from April 2010.

CHAPTER 31 Hospital managers' discharge power

31.1 This chapter gives guidance on the exercise of hospital managers' power to discharge detained and supervised community treatment (SCT) patients.

Reference Guide 12.117-12.120 (detention) and 15.115-15.117 (SCT)

The power to discharge

31.2 Section 23 of the Act gives hospital managers the power to discharge most detained patients and all SCT patients. They may not discharge patients remanded to hospital under sections 35 or 36 of the Act or subject to interim hospital orders under section 38, and they may not discharge restricted patients without the consent of the Secretary of State for Justice.

Exercise of power of discharge on behalf of managers

31.3 The hospital managers – meaning the organisation or individual in charge of the hospital – must either consider discharge themselves or arrange for their power to be exercised on their behalf by a "managers' panel".

31.4 A managers' panel may consist of three or more people who are:

Section 23(4)

- members of the organisation in charge of the hospital (eg the chair or non-executive directors of an NHS trust); or

- members of a committee or sub-committee which is authorised for the purpose.

31.5 In the case of an NHS foundation trust, a panel can consist of any three or more people appointed for the purpose by the trust whether or not they are members of the trust itself or any of its committees or sub-committees.

Section 23(6)

Section 23(5) 31.6 In NHS bodies (including NHS foundation trusts), none of the people on managers' panels may be employees (or, in the case of NHS trusts, officers) of the body concerned. (People do not become employees or officers simply because they are paid a fee for serving on managers' panels.)

31.7 In independent hospitals, managers' panels should not include people who are on the staff of the hospital or who have a financial interest in it.

31.8 In all cases, the board (or the equivalent) of the organisation concerned should ensure that the people it appoints properly understand their role and the working of the Act. It should also ensure that they receive suitable training to equip them to understand the law, work with patients and professionals, reach sound judgements and properly record their decisions. This should include training in how risk is assessed and how to comprehend a risk assessment report.

31.9 Appointments to managers' panels should be made for a fixed period. Reappointment (if permitted) should not be automatic and should be preceded by a review of the person's continuing suitability.

When to review detention or SCT

31.10 Hospital managers should ensure that all relevant patients are aware that they may ask to be discharged by the hospital managers and of the distinction between this and their right to apply for a Tribunal hearing.

31.11 Hospital managers:

- may undertake a review of whether or not a patient should be discharged at any time at their discretion;

- must undertake a review if the patient's responsible clinician submits to them a report under section 20 of the Act renewing detention or under section 20A extending SCT;

- should consider holding a review when they receive a request from (or on behalf of) a patient; and

- should consider holding a review when the responsible clinician makes a report to them under section 25 barring an order by the nearest relative to discharge a patient.

31.12 In the last two cases, when deciding whether to consider the case, managers' panels are entitled to take into account whether the Tribunal has recently considered the patient's case or is due to do so in the near future.

31.13 It is desirable that a managers' panel considers a report made under section 20 or section 20A and decides whether to exercise its discharge power, before the current period of detention or SCT ends. However, the responsible clinician's report itself provides authority for the patient's continued detention or SCT, even if a managers' panel has not yet considered the case or reached a decision.

Criteria to be applied

31.14 The Act does not define specific criteria that the hospital managers must use when considering discharge. The essential yardstick is whether the grounds for continued detention or continued SCT under the Act are satisfied. To ensure that this is done in a systematic and consistent way, managers' panels should consider the questions set out below, in the order stated.

31.15 For patients detained for assessment under sections 2 or 4 of the Act:

- is the patient still suffering from mental disorder?

- if so, is the disorder of a nature or degree which warrants the continued detention of the patient in hospital?

- ought the detention to continue in the interests of the patient's health or safety or for the protection of other people?

31.16 For other detained patients:

- is the patient still suffering from mental disorder?

- if so, is the disorder of a nature or degree which makes treatment in a hospital appropriate?

- is continued detention for medical treatment necessary for the patient's health or safety or for the protection of other people?

- is appropriate medical treatment available for the patient?

31.17 For patients on SCT:

- is the patient still suffering from mental disorder?

- if so, is the disorder of a nature or degree which makes it appropriate for the patient to receive medical treatment?

- if so, is it necessary in the interests of the patient's health or safety or the protection of other people that the patient should receive such treatment?

- is it still necessary for the responsible clinician to be able to exercise the power to recall the patient to hospital, if that is needed?

- is appropriate medical treatment available for the patient?

31.18 If three or more members of the panel (who between them make up a majority) are satisfied from the evidence presented to them that the answer to any of the questions set out above is "no", the patient should be discharged.

31.19 Where the answer to all the relevant questions above is "yes", but the responsible clinician has made a report under section 25 barring a nearest relative's attempt to discharge the patient, the managers should also consider the following question:

- would the patient, if discharged, be likely to act in a manner that is dangerous to other people or to themselves?

31.20 This last question provides a more stringent test for continuing detention or SCT (see **chapter 29**).

31.21 If three or more members of the panel (being a majority) disagree with the responsible clinician and decide that the answer to this question is "no", the panel should usually discharge the patient. However, the hospital managers retain a residual discretion not to discharge in these cases, so panels should always consider whether there are exceptional reasons why the patient should not be discharged.

31.22 In all cases, hospital managers have discretion to discharge patients even if the criteria for continued detention or SCT are met. Managers' panels must therefore always consider whether there are other reasons why the patient should be discharged despite the answers to the questions set out above.

Procedure for reviewing detention or SCT

31.23 The Act does not define the procedure for reviewing a patient's detention or SCT. However, the exercise of this power is subject to the general law and to public law duties which arise from it. Hospital managers' conduct of reviews must satisfy the fundamental legal requirements of fairness, reasonableness and lawfulness. Managers' panels should therefore:

- adopt and apply a procedure which is fair and reasonable;

- not make irrational decisions – that is, decisions which no managers' panel, properly directing itself as to the law and on the available information, could have made; and

- not act unlawfully – that is, contrary to the provisions of the Act and any other legislation (including the Human Rights Act 1998 and relevant equality and anti-discrimination legislation).

Conduct of reviews where detention or SCT is contested

31.24 Reviews should be conducted in such a way as to ensure that the case for continuing the patient's detention or SCT is properly considered against the questions set out above and in the light of all the relevant evidence. This means that managers' panels need to have before them sufficient information about the patient's past history of care and treatment, and details of any future plans. The main source of this is likely to be the patient's documentation and care plan under the Care Programme Approach (CPA) (or its equivalent). It is essential that panels are fully informed about any history of violence or self-harm and that a recent risk assessment is provided to the panel.

31.25 In advance of the hearing, managers' panels should be provided with written reports from the patient's responsible clinician and from other key individuals directly involved in the patient's care who they think are appropriate, such as the patient's care co-ordinator, named nurse, social worker, occupational therapist or clinical psychologist.

31.26 The patient should be provided with copies of the reports as soon as they are available, unless (in the light of any recommendation made by their authors) panels are of the opinion that disclosing the information would be likely to cause serious harm to the physical or mental health of the patient or any other individual. The patient's legal or other representative should also receive copies of these reports.

31.27 Reports should be provided in good time so that patients and their representatives can consider them and, where relevant, draw the panels' attention to any apparent inaccuracies. Any decision to withhold a report (in whole or part) should be recorded, with reasons.

31.28 The nearest relative should normally be informed when managers' panels are to consider a patient's case, unless the patient objects, subject to the normal considerations about involving nearest relatives (see **paragraphs 2.27-2.33**).

31.29 Panels should be prepared to consider the views of the patient's relatives and carers, and other people who know the patient well, either at the patient's request or where such people offer their views on their own initiative. Relatives, carers and any other relevant people may be invited to put their views to the managers' panel in person. If the patient objects to this, a suitable member of the professional care team should be asked to include the person's views in their report.

31.30 The report submitted by the responsible clinician should cover the history of the patient's care and treatment and details of their care plan, including all risk assessments. Where the review is being held because the responsible clinician has made a report under section 20, 20A or 21B renewing detention or extending SCT, panels should also have a copy of the report itself before them. This should be supplemented by a record of the consultation undertaken by the responsible clinician in accordance with those sections before making the report. The written reports should be considered by the panel alongside documentation compiled under the CPA (or its equivalent).

31.31 Where relevant, panels should also have in front of them any order made by the responsible clinician under section 25 barring a patient's discharge by their nearest relative.

31.32 The procedure for the conduct of any hearing is for managers' panels themselves to decide, but generally it needs to balance informality against the rigour demanded by the importance of the task. Key points are:

- the patient should be given a full opportunity, and any necessary help, to explain why they should be no longer be detained or on SCT;

- the patient should be allowed to be accompanied by a representative of their own choosing to help in putting their point of view to the panel;

- the patient should also be allowed to have a relative, friend or advocate attend to support them; and

- the responsible clinician and other professionals should be asked to give their views on whether the patient's continued detention or SCT is justified and to explain the grounds on which those views are based.

31.33 It is also for hospital managers themselves to decide where hearings should take place. For SCT patients, and patients currently on leave of absence from hospital, the hospital itself may not be the most convenient or acceptable place for the patient. Hospital managers should be prepared to consider whether there are more appropriate locations which it would be feasible to use.

31.34 The patient and the other people giving views to the panel should, if the patient wishes it, be able to hear each other's statements to the panel and to put questions to each other, unless the panel believes that would be likely to cause serious harm to the physical or mental health of the patient or any other individual. Unless, exceptionally, it is considered too unsafe, patients should always be offered the opportunity of speaking to the panel alone (with or without their representative and anyone else they have asked to attend to support them at the hearing).

31.35 Members of managers' panels will not normally be qualified to form clinical assessments of their own. They must give full weight to the views of all the professionals concerned in the patient's care. If there is a divergence of views among the professionals about whether the patient meets the clinical grounds for continued detention or SCT, managers' panels should consider adjourning to seek further medical or other professional advice.

31.36 In considering the questions set out earlier in this chapter and deciding in the light of them whether or not to discharge the patient from detention, managers' panels need to consider very carefully the implications for the patient's subsequent care. Before a managers' panel considers a case, the responsible clinician, in consultation with the multi-disciplinary team, should have considered what services and other arrangements might be put in place for the patient if discharged and whether those arrangements would be sufficient to make continued detention or SCT (as the case may be) no longer necessary.

31.37 The presence or absence of adequate community care arrangements may be critical in deciding whether continued detention (in particular) is necessary. If managers' panels believe they have not been provided with sufficient information about arrangements that could be made were the patient discharged, they should consider adjourning and requesting further information.

31.38 If panels conclude that the patient ought to be discharged, but practical steps to put after-care in place need to be taken first, they may adjourn the panel for a brief period to enable that to happen before formally discharging the patient. Alternatively, they may order the patient's discharge from a specified date in the near future. They may not discharge patients provisionally but defer the final decision to discharge until certain conditions have been met.

Uncontested renewals

31.39 If a patient's detention or SCT is renewed or extended by their responsible clinician, the hospital managers must always decide whether the patient should be discharged anyway, even if the patient has indicated that they do not wish to challenge the renewal or extension.

31.40 It is for hospital managers to decide whether to adopt a different procedure in uncontested cases. Some hospitals, as a matter of policy, do not differentiate between contested and uncontested cases.

31.41 Where a different procedure is used, patients should be interviewed by at least one member of the managers' panel considering their case, if they request it, or if the panel thinks it desirable after reading the renewal or extension report.

31.42 Otherwise, managers' panels may consider the case on the papers, if they wish. But they should hold a full hearing if they have reason to suspect that the patient may, in fact, wish to be discharged, or there are prima facie grounds to think that the responsible clinician's decision to renew detention or extend SCT is not correct. The mere fact that patients have not said they object to the renewal or extension should not be taken as evidence that they agree with it, or that it is the correct decision.

Decisions

31.43 Hospital managers have a common law duty to give reasons for their decisions. The decisions of managers' panels, and the reasons for them, should be fully recorded at the end of each review. The decision should be communicated as soon as practicable, both orally and in writing, to the patient, to the nearest relative (where relevant) and to the professionals concerned.

31.44 If the patient is not to be discharged, at least one member of the panel should offer to see the patient to explain in person the reasons for the decision. Copies of the papers relating to the review, and the formal record of the decision, should be kept in the patient's notes.

Reference Guide 12.121-12.122 (detention) and 15.118-15.119 (SCT)

NHS patients treated by independent hospitals

31.45 NHS bodies have the power to discharge:

- NHS patients who are detained in independent hospitals; and

- NHS SCT patients whose responsible hospital is an independent hospital.

This is in addition to the power of the managers of the independent hospitals themselves. The NHS body concerned is the one which has contracted with the independent hospital in respect of the patient.

31.46 NHS bodies may take the decision themselves, delegate it to a panel of three or more members of their board or of a committee or sub-committee which is approved for that purpose, or (in the case of an NHS foundation trust) delegate it to any three or more people appointed for the purpose. The members of the panel must not be employees of the body (or officers, if the body is an NHS trust).

31.47 As a general rule, NHS bodies are entitled to expect that the managers' panel arrangements in independent hospitals will be sufficient. They do not need to arrange a panel hearing of their own simply because they are requested to do so. But they (or a panel on their behalf) must consider whether there are any special circumstances which would make it unfair to a patient for them not to hold a hearing. As a result, NHS bodies contracting with independent hospitals should take steps to satisfy themselves that the independent hospital's own arrangements for taking discharge decisions are adequate to protect the rights of NHS patients.

CHAPTER 32
The Tribunal

32.1   This chapter provides guidance on the role of the Tribunal[1] and related duties on hospital managers and others.

Reference Guide chapters 20 and 21

Purpose of the Tribunal

32.2   The Tribunal is an independent judicial body. Its main purpose is to review the cases of detained, conditionally discharged, and supervised community treatment (SCT) patients under the Act and to direct the discharge of any patients where it thinks it appropriate. It also considers applications for discharge from guardianship.

32.3   The Tribunal provides a significant safeguard for patients who have had their liberty curtailed under the Act. Those giving evidence at hearings should do what they can to help enable Tribunal hearings to be conducted in a professional manner, which includes having regard to the patient's wishes and feelings and ensuring that the patient feels as comfortable with the proceedings as possible.

32.4   It is for those who believe that a patient should continue to be detained or remain an SCT patient to prove their case, not for the patient to disprove it. They will therefore need to present the Tribunal with sufficient evidence to support continuing liability to detention or SCT. Clinical and social reports form the backbone of this evidence. Care should be given to ensure that all information is as up to date as possible to avoid adjournment. In order to support the Tribunal in making its decision all information should be clear and concise.

---

[1] At the time of publication, the Tribunal is the Mental Health Review Tribunal (MHRT). However, the MHRT is intended to be replaced in England by a new First-Tier Tribunal established under the Tribunals, Courts and Enforcement Act 2007. There is also intended to be a right of appeal, on a point of law, from that Tribunal to a new Upper Tribunal.

Informing the patient and nearest relative of rights to apply to the Tribunal

32.5 Hospital managers and the local social services authority (LSSA) are under a duty to take steps to ensure that patients understand their rights to apply for a Tribunal hearing. Hospital managers and the LSSA should also advise patients of their entitlement to free legal advice and representation. They should do both whenever:

- patients are first detained in hospital, received into guardianship or discharged to SCT;

- their detention or guardianship is renewed or SCT is extended; and

- their status under the Act changes – for example, if they move from detention under section 2 to detention under section 3 or if their community treatment order is revoked.

32.6 Unless the patient requests otherwise, the information should normally also be given to their nearest relative (subject to the normal considerations about involving nearest relatives see – **paragraphs 2.27-2.33**).

32.7 Hospital managers and professionals should enable detained patients to be visited by their legal representatives at any reasonable time. This is particularly important where visits are necessary to discuss a Tribunal application. Where the patient consents, legal representatives and independent doctors should be given prompt access to the patient's medical records. Delays in providing access can hold up Tribunal proceedings and should be avoided.

32.8 In connection with an application (or a reference) to the Tribunal, an independent doctor or approved clinician authorised by (or on behalf of) a patient has a right to visit and examine the patient in private. Those doctors and approved clinicians also have a right to inspect any records relating to the patient's detention, treatment and

Sections 67 and 76

(where relevant) after-care under section 117. Where nearest relatives have a right to apply to the Tribunal, they too may authorise independent doctors or approved clinicians in the same way. The patient's consent is not required for authorised doctors or approved clinicians to see their records, and they should be given prompt access to the records they wish to see.

Hospital managers' duty to refer cases to the Tribunal

32.9 The hospital managers have various duties to refer patients to the Tribunal. They may also request the Secretary of State to refer a patient, and there are certain circumstances where they should always consider doing so. (See **chapter 31**.)

Reports – general

32.10 Responsible authorities (that is the managers of the relevant hospital or the LSSA responsible for a guardianship patient) should be familiar with the Tribunal's rules and procedures. The rules place a statutory duty on the responsible authority to provide the Tribunal with a statement of relevant facts together with certain reports.

32.11 It is important that documents and information are provided in accordance with the Tribunal's rules and procedures in good time for any Tribunal hearing. Missing, out-of-date or inadequate reports can lead to adjournments or unnecessarily long hearings. Where responsible clinicians, social workers or other professionals are required to provide reports, they should do this promptly and within the statutory timescale.

32.12 In the case of a restricted patient, if the opinion of the responsible clinician or other professional changes from what was recorded in the original Tribunal report(s), it is vital that this is communicated in writing, prior to the hearing, to the Tribunal office and the Mental Health Unit of the Ministry of Justice to allow them the opportunity to prepare a supplementary statement.

32.13 If a Tribunal panel feels that it needs more information on any report, it may request it, either in the form of a supplementary report or by questioning a witness at the hearing itself.

32.14 In some circumstances, the Tribunal will not sit immediately after receiving the report. In these cases, the report writers should consider whether anything in the patient's circumstances have changed and should produce a concise update to the report. This is especially important if the patient's status changes – for example, if a patient becomes an SCT patient or moves from detention under section 2 to section 3.

32.15 In those cases, the application will need to be considered under the new circumstances, and the report will need to provide a justification for continued detention or liability to recall under the new circumstances. The Tribunal may ask the author of the report to talk through it, so it is good practice for the authors to re-familiarise themselves with the content of any report before the hearing. If the author of the report is unable to attend, it is important that anyone attending in their place should, wherever possible, also have a good knowledge of the patient's case.

32.16 Hospital managers (or LSSAs in guardianship cases) should ensure that the Tribunal is notified immediately of any events or changes that might have a bearing on Tribunal proceedings – for example, where a patient is discharged or one of the parties is unavailable.

32.17 If the author of a report prepared for the Tribunal is aware of information they do not think the patient should see, they should follow the Tribunal's procedure for the submission of such information. Ultimately, it is for the Tribunal to decide what should be disclosed to the patient.

32.18 Reports should be sent to the appropriate Tribunal office, preferably by secure e-mail, otherwise by post.

32.19 The responsible authority must ensure that up-to-date reports prepared specifically for the Tribunal are provided in accordance with the Tribunal's rules and procedures. In practice, this will normally include a report completed by the patient's responsible clinician. Where the patient is under the age of 18 and the responsible clinician is not a child and adolescent mental health service (CAMHS) specialist, hospital managers should ensure that a report is prepared by a CAMHS specialist.

32.20 Where possible, reports should be written by the professionals with the best overall knowledge of the patient's situation.

32.21 The reports should be submitted in good time to enable all parties, including the Secretary of State in restricted cases, to fulfil their responsibilities.

Medical examination

32.22 A medical member of the Tribunal may want to examine the patient at any time before the hearing. Hospital managers must ensure that the medical member can see patients who are in hospital in private and examine their medical records. It is important that the patient is told of the visit in advance so that they can be available when the medical member visits.

Withdrawing the application

32.23 A request to withdraw an application may be made by the applicant in accordance with the Tribunal rules. The applicant may not withdraw a reference made by the Secretary of State.

32.24 An application will also be considered to be withdrawn if the patient is discharged. If this happens outside office hours, someone acting on behalf of the hospital managers (or the LSSA, if it is a guardianship case) should contact the Tribunal office as soon as possible, to inform them. For detained patients, this could be done by a member of the ward staff.

Representation

32.25 Hospital managers (or LSSAs, as the case may be) should inform patients of their right to present their own case to the Tribunal and their right to be represented by someone else. Staff should be available to help patients make an application. This is especially important for SCT patients who may not have daily contact with professionals.

The hearing

Attendance at hearings

32.26 Normally, a patient will be present throughout their Tribunal hearing. Patients do not need to attend their hearing, but professionals should encourage them to attend unless they judge that it would be detrimental to their health or wellbeing.

32.27 It is important that the patient's responsible clinician attends the Tribunal, supported by other staff involved in the patient's care where appropriate, as their evidence is crucial for making the case for the patient's continued detention or SCT under the Act. Wherever possible, the responsible clinician, and other relevant staff, should attend for the full hearing so that they are aware of all the evidence made available to the Tribunal and of the Tribunal's decision and reasons.

32.28 A responsible clinician can attend the hearing solely as a witness or as the nominated representative of the responsible authority. As a representative of the responsible authority, the responsible clinician has the ability to call and cross-examine witnesses and to make submissions to the Tribunal. However, this may not always be desirable where it is envisaged that the responsible clinician will have to continue working closely with a patient.

32.29 Responsible authorities should therefore consider whether they want to send an additional person to represent their interests, allowing the responsible clinician to appear solely as a witness. Responsible clinicians should be clear in what capacity they are attending the Tribunal, as they may well be asked this by the panel.

32.30 It is important that other people who prepare reports submitted by the responsible authority attend the hearing to provide further up-to-date information about the patient, including (where relevant) their home circumstances and the after-care available in the event of a decision to discharge the patient.

32.31 Increasingly, Tribunal hearings find it helpful to speak to a nurse, particularly a nurse who knows the patient. It is often helpful for a nurse who knows the patient to accompany them to the hearing.

32.32 Hospital managers should ensure that all professionals who attend Tribunal hearings are adequately prepared.

Accommodation for hearings

32.33 The managers of a hospital in which a Tribunal hearing is to be held should provide suitable accommodation for that purpose. The hearing room should be private, quiet, clean and adequately sized and furnished. It should not contain confidential information about other patients. If the room is also used for other purposes, care should be taken to ensure that any equipment (such as a video camera or a two-way mirror) would not have a disturbing effect on the patient.

32.34 The patient should have access to a separate room in which to hold any private discussions that are necessary – for example, with their representative – as should the Tribunal members, so that they can discuss their decision.

32.35 Where a patient is being treated in the community, the hospital managers should consider whether a hospital venue is appropriate. They may wish to discuss alternatives with the Tribunal office.

Interpretation

32.36 Where necessary, the Tribunal will provide, free of charge, interpretation services for patients and their representatives. Where patients or their representatives are hard of hearing or have speech difficulties (or both), the Tribunal will provide such services of sign language interpreters, lip speakers or palantypists as may be necessary. Hospital managers and LSSAs should inform the Tribunal well in advance if they think any such services might be necessary.

Communication of the decision

32.37 The Tribunal will normally communicate its decision to all parties orally at the end of the hearing. Provided it is feasible to do so, and the patient wishes it, the Tribunal will speak to them personally. Otherwise, the decision will be given to the patient's representative (if they have one). If the patient is unrepresented, and it is not feasible to discuss matters with them after the hearing, the hospital managers or LSSA should ensure that they are told the decision as soon as possible. Copies of the decision can be left at a hospital on the day of the hearing. All parties to the hearing should receive a written copy of the reasons for the decision.

Complaints

32.38 Complaints from users about the Tribunal should be sent to the Tribunal office. The Tribunal has procedures in place to deal with complaints promptly.

Further information on the Tribunal

32.39 The Tribunal itself publishes further information and guidance about its procedures and operations.

CHAPTER 33
Patients concerned with criminal proceedings

Reference Guide chapters 3-11

33.1 This chapter offers guidance on the use of the Act to arrange treatment for mentally disordered people who come into contact with the criminal justice system.

Assessment for potential admission to hospital

33.2 People who are subject to criminal proceedings have the same rights to psychiatric assessment and treatment as anyone else. Any person who is in police or prison custody or before the courts charged with a criminal offence and who is in need of medical treatment for mental disorder should be considered for admission to hospital.

33.3 Wherever possible, people who appear to the court to be mentally disordered should have their treatment needs considered at the earliest possible opportunity, by the court mental health assessment scheme where there is one. Such people may be at greatest risk of self-harm while in custody. Prompt access to specialist treatment may prevent significant deterioration in their condition and is likely to assist in a speedier trial process, helping to avoid longer-term harm or detention in an unsuitable environment.

33.4 If criminal proceedings are discontinued, it may be appropriate for the relevant local social services authority (LSSA) to arrange for an approved mental health professional (AMHP) to consider making an application for admission under Part 2 of the Act.

33.5 A prison healthcare centre is not a hospital within the meaning of the Act. The rules in Part 4 of the Act about medical treatment of detained patients do not apply and treatment cannot be given there under the Act without the patient's consent (see **chapter 23**).

CHAPTER

33

Patients
concerned
with
criminal
proceedings

Agency responsibilities

33.6   Primary care trusts (PCTs) should:

- provide the courts, in response to a request under section 39 of the Act, with comprehensive information on the range of facilities available for the admission of patients subject to the criminal justice process. In particular, PCTs should provide the courts with comprehensive information regarding child and adolescent mental health service (CAMHS) beds that are (or could be made) available for patients;

- appoint a named person to respond to requests for information; and

- ensure that prompt medical assessment of defendants is provided to assist in the speedy completion of the trial process and the most suitable disposal for the offender.

33.7   Section 39A requires an LSSA to inform the court, if requested, whether it, or any person approved by it, is willing to receive an offender into guardianship and how the guardian's powers would be exercised. LSSAs should appoint a named person to respond to requests from the courts about mental health services provided in the community, including under guardianship.

Assessment by a doctor

33.8   A doctor who is asked to provide evidence in relation to a possible admission under Part 3 of the Act should bear in mind that the request is not for a general report on the defendant's condition but for advice on whether or not the patient should be diverted from prison by way of a hospital order (or a community order with a mental health treatment requirement under criminal justice legislation).

33.9   Doctors should:

- identify themselves to the person being assessed, explain who has requested the report and make clear the limits of confidentiality in relation to the report. They should explain that any information disclosed, and the medical opinion, could be relevant not only to medical disposal by the court but also to the imposition of a punitive sentence, or to its length; and

- request relevant pre-sentence reports, the Inmate Medical Record, if there is one, and previous psychiatric reports, as well as relevant documentation regarding the alleged offence. If any of this information is not available, the doctor's report should say so clearly.

33.10 The doctor, or one of them if two doctors are preparing reports, should have access to a bed, or take responsibility for referring the case to another clinician who does, if they propose to recommend admission to hospital. In the case of a defendant under the age of 18, the doctor should ideally have specialist knowledge of CAMHS and the needs of young people.

33.11 The doctor should, where possible, identify and access other independent sources of information about the person's previous history (including convictions). This should include information from GP records, previous psychiatric treatment and patterns of behaviour.

33.12 Assessment for admission of the patient is the responsibility of the doctor, but other members of the clinical team who would be involved with the person's care and treatment should also be consulted. A multi-disciplinary assessment should usually be undertaken if admission to hospital is likely to be recommended. The doctor should also contact the person who is preparing a pre-sentence report, especially if psychiatric treatment is recommended as a condition of a community order.

33.13 In cases where the doctor cannot state with confidence at the time of sentencing whether a hospital order will be appropriate, they should consider recommending an interim hospital order under section 38 of the Act. This order provides for the person to be admitted to hospital for up to 12 weeks (which may be extended for further

CHAPTER

33

Patients
concerned
with
criminal
proceedings

periods of up to 28 days to a maximum total period of 12 months) so that the court can reach a conclusion on the most appropriate and effective disposal.

Independent medical assessment

33.14 A patient who is remanded to hospital for a report (section 35) or for treatment (section 36) is entitled to obtain, at their own expense, or where applicable through legal aid, an independent report on their mental condition from a doctor or other clinician of their choosing, for the purpose of applying to court for the termination of the remand. The hospital managers should help in the exercise of this right by enabling the patient to contact a suitably qualified and experienced solicitor or other adviser.

Reports to the court

33.15 Clinical opinion is particularly important in helping courts to determine the sentence to be passed. In particular, it will help to inform the decision whether to divert the offender from punishment by way of a hospital order, or whether a prison sentence is the most suitable disposal.

33.16 A medical report for the court should set out:

- the material on which the report is based;

- how that material relates to the opinion given;

- where relevant, how the opinion may relate to any other trial issue;

- factors relating to the presence of mental disorder that may affect the risk that the patient poses to themselves or to others, including the risk of re-offending; and

- if admission to hospital is recommended, what, if any, special treatment or security is recommended and whether the doctor represents an organisation that is able to provide what is required.

The report should not speculate about guilt or innocence.

33.17 Section 157 of the Criminal Justice Act 2003 requires the court to obtain a medical report before passing a custodial sentence other than one fixed by law. Before passing such a sentence, the court must consider any information before it which relates to the offender's mental condition and the likely effect of such a sentence on that condition and on any treatment that may be available for it.

33.18 It may, therefore, be appropriate to include recommendations on the disposal of the case. In making recommendations for disposal, the doctor should consider the longer-term, as well as immediate, consequences. Factors to be taken into account include:

- whether the court may wish to make a hospital order subject to special restrictions;

- whether, for restricted patients, the order should designate admission to a named unit within the hospital;

- whether, in the event of the court concluding that a prison sentence is appropriate, the offender should initially be admitted to hospital by way of a hospital direction under section 45A; and

- whether a community order with a mental health treatment requirement may be appropriate.

33.19 Where an offender is made subject to special restrictions ("restricted patients"), the court, or the Secretary of State for Justice in some circumstances, may specify that the person be detained in a named unit within a hospital. This is to ensure an appropriate level of security.

33.20 A named hospital unit can be any part of a hospital which is treated as a separate unit. It will be for the court (or the Secretary of State, as the case may be) to define what is meant in each case where it makes use of the power. Admission to a named unit will mean that the consent of the Secretary of State will be required for any leave of absence or transfer from the named unit, whether the transfer is to another part of the same hospital or to another hospital.

CHAPTER

33

Patients
concerned
with
criminal
proceedings

33.21 The need to consider the longer-term implications of a recommended disposal is particularly important where an extended or indeterminate sentence for public protection is indicated under the Criminal Justice Act 2003. Either a hospital order under section 37 or attachment of a hospital direction to the prison sentence under section 45A is available to the court. Discretion lies with the court.

33.22 A hospital order, with or without restrictions, diverts the offender from punishment to treatment. There is no tariff to serve, and the period of detention will be determined by the disorder and the risk of harm which attaches to it.

33.23 A hospital direction, by contrast, accompanies a prison sentence and means that, from the start of the sentence, the offender will be managed in hospital in the same way as a prisoner who has been transferred to hospital subject to special restrictions under sections 47 and 49 of the Act (see **paragraph 33.34**). The responsible clinician can propose transfer to prison to the Secretary of State for Justice at any time before the prisoner's release date if, in their opinion, no further treatment is necessary or likely to be effective.

Availability of places

33.24 If the medical evidence is that the person needs treatment in hospital, but the medical witness cannot identify a suitable facility where the person could be admitted immediately, they should seek advice from the PCT for the person's home area. If the person has no permanent address, responsibility lies with the PCT for the area where they are registered with a GP or, if they are not registered with a GP, where the offence was committed for which sentence is being passed.

Transport to and from court

33.25 For patients remanded to hospital under sections 35 or 36 of the Act, or subject to a hospital order or an interim hospital order, the court has the power to direct who is to be responsible for conveying the defendant from the court to the receiving hospital. In practice, when remand orders are first made, patients are usually returned to the holding prison, and arrangements are then made to admit them to hospital within the statutory period.

33.26 When a patient has been admitted on remand or is subject to an interim hospital order, it is the responsibility of the hospital to return the patient to court as required. The court should give adequate notice of hearings. The hospital should liaise with the court in plenty of time to confirm the arrangements for escorting the patient to and from the court. The hospital will be responsible for providing a suitable escort for the patient when travelling from the hospital to the court and should plan for the provision of necessary staff to do this. The assistance of the police may be requested, if necessary. If possible, and having regard to the needs of the patient, medical or nursing staff should remain with the patient on court premises, even though legal accountability while the patient is detained for hearings remains with the court.

33.27 For further guidance on conveyance of patients under the Act, see **chapter 11**.

Section 56

Treatment without consent – patients remanded for report

33.28 The rules in Part 4 of the Act about medical treatment of detained patients do not apply to patients remanded to hospital under section 35 for a report on their mental condition. As a result, treatment can be administered only with their consent, or, in the case of a patient aged 16 or over who lacks capacity to consent, in accordance with the Mental Capacity Act 2005 (see **chapter 23**).

33.29 Where a patient remanded under section 35 is thought to be in need of medical treatment for mental disorder which cannot otherwise be given, the patient should be referred back to court by the clinician in charge of their care as soon as possible, with an appropriate recommendation and with an assessment of whether they are in a fit state to attend court.

CHAPTER

33

Patients
concerned
with
criminal
proceedings

33.30 If there is a delay in securing a court date, consideration should be given to whether the patient meets the criteria for detention under Part 2 of the Act to enable compulsory treatment to be given. This will be concurrent with, and not a replacement for, the remand made by the court.

Transfer of prisoners to hospital

33.31 The need for in-patient treatment for a prisoner should be identified and acted upon quickly, and prison healthcare staff should make contact immediately with the responsible PCT. Responsible NHS commissioners should aim to ensure that transfers of prisoners with mental disorders are carried out within a timeframe equivalent to levels of care experienced by patients who are admitted to mental healthcare services from the community. Any unacceptable delays in transfer after identification of need should be actively monitored and investigated.

33.32 Prisoners with a diagnosis of severe and enduring mental disorder who have given informed consent to treatment should also be considered for transfer to hospital for treatment if the prison environment is considered to be contributing to their disorder. An assessment of need and regular review should consider whether the prison healthcare centre is capable of providing for the prisoner's care if they are considered to be too unwell or vulnerable to return to residential wings.

33.33 Prisoners transferred to hospital under sections 47 or 48 should not be remitted to prison unless clinical staff from the hospital and prison have met to plan the prisoner's future care. This is often called a "section 117 meeting". Appropriate staff from the receiving prison should be invited to attend the review meeting prior to the prisoner's discharge back to prison.

Patients transferred from prison subject to special restrictions

33.34 When a person is transferred from prison to hospital under sections 47 or 48 as a restricted patient, it is the responsibility of the hospital managers and the responsible clinician to ensure that the patient has received, and as far as possible has understood, the letter from the Ministry of Justice explaining the roles of hospital managers and responsible clinicians in relation to restricted patients.

33.35 When prisoners have been transferred under section 47 and remain detained in hospital after their release date, they cease to be restricted patients but remain detained as if on a hospital order without restrictions. The responsible clinician's options under the Act are modified accordingly, and the patient may, for example, be discharged onto supervised community treatment (SCT).

Further guidance on the management of restricted patients

33.36 Professionals should approach the Mental Health Unit of the Ministry of Justice for more detailed guidance about the management of restricted patients.

Related material

- *Notes for the Guidance of Social Supervisors – Supervision and After-care of Conditionally Discharged Restricted Patients*, Home Office, 2007

- *Mental Health Act 2007 – Guidance for the Courts and Sentencing Powers for Mentally Disordered Offenders*, March 2008

- Prison Service Instruction 3/2006, which gives comprehensive guidance on the transfer process, professional roles and timescales

- Criminal Justice Act 2003

- *Guidance for Supervising Psychiatrists – Supervision and After-care of Conditionally Discharged Restricted Patients*, Home Office, June 2006

This material does not form part of the Code. It is provided for assistance only.

CHAPTER 34 **People with learning disabilities or autistic spectrum disorders**

34.1　This chapter deals with issues of particular relevance to patients with learning disabilities, autistic spectrum disorders or both.

Learning disabilities

34.2　For the purposes of the Act, a learning disability is defined as "a state of arrested or incomplete development of the mind which includes significant impairment of intelligence and social functioning". Section 1(4)

34.3　Although defined as a mental disorder in this way, learning disability shares few features with the serious mental illnesses that are the most common reason for using the Act. Relatively few people with learning disabilities are detained under the Act, and where they are, it is not usually solely because of their learning disability itself.

34.4　The identification of an individual with a learning disability is a matter for clinical judgement, guided by current professional practice. Those assessing the patient must be satisfied that they display a number of characteristics. The following is general guidance in relation to the key factors in the definition of learning disability for the purposes of the Act.

> *Arrested or incomplete development of mind:* An adult with arrested or incomplete development of mind is one who has experienced a significant impairment of the normal process of maturation of intellectual and social development that occurs during childhood and adolescence. By using these words in its definition of learning disability, the Act embraces the general understanding that features which qualify as a learning

disability are present prior to adulthood. For the purposes of the Act, learning disability does not include people whose intellectual disorder derives from accident, injury or illness occurring after they completed normal maturation (although such conditions do fall within the definition of mental disorder in the Act).

Significant impairment of intelligence: The judgement as to the presence of this particular characteristic must be made on the basis of reliable and careful assessment. It is not defined rigidly by the application of an arbitrary cut-off point such as an IQ of 70.

Significant impairment of social functioning: Reliable and recent observations will be helpful in determining the nature and extent of social competence, preferably from a number of sources who have experience of interacting with the person in social situations, including social workers, nurses, speech and language and occupational therapists, and psychologists. Social functioning assessment tests can be a valuable tool in determining this aspect of learning disability.

34.5　It is important to assess the person as a whole. It may be appropriate to identify learning disability in someone with an IQ somewhat higher than 70 if their social functioning is severely impaired. A person with a low IQ may be correctly diagnosed as having a learning disability even if their social functioning is relatively good.

Abnormally aggressive and seriously irresponsible behaviour

Section 1(2A) and (2B)
Reference Guide 1.12-1.15

34.6　An application for detention for treatment, or for reception into guardianship, on the basis of a learning disability without another concomitant mental disorder may be made only where it is associated with one or both of the following further features:

- abnormally aggressive behaviour; or

- seriously irresponsible conduct.

CHAPTER

34

People with
learning
disabilities
or autistic
spectrum
disorders

34.7 Neither term is defined in the Act, and it is not possible to state with any precision exactly what type of conduct could be considered to fall into either category. It will, inevitably, depend not only on the nature of the behaviour and the circumstances in which it is exhibited, but also on the extent to which that conduct gives rise to a serious risk to the health or safety of the patient or to the health or safety of other people, or both.

34.8 In assessing whether a patient's learning disability is associated with conduct that could not only be categorised as aggressive but as abnormally so, relevant factors may include:

- when such aggressive behaviour has been observed, and how persistent and severe it has been;

- whether it has occurred without a specific trigger or seems out of proportion to the circumstances that triggered it;

- whether, and to what degree, it has in fact resulted in harm or distress to other people, or actual damage to property;

- how likely, if it has not been observed recently, it is to recur; and

- how common similar behaviour is in the population generally.

34.9 Similarly, in assessing whether a patient's learning disability is associated with conduct that is not only irresponsible but seriously so, relevant factors may include:

- whether behaviour has been observed that suggests a disregard or an inadequate regard for its serious or dangerous consequences;

- how recently such behaviour has been observed and, when it has been observed, how persistent it has been;

- how seriously detrimental to the patient, or to other people, the consequences of the behaviour were or might have been;

- whether, and to what degree, the behaviour has actually resulted in harm to the patient or the patient's interests, or in harm to other people or to damage to property; and

- if it has not been observed recently, how likely it is to recur.

34.10 When assessing whether a patient with a learning disability should be detained for treatment under the Act, it is important to establish whether any abnormally aggressive or seriously irresponsible conduct identified stems from difficulties in communication. If, for example, the patient is displaying such conduct as their only way of drawing attention to an underlying physical health problem, it would be wrong to interpret the behaviour as an indication of a worsening of their mental disorder, and treatment under the Act would not be an appropriate response.

Practice considerations

34.11 Unless urgent action is required, it would not be good practice to diagnose a patient who has a learning disability as meeting either of these additional conditions without an assessment by a consultant psychiatrist in learning disabilities and a formal psychological assessment. Ideally, this would be part of a complete appraisal by medical, nursing, social work, speech and language therapy, occupational therapy and psychology professionals with experience in learning disabilities, in consultation with a relative, friend or supporter of the patient. Wherever possible, an approved mental health professional (AMHP) who assesses a patient with a learning disability under the Act should have training and experience in working with people with learning disabilities. The patient's person-centred plan and health action plan may also inform the assessment process.

34.12 All those involved in examining, assessing, treating or taking other decisions in relation to people with learning disabilities should bear in mind that there are particular issues that people with learning disabilities may face.

These include:

- incorrect assumptions that they do not have capacity to make decisions for themselves and a tendency to be over-protective;

- over-reliance on family members, both for support and for decision-making. Although the considerable expertise that family members often have should be acknowledged, this may put them in the difficult position of having to take decisions inappropriately on behalf of the patient;

- a lack of appreciation of the potential abilities of people with learning disabilities, including their potential to speak up for themselves;

- being denied access to decision-making processes, not being included in meetings about them, information made inaccessible to them, and decisions being made in their absence;

- limited life experiences to draw on when making choices; and

- their learning disability being seen as the explanation for all their physical and behavioural attributes when there may, in fact, be an underlying cause relating to a separate issue of physical or mental health (diagnostic overshadowing).

34.13 Those working under the Act with people with learning disabilities should bear in mind the following general points:

- people with learning disabilities may use non-verbal communication rather than spoken language. This non-verbal communication may include behaviour, gestures, posture and body language, ways of moving, signing, noises and pointing. It is important to recognise people's communication in all its forms and to avoid assuming that people's behaviour is a symptom of their mental disorder, when it may be an attempt to communicate feelings or physical pain or discomfort.

- people with learning disabilities may find new environments, such as a medical setting, frightening. All "reasonable adjustments" (as required by the Disability Discrimination Act 1995) need to be made to adapt and respond to each individual's needs. This may mean offering a quiet space, for example, or having one link person assigned who speaks with the person.

- the most appropriate method of communication for each person with learning disabilities should be identified as soon as possible, and the help of a speech and language therapist should be sought wherever appropriate. It is helpful to identify a specific person who will undertake this task.

- some people with learning disabilities may prefer to have written material in simple language with images or symbols to assist, and this could be reinforced orally, through personal contact or other means. It can be helpful to repeat information and leave a record of the information that has been passed on, so that the person can consult it and ask others to clarify anything that is difficult to understand.

CHAPTER

34

People with
learning
disabilities
or autistic
spectrum
disorders

- it is important to set aside sufficient time for preparation of suitable information and for preparation before meetings. Meetings should be held in an environment that is not intimidating, in order to allow the patient every chance to understand the information given.

34.14 People with learning disabilities may also encounter problems in:

- understanding what is being explained to them and communicating their views (in situations that increase their levels of anxiety they may find it even more difficult to understand what is said to them); and

- in being understood, particularly where lack of spoken language makes it hard for them to provide explanations of pain or other symptoms that might aid diagnosis of physical or mental illness.

34.15 Where information relates to their right to have their case reviewed by the Tribunal, the information will need to be designed to help people with learning disabilities understand the Tribunal's role. They may well need support to make an informed decision about whether and when to make an application.

34.16 Where professionals taking decisions under the Act have limited expertise with people with learning disabilities, it is good practice to seek advice from the local specialist service, which can provide details of alternatives to compulsory treatment and give advice on good communication. But any problem with availability of such services should not be allowed to delay action that is immediately necessary. It is desirable that, during examination or assessment, people with learning disabilities have someone with them whom they know well and with whom they have good communication (subject to the normal considerations of patient confidentiality).

34.17 The potential of co-morbidity with mental illness and personality disorder should also be kept in mind, in order that the skills of clinicians and others with appropriate expertise can be brought into play at all points in the assessment, treatment and care pathway. The possibility of physical health problems underlying the presentation of abnormally aggressive or seriously irresponsible behaviour should similarly always be kept in mind.

Autistic spectrum disorders

34.18 The Act's definition of mental disorder includes the full range of autistic spectrum disorders, including those existing alongside a learning disability or any other kind of mental disorder. While it is possible for someone on the autistic spectrum to meet the conditions for treatment under the Act without having any other form of mental disorder, even if it is not associated with abnormally aggressive or seriously irresponsible behaviour, this is likely to happen only very rarely. Compulsory treatment in a hospital setting is rarely likely to be helpful for a person with autism, who may be very distressed by even minor changes in routine and is likely to find detention in hospital anxiety provoking. Sensitive, person-centred support in a familiar setting will usually be more helpful. Wherever possible, less restrictive alternative ways of providing the treatment or support a person needs should be found.

34.19 Autistic spectrum disorders are disorders occurring from early stages in development in which the person shows marked difficulties with social communication, social interaction and social imagination. They may be preoccupied with a particular subject of interest.

CHAPTER

34

People with
learning
disabilities
or autistic
spectrum
disorders

34.20 These disorders are developmental in nature and are not mental illnesses in themselves. However, people with an autistic spectrum disorder may have additional or related problems, which frequently include anxiety. These may be related to social factors associated with frustration or communication problems or to patterns of thought and behaviour that are rigid or literal in nature. As with people with learning disabilities, it should be borne in mind that people with autistic spectrum disorders may also have co-morbid mental disorders, including mood disorders and, occasionally, personality disorders.

34.21 A person with an autistic spectrum disorder may have additional sensory and motor difficulties that make them behave in an unusual manner and that might be interpreted as a mental illness but are in fact a coping mechanism. These include sensitivity to light, sound, touch and balance and may result in a range of regulatory behaviours, including rocking, self-injury and avoidance, such as running away.

34.22 A person with an autistic spectrum disorder is likely to behave in ways that seem odd to other people. But mere eccentricity, in anyone, is not in itself a reason for compulsory measures under the Act.

34.23 There can also be a repetitive or compulsive element to much of the behaviour of people with autistic spectrum disorders. The person may appear to be choosing to act in a particular way, but their behaviour may be distressing even to themselves. It may be driven or made worse by anxiety and could lead to harm to self or others. Repetitive behaviour does not in itself constitute a mental disorder.

34.24 The examination or assessment of someone with an autistic spectrum disorder requires special consideration of how to communicate effectively with the person being assessed. Whenever possible, the people carrying out assessments should have experience and training in working with people with these disorders. If this is not possible, they should seek assistance from specialists with appropriate expertise, but this should not be allowed to delay action that is immediately necessary. Assessment should ideally be part of a complete appraisal – a multi-disciplinary process involving medical, nursing, social work, occupational therapy, speech and language therapy and psychology professionals (as necessary) with relevant specialist experience.

34.25 Where appropriate, someone who knows the person with an autistic spectrum disorder should be present at an initial examination and assessment (subject to the normal considerations of patient confidentiality). Knowledge of the person's early developmental history and usual pattern of behaviour will help prevent someone with an autistic spectrum disorder from being wrongly made subject to compulsory measures under the Act, or treated inappropriately with psychopharmacological agents.

34.26 A person with an autistic spectrum disorder may show a marked difference between their intellectual and their emotional development, associated on occasion with aggressive or seriously irresponsible behaviour. They may be able to discuss an action intellectually and express a desire to do it (or not, as the case may be) but not have the instinctive social empathy to keep to their intentions. This should be understood and responded to by professionals, who should recognise that the nature of the communication problems may require specialist structured approaches to communication. However, when the person is unable to prevent themselves from causing severe harm to themselves or others, compulsory measures under the Act may become necessary.

CHAPTER

34

People with
learning
disabilities
or autistic
spectrum
disorders

34.27 If people with autistic spectrum disorders do need to be detained under the Act, it is important that they are treated in a setting that can accommodate their social and communication needs as well as being able to treat their mental disorder.

Related material

- *Valuing People – A New Strategy for the 21st Century* (Cm 5086), The Stationery Office, March 2001

- *Valuing People: A New Strategy for Learning Disability for the 21st Century: Planning with People towards Person Centred Approaches – Guidance for Partnership Boards*, Department of Health, 28 January 2002

- *Action for Health, Health Action Plans and Health Facilitation Detailed Good Practice Guidance on Implementation for Learning Disability Partnership Boards*, Department of Health, 6 August 2002

This material does not form part of the Code. It is provided for assistance only.

APPLYING THE PRINCIPLES

This scenario is not intended to provide a template for decisions in applying the principles in similar situations. The scenario itself is only illustrative and does not form part of the Code itself.

AUTISM AND LEARNING DISABILITY

Albert is a 22 year old man with profound and multiple learning disabilities. He is six feet four inches tall and very powerfully built. As a child, he was also diagnosed with Kanner syndrome – a severe form of autistic spectrum disorder. He is unable to speak.

Albert lives in a residential care home. Following the recent death of a close friend, Albert became withdrawn and uncommunicative. His GP diagnosed depression and prescribed medication.

After a few weeks on this medication, Albert's mood changed. He was no longer withdrawn but began to display aggressive behaviour and, in particular, began banging the side of his head against the door handle. Staff at the group house felt he was becoming a risk to himself and to other people who came into contact with him and asked for a Mental Health Act assessment.

In considering whether admission to hospital under the Act is appropriate for Albert, the doctors and the AMHP should consider the principles and how they might be applied.

Among the things they might wish to consider in making a decision in these circumstances are the following.

Purpose principle
- What factors need to be considered in assessing for Albert's safety and wellbeing?

- Have any physical health factors been considered?

- Are there any social, occupational, psychological or sensory issues that may be influencing Albert's behaviour?

CHAPTER

34

People with
learning
disabilities
or autistic
spectrum
disorders

- Are there any issues of risk? If so, is the risk to Albert or to other people? Or both?

- If Albert were to be detained, how may the resultant change of environment impact on his condition?

Least restriction principle

- What are the possible alternatives to admission under the Act? Additional support to Albert in the residential care home? Further assessment, including investigation of possible underlying physical health problems?

Respect principle

- Is any aspect of Albert's behaviour an attempt to communicate what is wrong or express any views about what he would want to happen?

- How has he communicated his views in the past?

- Given that Albert is young and strong, are any assumptions being made about the risk his behaviour poses and, if so, how might they be affecting the options being considered?

Participation principle

- What methods have been employed to try to ascertain Albert's view about his care and treatment?

- Have Albert's family been contacted?

- What do they know about Albert that might inform an evaluation of his condition and the likely effectiveness of the various possible responses?

- What do they want and what do they know about him that might inform what he might want?

- Have the staff at the residential care home been asked what they think Albert's behaviour might mean and whether they have any information that might inform an evaluation of his condition and the likely effectiveness of the various possible responses?

- Do the staff know what Albert might want?

- Does Albert have access to an advocate or other support mechanism that can help interpret his behaviour?

- Has Albert's GP been contacted? What is the GP's view about Albert's condition and what is their view about what Albert might want?

Effectiveness, efficiency and equity principle

- Is there someone with specialist knowledge of learning disability and autism available to be involved in the assessment? If so, given the circumstances, can the assessment wait until they can attend?

CHAPTER 35 **People with personality disorders**

This chapter deals with issues of particular relevance to people with a personality disorder.

Personality disorders – general points

35.1   The Act applies equally to all people with mental disorders, including those with either primary or secondary diagnoses of personality disorder.

35.2   Generally, people who have personality disorders present a complex range of mental health and other problems:

- many people may have a diagnosis of more than one personality disorder, and they may also have other mental health problems such as depression, anxiety or post-traumatic stress syndrome;

- suicidality, self-harm, substance misuse problems and eating disorders are also common in people with personality disorders;

- some individuals experience very severe, periodic emotional distress in response to stressful circumstances and crisis, particularly people with borderline personality disorder;

- some individuals can at times display a form of psychosis that is qualitatively different from that displayed by people with a diagnosis of mental illness;

- people with personality disorders usually have long-standing and recurrent relationship difficulties;

- people with personality disorders are more likely than other population groups to experience housing problems and long-term unemployment;

- a very small subgroup of people with personality disorders may be anti-social and dangerous;

- anti-social personality disorder is strongly associated with offending, and it is estimated that personality disorders have a high prevalence within offender populations.

Personality disorders and mental health legislation

35.3 People with personality disorders who are subject to compulsory measures under the Act may include individuals who:

- have a primary diagnosis of personality disorder and present a serious risk to themselves or others (or both);

- have complex mental disorders, including personality disorder, and present a serious risk to themselves or to others (or both);

- have a primary diagnosis of personality disorder or complex disorders including personality disorder and are transferred from prison for treatment in secure psychiatric or personality disorder in patient services;

- are transferred from prison or other secure settings for treatment within designated dangerous and severe personality disorder (DSPD) units in hospitals; and

- are personality disordered offenders who have completed in-patient treatment in DSPD units, or other secure settings, but who may need further treatment in the community.

Practice considerations

Assessment

35.4 People with personality disorders may present and behave in very different ways from those with other mental disorders. It is important that such behaviours and presentations are properly understood if the Act is to be used appropriately.

35.5   Especially in times of crisis, decisions about the use of the
        Act for people with personality disorders will often have
        to be made by professionals who are not specialists in the
        field. It is therefore important that approved mental health
        professionals and doctors carrying out initial assessments
        have a sufficient understanding of personality disorders as
        well as other forms of mental disorder.

35.6   Individuals who have historically been labelled by various
        local agencies as having a personality disorder may never,
        in fact, have had a thorough clinical assessment and
        formulation. A number of validated assessment tools
        enable a more precise identification to be made.
        Professionals will need to ensure that any treatment and
        after-care plans are shaped by appropriate clinical
        assessments conducted by suitably trained practitioners.

35.7   In emergency or very high-risk situations, where such
        an assessment has not already been carried out and an
        application for detention under the Act is being considered,
        then responding to the immediate risk to the health or
        safety of the patient or to other people is the first priority.
        However, achieving an appropriate clinical assessment and
        formulation should be an immediate aim of detention.

Appropriate medical treatment

35.8   What constitutes appropriate medical treatment for a
        particular patient with a personality disorder will depend
        very much on their individual circumstances. First and
        foremost, that calls for a clinical judgement by the
        clinicians responsible for their assessment or treatment.

35.9   A proposed care plan will not, of course, meet the Act's
        definition of appropriate medical treatment unless it is for
        the purpose of alleviating or preventing a worsening of
        the patient's mental disorder, its symptoms or
        manifestations (see **chapter 6**).

35.10 Generally, treatment approaches for personality disorders
        need to be relatively intense and long term, structured and
        coherent. Sustainable long-term change is more likely to
        be achieved with the voluntary engagement of the patient.

35.11 People with personality disorders may take time to engage and develop motivation for such longer-term treatment. But even patients who are not engaged in that kind of treatment may need other forms of treatment, including nurse and specialist care, to manage the continuing risks posed by their disorders, and this may constitute appropriate medical treatment.

35.12 In the majority of cases, the primary model of intervention for personality disorders is rooted in a psycho-social model.

35.13 Patients who have been detained may often need to continue treatment in a community setting on discharge. Where there are continuing risks that cannot otherwise be managed safely, supervised community treatment, guardianship or (for restricted patients) conditional discharge may provide a framework within which such patients can continue their treatment in the community.

35.14 In deciding whether treatment under the Act can be delivered safely in the community, account should be taken of:

- where the specific model of treatment intervention can be delivered most effectively and safely;

- if management of personal and social relationships is a factor in the intervention, how the appropriate day-to-day support and monitoring of the patient's social as well as psychological needs can be provided;

- to what degree the psycho-social model of intervention requires the active participation of the patient for an effective and safe outcome;

- the degree to which the patient has the ability to take part in a psycho-social intervention that protects their own and others' safety;

- the degree to which 24-hour access to support will be required; and

- the need for the intervention plan to be supervised by a professional who is appropriately qualified in the model of intervention and in risk assessment and management in the community.

35.15 In the case of personality disordered offenders who may already have received long-term treatment programmes within secure or prison settings, treatment in the community may well still be required while they resettle in the community.

Related material

- *Personality disorder: No longer a diagnosis of exclusion. Policy implementation guidance for the development of services for people with personality disorder,* Department of Health, January 2003

  This material does not form part of the Code. It is provided for assistance only.

CHAPTER 36 Children and young people under the age of 18

Reference Guide
chapter 36

36.1   This chapter provides guidance on particular issues arising in relation to children (less than 16 years old) and young people (16 or 17 years old).

36.2   This chapter sets out some of the key factors that need to be borne in mind and their interconnections, including:

- some of the main concepts that need to be considered when dealing with patients who are under 18, such as who has parental responsibility, and the parental zone of control;

- when the Mental Health Act should be used and when the Children Act should be used;

- what it means for children and young people to be capable of consent;

- how to make decisions about admission or treatment of informal patients of 16 or 17 year olds;

- how to deal with informal patients under 16 years old;

- how treatment for under 18s is regulated by the Mental Health Act;

- when an application to the court should be made;

- the need to provide age-appropriate services;

- applications and references to the Tribunal; and

- general duties concerning, for example, local authorities visiting children and young people in hospital.

CHAPTER

36

Children
and young
people
under the
age of 18

General considerations

36.3   The legal framework governing the admission to hospital and treatment of children is complex, and it is important to remember a number of factors. Those responsible for the care of children and young people in hospital should be familiar with other relevant legislation, including the Children Acts 1989 and 2004, Mental Capacity Act 2005 (MCA), Family Law Reform Act 1969, Human Rights Act 1998 and the United Nations Convention on the Rights of the Child, as well as relevant case law, common law principles and relevant codes of practice.

36.4   When taking decisions under the Act about children and young people, the following should always be borne in mind:

- the best interests of the child or young person must always be a significant consideration;

- children and young people should always be kept as fully informed as possible, just as an adult would be, and should receive clear and detailed information concerning their care and treatment, explained in a way they can understand and in a format that is appropriate to their age;

- the child or young person's views, wishes and feelings should always be considered;

- any intervention in the life of a child or young person that is considered necessary by reason of their mental disorder should be the option that is least restrictive and least likely to expose them to the risk of any stigmatisation, consistent with effective care and treatment, and it should also result in the least possible separation from family, carers, friends and community or interruption of their education, as is consistent with their wellbeing;

- all children and young people should receive the same access to educational provision as their peers;

- children and young people have as much right to expect their dignity to be respected as anyone else; and

- children and young people have as much right to privacy and confidentiality as anyone else.

People with parental responsibility

36.5 Those with parental responsibility will usually, but not always, be the parents of the child or young person. Legally, under the Children Act 1989, consent to treat a child or young person is needed from only one person with parental responsibility, although it is good practice to involve both parents and others close to the child or young person in the decision-making process. However, if one person with parental responsibility strongly disagreed with the decision to treat and was likely to challenge it in court, it might be appropriate to seek authorisation from the court before relying on the consent of another person with parental responsibility.

36.6 It is essential that those taking decisions under the Mental Health Act are clear about who has parental responsibility and that they always request copies of any court orders for reference on the child or young person's medical or social service file. These orders may include care orders, residence orders, contact orders, evidence of appointment as the child or young person's guardian, parental responsibility agreements or orders under section 4 of the Children Act and any order under wardship. If the parents of a child or young person are separated, and the child or young person is living with one parent, the person responsible for the care and treatment of the patient should try to establish whether there is a residence order and, if so, in whose favour.

36.7 Once it is established who has parental responsibility for the child or young person, the person responsible for the care and treatment of the patient must determine whether a person with parental responsibility has the capacity, within the meaning of the MCA, to take a

CHAPTER

36

Children
and young
people
under the
age of 18

decision about the child or young person's treatment and whether the decision is within the zone of parental control (see **paragraphs 36.9-36.15**).

Children looked after by the local authority

36.8   Where children or young people are looked after by the local authority (see section 22 of the Children Act 1989), treatment decisions should usually be discussed with the parent or other person with parental responsibility who continues to have parental responsibility for the child. If a child or young person is voluntarily accommodated by the local authority, parents or other people with parental responsibility have the same rights and responsibilities in relation to treatment as they would otherwise. If the child or young person is subject to a care order, the parents (or others with parental responsibility) share parental responsibility with the local authority, and it will be a matter for negotiation and agreement between them as to who should be consulted about treatment decisions. However, local authorities can, in the exercise of their powers under section 33(3)(b) of the Children Act 1989, limit the extent to which parents (or others) may exercise their parental responsibility. (See also **paragraphs 36.80-36.82** for the duties of local authorities in relation to hospital patients.)

Zone of parental control

36.9   People with parental responsibility may in certain circumstances (see below) consent on behalf of a child under 16 to them being given medical treatment or being admitted informally for such treatment. Even in these circumstances, mental health professionals can rely on such consent only where it is within what in this guidance is called the "zone of parental control". This may also apply to young people of 16 or 17 years of age who are given medical treatment for mental disorder and who lack the ability to consent for themselves, and to decisions about such young people being admitted for such treatment informally if they lack capacity. The concept of the zone of parental control derives largely from case law from the European Court of Human Rights in Strasbourg.[1] It is difficult to have clear rules about what may fall in the zone, when so much depends on the particular facts of each case. Certain guidelines are set out below, but where there is doubt professionals should take legal advice so that account may be taken of the most recent case law.

36.10 In assessing whether a particular decision falls within the parameters of the zone of parental control, two key questions must be considered:

- firstly, is the decision one that a parent would be expected to make, having regard both to what is considered to be normal practice in our society and to any relevant human rights decisions made by the courts?; and

- secondly, are there no indications that the parent might not act in the best interests of the child or young person?

36.11 The less confident a professional is that they can answer both questions in the affirmative, the more likely it will be that the decision in question falls outside the zone.

36.12 The parameters of the zone will vary from one case to the next: they are determined not only by social norms, but also by the circumstances and dynamics of a specific parent and child or young person. In assessing where the boundaries lie in any particular case, and so whether a parent's consent may be relied upon, mental health professionals might find it helpful to consider the following factors:

- the nature and invasiveness of what is to be done to the patient (including the extent to which their liberty will be curtailed) – the more extreme the intervention, the more likely it will be that it falls outside the zone;

[1]For example Nielsen v Denmark (1989) 11 EHRR 175.

CHAPTER

36

Children
and young
people
under the
age of 18

- whether the patient is resisting – treating a child or young person who is resisting needs more justification;

- the general social standards in force at the time concerning the sorts of decisions it is acceptable for parents to make – anything that goes beyond the kind of decisions parents routinely make will be more suspect;

- the age, maturity and understanding of the child or young person – the greater these are, the more likely it will be that it should be the child or young person who takes the decision; and

- the extent to which a parent's interests may conflict with those of the child or young person – this may suggest that the parent will not act in the child or young person's best interests.

36.13 For example, in a case where the parents had gone through a particularly acrimonious divorce, it might not be possible to separate the decision about whether to admit the child to hospital from the parents' own hostilities, and it might not be possible to treat the parents as able to make an impartial decision. It might also not be appropriate to rely on the consent of a parent in circumstances where the mental health of the child or young person has led to chronic battles over control in the home. In another case, there might be concerns about the mental capacity of the person with parental responsibility, and whether they have capacity to take a decision about the child's treatment.

36.14 It is also possible that a decision on treatment could be outside the zone of parental control simply because of the nature of the proposed treatment, eg where, like electro-convulsive therapy (ECT), it could be considered particularly invasive or controversial.

36.15 In any case where reliance could not be placed on the consent of a person with parental responsibility, or on that of the child or young person, consideration should be given to alternative ways to treat them. One way would be to apply to have the child or young person detained under the Mental Health Act, but this is available only where they meet all the criteria for such detention. In cases where they do not meet the criteria, it may be appropriate to seek authorisation from the court.

Care for children whose liberty must be restricted – when might the Mental Health Act or the Children Act be appropriate?

36.16 There is no minimum age limit for detention in hospital under the Mental Health Act. It may be used to detain children or young people where that is justified by the risk posed by their mental disorder and all the relevant criteria are met.

36.17 However, where the child or young person with a mental disorder needs to be detained, but the primary purpose is not to provide medical treatment for mental disorder, consideration should be given to using section 25 of the Children Act 1989.

36.18 For example, if a child or young person is seriously mentally ill, they may require to be admitted for treatment under the Mental Health Act. But if they are behaviourally disturbed, and there is no need for them to be hospitalised, their needs might be more appropriately met within secure accommodation under the Children Act. Professionals who address these questions should:

- be aware of the relevant statutory provisions and have easy access to competent legal advice;

- keep in mind the importance of ensuring that the care and treatment of the child or young person are managed with clarity and consistency and within a recognisable framework (such as the child and adolescent mental health services (CAMHS) Care Programme Approach); and

CHAPTER

36

Children
and young
people
under the
age of 18

- attempt to select the option that reflects the predominant needs of the child or young person at that time, whether that is to provide specific mental healthcare and treatment or to achieve a measure of safety and protection. In any event, the least restrictive option consistent with the care and treatment objectives for the child or young person should be adopted.

Decisions on admission and treatment of under 18s

36.19 The decision to admit a child or young person to hospital is inextricably linked to the decision to treat them once they have been admitted. But they may need to be considered separately in light of the different provisions that are relevant to each decision.

36.20 At least one of the people involved in the assessment of a person who is under 18 years old, ie one of the two medical practitioners or the approved mental health professional (AMHP), should be a clinician specialising in CAMHS. Where this is not possible, a CAMHS clinician should be consulted as soon as possible. In cases where the child or young person has complex or multiple needs, other clinicians may need to be involved, eg a learning disability CAMHS consultant where the child or young person has a learning disability. See **chapter 4** for fuller information on the assessment process.

Informal admission and treatment of 16 or 17 year olds

36.21 The law about admission and treatment of young people aged 16 or 17 differs from that for children under 16. But in both cases, whether they are capable of consenting to what is proposed is of central importance.

Informal admission of 16 and 17 year olds with capacity to consent

36.22 A decision about admission for informal treatment of a 16 or 17 year old who has capacity must be made in accordance with section 131 of the Mental Health Act. Section 131 of the Act provides that where a patient who is 16 or 17 years old has capacity (as defined in the MCA) to consent to being admitted to hospital for treatment of a mental disorder, they themselves may consent or not consent to being admitted, regardless of the views of a person with parental responsibility. This means that if a young person who is 16 or 17 years old, and who has the capacity to make such a decision, consents to being admitted for treatment, they can be treated as an informal patient in accordance with section 131, even if a person with parental responsibility is refusing consent.

36.23 Section 131 also applies to a patient who is 16 or 17 years old and has capacity but does not consent (for whatever reason, including being overwhelmed by the implications of the decision) or who refuses consent, so in these circumstances a person with parental responsibility cannot consent on their behalf. In such cases, consideration should be given to whether the patient satisfies all the criteria for detention under the Act. If those criteria are not satisfied, but treatment in hospital is thought to be in the patient's best interests, it may be necessary to seek authorisation from the court instead.

36.24 If the young person is admitted informally, the considerations set out in **paragraphs 36.27** onwards will apply to their treatment.

Informal admission of 16 and 17 year olds who lack capacity to consent

36.25 Different considerations apply to a decision to informally admit a young person aged 16 or 17 where the young person lacks capacity. Section 131 of the Act does not apply. The MCA may apply in the same way as it does to those who are aged 18 or over, unless the admission and treatment amounts to a deprivation of liberty. If there is a deprivation of liberty, admission of a 16 or 17 year old cannot be authorised under the MCA, and the legality of any such admission should be assessed under common law principles.

CHAPTER

36

Children
and young
people
under the
age of 18

36.26 Common law principles allow a person with parental responsibility in these circumstances to consent, but only if the matter is within the zone of parental control. If it is outside the zone, then consideration should be given to whether the young person meets all the criteria for detention under the Mental Health Act. If the Act is not applicable, it may be necessary to seek authorisation from the court.

Informal treatment of 16 and 17 year olds who are capable of consenting

36.27 Special provision is made for the treatment of young people. By virtue of section 8 of the Family Law Reform Act 1969, people who are 16 or 17 years old are presumed to be capable of consenting to their own medical treatment and to any ancillary procedures involved in that treatment, such as an anaesthetic.

36.28 This test is different from that in section 131 of the Mental Health Act. A young person who has capacity to consent (within the meaning of the MCA) may nonetheless not be capable of consenting in a particular case, for example because they are overwhelmed by the implications of the relevant decision.

36.29 As would apply in the case of an adult, consent will be valid only if it is given voluntarily by an appropriately informed patient capable of consenting to the particular intervention. However, unlike in the case of an adult, the refusal by a person aged 16 or 17 to consent may in certain circumstances be overridden by a court.

36.30 Section 8 of the Family Law Reform Act applies only to the young person's own treatment. It does not apply to an intervention that is not potentially of direct health benefit to the young person, such as non-therapeutic research into the causes of a disorder. However, a young person may be able to consent to such an intervention if they have the understanding and ability to do so.

36.31 When assessing whether a young person is capable of consent, the same criteria should be used as for adults.

36.32 If the young person is capable of giving valid consent and does so, then it is not legally necessary to obtain consent from a person with parental responsibility as well. It is, however, good practice to involve the young person's family in the decision-making process, if the young person consents to their information being shared.

36.33 When a young person refuses consent, the courts in the past have found that a person with parental responsibility can overrule their refusal in non-emergency cases. However, there is no post-Human Rights Act decision on this, and the trend in recent cases is to reflect greater autonomy for under 18s in law. In the Department of Health's view, it is not wise to rely on the consent of a person with parental responsibility to treat a young person who refuses in these circumstances. Consideration should be given to whether the young person meets all the criteria for detention under the Mental Health Act. If they do not, it may be necessary to seek authorisation from the court.

36.34 In an emergency, where a 16 or 17 year old who is capable of consenting refuses to have treatment, it is likely that the young person's decision could be overruled and the clinician could act without anyone's consent if the refusal would in all likelihood lead to their death or to severe permanent injury.

Informal treatment of 16 and 17 year olds who are not capable of consenting

36.35 Different considerations also apply to a decision to treat a young person aged 16 or 17 informally where the young person lacks capacity or is otherwise not capable of consenting. Where the young person lacks capacity, the MCA will apply in the same way as it does to those aged 18 and over, unless the treatment amounts to a deprivation of liberty.

CHAPTER

36

Children
and young
people
under the
age of 18

36.36 If the treatment amounts to a deprivation of liberty, it cannot be authorised under the MCA for a 16 or 17 year old, and the legality of any such treatment should be assessed under common law principles.

36.37 Common law principles will also apply if the young person has capacity to consent (as defined in the MCA) but for some other reason is not capable of consenting, for example because they are overwhelmed by the implications of the decision. This means that a person with parental responsibility could consent on their behalf if the matter is within the zone of parental control. If it is not, then consideration should be given to whether the young person meets all the criteria for detention under the Mental Health Act. If they do not, it may be necessary to seek authorisation from the court.

Under 16s

What is Gillick competence?

36.38 In the case of Gillick,[2] the court held that children who have sufficient understanding and intelligence to enable them to understand fully what is involved in a proposed intervention will also have the competence to consent to that intervention. This is sometimes described as being "Gillick competent". A child may be Gillick competent to consent to admission to hospital, medical treatment, research or any other activity that requires their consent.

36.39 The concept of Gillick competence is said to reflect the child's increasing development to maturity. The understanding required for different interventions will vary considerably. A child may have the competence to consent to some interventions but not others. The child's competence to consent should be assessed carefully in relation to each decision that needs to be made.

[2]Gillick v West Norfolk and Wisbech Area Health Authority [1986] A.C.112.

36.40 In some cases, for example because of a mental disorder, a child's mental state may fluctuate significantly, so that on some occasions the child appears to be Gillick competent in respect of a particular decision and on other occasions does not. In cases such as these, careful consideration should be given to whether the child is truly Gillick competent at any time to take a relevant decision.

36.41 If the child is Gillick competent and is able to give voluntary consent after receiving appropriate information, that consent will be valid and additional consent by a person with parental responsibility will not be required. It is, however, good practice to involve the child's parents, guardian or carers in the decision-making process, if the child consents to their information being shared.

Informal admission and treatment of under 16s who are Gillick competent

36.42 Where a child who is Gillick competent consents, they may be admitted to hospital as an informal patient. Where a child who is Gillick competent to do so has consented to being admitted informally, they may be given treatment if they are competent to consent to it and do consent. Consent should be sought for each aspect of the child's care and treatment as it arises. "Blanket" consent forms should not be used.

36.43 Where a child who is Gillick competent refuses to be admitted for treatment, in the past the courts have held that a person with parental responsibility can overrule their refusal. However, there is no post-Human Rights Act decision on this. The trend in recent cases is to reflect greater autonomy for competent under 18s, so it may be unwise to rely on the consent of a person with parental responsibility.

36.44 Consideration should be given to whether the child meets all the criteria for detention under the Mental Health Act. If they do not, it may be appropriate to seek authorisation from the court, except in cases where the child's refusal would be likely to lead to their death or to severe

CHAPTER

36

Children
and young
people
under the
age of 18

permanent injury, in which case the child could be admitted to hospital and treated without consent.

Informal admission and treatment of under 16s who are not Gillick competent

36.45 Where a child is not Gillick competent, it will usually be possible for a person with parental responsibility to consent on their behalf to their informal admission to hospital for treatment for mental disorder.

36.46 Before relying on parental consent in relation to a child who is under 16 years old and who is not Gillick competent, an assessment should be made of whether the matter is within the zone of parental control.

36.47 A child's views should be taken into account, even if they are not Gillick competent. How much weight the child's views should be given will depend on how mature the child is. Where a child has been Gillick competent to make a decision but then loses competence, any views they expressed before losing competence should be taken into account and may act as parameters limiting the zone of parental control. For example, if a child has expressed willingness to receive one form of treatment but not another while Gillick competent but then loses competence, it might not be appropriate to give the treatment to the child as an informal patient where the child has previously refused it, even if a person with parental responsibility consents.

36.48 If the decision regarding the admission and treatment of a child (including how the child is to be kept safely in one place) is within the zone of parental control, and consent is given by a person with parental responsibility, then the clinician may rely on that consent and admit and treat the child as an informal patient on that basis.

36.49 The fact that a parent or other person with parental responsibility has informally admitted a child should not lead professionals to assume that consent has been given to all components of a treatment programme regarded as "necessary". Consent should be sought for each aspect of the child's care and treatment as it arises. "Blanket" consent forms should not be used.

36.50 If the decision is not within the zone of parental control, or the consent of a person with parental responsibility is not given, the child cannot be admitted and treated informally on the basis of the parent's consent. An application can be made under the Mental Health Act if the child meets all the criteria for detention under the Act. If the criteria are not met, it may be necessary to seek authorisation from the court.

Emergency treatment

36.51 A life-threatening emergency may arise when a patient who is under 18 is capable of consenting to a treatment but refuses to do so, or where a person with parental responsibility could consent but there is no time to seek their consent, or where they are refusing consent and there is no time to seek authorisation from the court. In such cases, the courts have stated that doubt should be resolved in favour of the preservation of life, and it will be acceptable to undertake treatment to preserve life or prevent irreversible serious deterioration of the patient's condition.

Treatments for under 18s regulated by the Mental Health Act

36.52 Treatment for mental disorder for under 18s is regulated by the Act when the patient is:

- detained;

- on supervised community treatment (SCT); or

- for some treatments, an informal patient.

36.53 Even where treatment under the Act does not require consent, the safeguards differ depending on whether the patient is able to and does consent, so it is important to know whether the patient is able to and does consent.

CHAPTER

36

Children
and young
people
under the
age of 18

Treatment requiring the patient's consent (section 57)

36.54 Treatment covered by section 57 of the Act (primarily
neurosurgery for mental disorder) cannot be given to a
child or young person who does not personally consent
to it, whether they are detained or not. These treatments
cannot, therefore, be given to any young person or child
who is not capable of consenting, even if a person with
parental responsibility consents.

Electro-convulsive therapy (section 58A)

36.55 There is provision in the Act about treatment with ECT of
patients who are under 18 which applies whether they are
being informally treated or are detained under the Act.

36.56 Detained patients cannot be given ECT without their
consent, if they are capable of consenting to the
treatment, unless it is an emergency. If they are not
capable of consenting, or if it is an emergency, they may
be given ECT without their consent in accordance with
rules described in **chapter 24**.

36.57 The same applies to SCT patients, except that, even in
emergencies, if they have capacity or competence they
may be given ECT without consent only if they have been
recalled to hospital.

36.58 In addition, no child or young person under the age
of 18 may be given ECT without the approval of a
second opinion appointed doctor (SOAD), unless it is
an emergency, even if they consent to it.

36.59 There is nothing in the Act itself to prevent a person with
parental responsibility consenting to ECT on behalf of a
child or young person who lacks the ability to consent for
themselves and who is neither detained nor an SCT
patient.

36.60 However, although there is no case law at present directly
on this point, it would not be prudent to rely on such
consent, because it is likely to lie outside the parental
zone of control. Therefore, if a child under 16 who is not

detained or an SCT patient needs ECT, court authorisation should be sought, unless it is an emergency. This should be done before a SOAD is asked to approve the treatment. In practice, the issues the court is likely to address will mirror those that the SOAD is required to consider.

36.61 This will also be the case for young people of 16 or 17 who are not detained or SCT patients and who lack the ability to consent for themselves, except where the MCA could be used to provide the necessary authority. The MCA can be used for this only where it is not necessary to deprive the young person of liberty.[3] As in cases where court authorisation is obtained, a SOAD certificate will still be needed, unless it is an emergency.

36.62 Children and young people who are not detained under the Act but may require ECT are eligible for access to independent mental health advocates.[4]

Other treatment under the Act – detained and SCT patients only

36.63 The Act itself sets out when detained and SCT patients (of all ages) can be given other types of treatment for mental disorder, such as the requirement in section 58 for consent or a second opinion before medication can be given to detained patients after the initial period of three months. People with parental responsibility are not required to consent to such treatment on behalf of children and young people in this position.

Supervised community treatment

36.64 There is no lower age limit for SCT. The number of children and young people whose clinical and family circumstances make them suitable to move from being detained to having SCT is likely to be small, but it should be used where appropriate.

36.65 Parents (or other people with parental responsibility) may not consent on a child's behalf to treatment for mental disorder (or refuse it) while the child is on SCT. However,

[3]The word "not" was accidently omitted from the version of the code presented to Parliament, making the sentence factually incorrect. The MCA cannot be used to authorise deprivation of liberty of a person under 18.

[4]Independent mental health advocacy services under the Act are expected to be introduced in April 2009.

CHAPTER

36

Children
and young
people
under the
age of 18

if SCT patients under the age of 18 are living with one
or both parents, the person giving the treatment should
consult with the parent(s) about the particular treatment
(subject to the normal considerations of patient
confidentiality), bearing in mind that if there is something
that the parents would not accept, it would make it very
difficult for the patient to live with their parents while on
SCT. This dialogue should continue throughout the
patient's treatment on SCT. If a parent is unhappy with
the particular treatment or conditions attached to SCT,
and the child is not competent to consent, a review by
the patient's team should take place to consider whether
the treatment and care plan, and SCT in general, are still
appropriate for the child.

Applications to the High Court

36.66 In certain situations where decisions about admitting a
child or young person informally or giving treatment need
to be made, but the action cannot be taken under the
MCA and it is not appropriate to use the Mental Health
Act, the assistance of the High Court may be sought.
Consideration will need to be given to whether an
application should be made under the inherent jurisdiction
or for a section 8 order under the Children Act 1989. This
will depend on the facts of each case. Where a child is
under 16, an application should be considered, in
particular where the child:

- is not Gillick competent and where the person with
parental responsibility cannot be identified or is
incapacitated;

- is not Gillick competent and where one person with
parental responsibility consents but another strongly
disagrees and is likely to take the matter to court
themselves;

- is not Gillick competent and where there is concern
that the person with parental responsibility may not be
acting in the best interests of the child in making

treatment decisions on behalf of the child, eg where hostility between parents is a factor in any decision making or where there are concerns as to whether a person with parental responsibility is capable of making a decision in the best interests of the child;

- is not Gillick competent and where a person with parental responsibility consents but the decision is not within the zone of parental control, eg where the treatment in question is ECT; or

- is Gillick competent or is a young person who is capable of making a decision on their treatment and is refusing treatment.

Age-appropriate services[5]

36.67 Section 131A of the Act says that children and young people admitted to hospital for the treatment of mental disorder should be accommodated in an environment that is suitable for their age (subject to their needs).

36.68 This means that children and young people should have:

- appropriate physical facilities;

- staff with the right training, skills and knowledge to understand and address their specific needs as children and young people;

- a hospital routine that will allow their personal, social and educational development to continue as normally as possible; and

- equal access to educational opportunities as their peers, in so far as that is consistent with their ability to make use of them, considering their mental state.

36.69 Hospital managers should ensure that the environment is suitable, and in reaching their determination they must consult a person whom they consider to be suitable because they are experienced in CAMHS cases.

[5]This duty is expected to be in force from April 2010, but hospital managers should take all the steps they reasonably can to comply with the duty even before it comes into force. The Secretary of State recognises that some hospitals will not be able to do so fully immediately.

CHAPTER

36

Children
and young
people
under the
age of 18

36.70   If, exceptionally, a patient cannot be accommodated
in a dedicated child or adolescent ward, then discrete
accommodation in an adult ward, with facilities, security
and staffing appropriate to the needs of the child, might
provide the most satisfactory solution, eg young female
patients should be placed in single-sex accommodation.
Where possible, all those involved in the care and
treatment of children and young people should be child
specialists. Anyone who looks after them must always
have enhanced disclosure clearance from the Criminal
Records Bureau and that clearance must be kept up
to date.

36.71   In a small number of cases, the patient's need to be
accommodated in a safe environment could, in the short
term, take precedence over the suitability of that
environment for their age. Furthermore, it is also
important to recognise that there is a clear difference
between what is a suitable environment for a child or
young person in an emergency situation and what is a
suitable environment for a child or young person on a
longer-term basis. In an emergency, such as when the
patient is in crisis, the important thing is that the patient
is in a safe environment. Once the initial emergency
situation is over, hospital managers, in determining
whether the environment continues to be suitable, would
need to consider issues such as whether the patient can
mix with individuals of their own age, can receive visitors
of all ages and has access to education. Hospital
managers have a duty to consider whether a patient
should be transferred to more appropriate
accommodation and, if so, to arrange this as soon
as possible.

36.72   There will be times when the assessment concludes that
the best place for an under 18 year old is an adult ward.
This may happen when the young person is very close to
their 18th birthday, and placing the young person on a
CAMHS ward for a matter of weeks or days and then
transferring them to an adult ward would be counter-
therapeutic. In some cases the young person may express

a preference to be on an adult ward, such as when they are under the care of the early intervention psychosis team and they wish to go to the ward when the team rotates rather than to a unit with much younger children.

36.73 Where a young patient's presence on a ward with other children and young people might have a detrimental effect on the other young patients, the hospital managers need to ensure that the interests of other patients are protected. However, the needs of other patients should not override the need to provide accommodation in an environment that is suitable for the patient's age (subject to their needs) for an individual patient aged under 18.

36.74 Children and young people aged under 18 should also have access to age-appropriate leisure activities and facilities for visits from parents, guardians, siblings or carers.

The responsible clinician and others caring for and treating under 18s

36.75 Where possible, those responsible for the care and treatment of children and young people should be child specialists. Where this is not possible, it is good practice for the clinical staff to have regular access to and make use of a CAMHS specialist for advice and consultation.

Rights to apply to the Tribunal

36.76 Children and young people who are detained under the Mental Health Act have the same rights as other patients to apply to the Tribunal. It is important that children and young people are given assistance so that they get access to legal representation at an early stage. In addition, hospital managers should bear in mind that their duties to refer patients to the Tribunal are different in respect of patients who are under 18 years old. Where older patients must be referred after a three-year period without a Tribunal hearing, children and young people must be referred after one year.

CHAPTER

36

Children
and young
people
under the
age of 18

Education

36.77 No child or young person below the school leaving age should be denied access to learning merely because they are receiving medical treatment for a mental disorder. Young people over school leaving age should be encouraged to continue learning.

Confidentiality

36.78 All children and young people have a right to confidentiality. Under 16s who are Gillick competent and young people aged 16 or 17 are entitled to make decisions about the use and disclosure of information they have provided in confidence in the same way as adults. For example, they may be receiving treatment or counselling that they do not want their parents to know about. However, there are circumstances when the duty of care to the patient might require confidentiality to be breached to the extent of informing those with parental responsibility.

36.79 The decision to disclose information to parents and others with parental responsibility is complex for this age group and depends on a range of factors, including:

- the child or young person's age and developmental level;

- their maturity;

- their ability to take into account the future as well as the present;

- the severity of the mental disorder and the risks posed to themselves and to others;

- the degree of care and protection required;

- the degree of the parents' involvement in the care of the child or young person;

- the closeness of the relationship with the parents; and

- the current competence of the child or young person to make a decision about confidentiality.

In addition, it should be noted that competence to take a decision about information sharing, as with treatment, may change over time.

Duties of local authorities in relation to hospital patients

36.80 Local authorities should ensure that they arrange for visits to be made to:

- children and young people looked after by them who are in hospital, whether or not they are under a care order; and

- children and young people accommodated or intended to be accommodated for three months or more by NHS bodies, local education authorities or care homes.[6] This is in addition to their duty in respect of children and young people in their care in hospitals or nursing homes in England and Wales as required by section 116 of the Act. Local authorities should take such other steps in relation to the patient while they are in hospital or a nursing home as would be expected to be taken by the patient's parent(s).

36.81 Local authorities are under a duty in the Children Act 1989 to:

- promote contact between children and young people who are in need and their families, if they live away from home, and to help them get back together (paragraphs 10 and 15 of Schedule 2 to the Children Act); and

[6]See the Review of Children's Cases Regulations 1991 (Statutory Instrument 1991/895 as amended) and sections 85 and 86 of the Children Act 1989.

CHAPTER

36

Children
and young
people
under the
age of 18

- arrange for people (independent visitors) to visit and befriend children and young people looked after by the authority, wherever they are, if they have not been regularly visited by their parents (paragraph 17 of Schedule 2 to the Act).

36.82 Local authorities should be alerted if the whereabouts of the person with parental responsibility is not known or if that person has not visited the child or young person for a significant period of time. When alerted to this situation, the local authority should consider whether visits should be arranged.

Related material

- Children Act 1989 and guidance (particularly volumes 1, 4, 6 and 7)

- National Service Framework for Children, Young People and Maternity Services – Standard 9 (The Mental Health and Psychological Well-being of Children and Young People) issued by the Department for Education and Skills and the Department of Health in October 2004

- *Every Child Matters: Change for Children*, Department for Education and Skills, 2004

- *NHS Confidentiality Code of Practice*, Department of Health, 2003

- *Working Together to Safeguard Children*, HM Government, 2006

This material does not form part of the Code. It is provided for assistance only.

The following flow charts are for information only and do not form part of the Code, and they should be read in conjunction with the text in this chapter.

Informal admission and treatment of under 16s

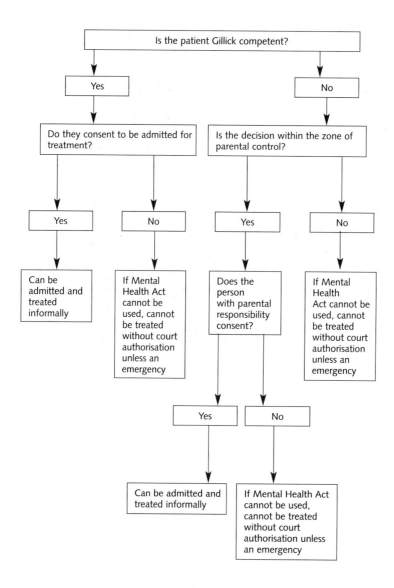

CHAPTER

36

Children
and young
people
under the
age of 18

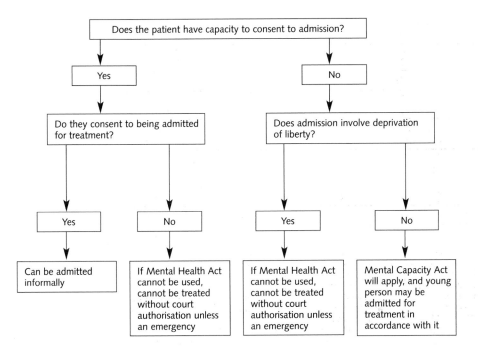

Informal admission of 16 and 17 year olds

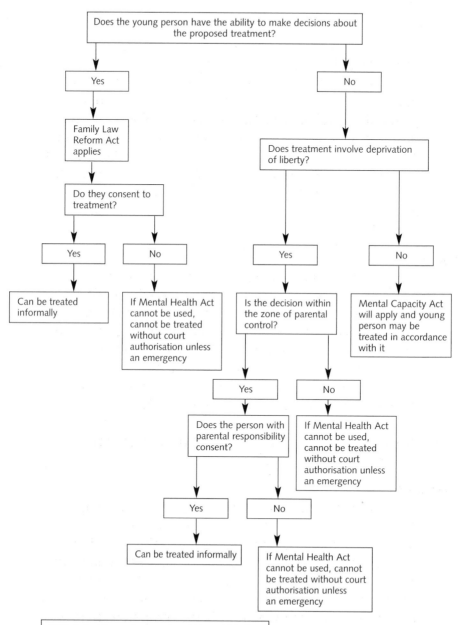

Informal treatment of 16 and 17 year olds

Does the young person have the ability to make decisions about the proposed treatment?

Yes → Family Law Reform Act applies → Do they consent to treatment?

- **Yes** → Can be treated informally
- **No** → If Mental Health Act cannot be used, cannot be treated without court authorisation unless an emergency

No → Does treatment involve deprivation of liberty?

- **Yes** → Is the decision within the zone of parental control?
  - **Yes** → Does the person with parental responsibility consent?
    - **Yes** → Can be treated informally
    - **No** → If Mental Health Act cannot be used, cannot be treated without court authorisation unless an emergency
  - **No** → If Mental Health Act cannot be used, cannot be treated without court authorisation unless an emergency
- **No** → Mental Capacity Act will apply and young person may be treated in accordance with it

Note: A decision on treatment could be outside the zone of parental control simply because of the nature of the proposed treatment, eg where, like ECT, it could be considered particularly invasive or controversial (see **paragraphs 36.9-36.15**)

CHAPTER

36

Children
and young
people
under the
age of 18

Examples

36.83 The following examples should be read in conjunction
with the preceding flow charts.

Example A

A 13 year old child is assessed as not being Gillick
competent. The primary purpose of the intervention is
to provide medical treatment for mental disorder. The
decision to authorise treatment falls within the zone of
parental control, as what is proposed is fairly standard,
but no person with parental responsibility consents. The
child cannot be admitted informally under section 131(1)
of the Mental Health Act. If the child meets the relevant
criteria, the child could be admitted to hospital for
assessment (section 2) or for treatment (section 3)
under the Act.

Example B

A 14 year old girl is assessed as not being Gillick
competent. The primary purpose of the intervention is
to provide medical treatment for mental disorder, but
she is severely anorexic and this will involve force feeding.
This is likely to take it outside the zone of parental
control, so even though a person with parental
responsibility consents, it is unlikely that the child can
be admitted informally under section 131(1). If the child
meets the relevant criteria, she could be admitted to
hospital for assessment (section 2) or for treatment
(section 3) under the Act.

Example C

A 15 year old child is assessed as being Gillick competent.
The primary purpose of the intervention is to provide
medical treatment for mental disorder. The child does not
consent to treatment in hospital. The child's parents are
keen for the child to be admitted to hospital and give
their consent. However, it is not considered safe to rely on
the parents' consent where a Gillick-competent child is
refusing. The child cannot be admitted informally under
section 131(1). If the child meets the relevant criteria,
the child could be admitted to hospital for assessment
(section 2) or for treatment (section 3) under the Act.

Example D

> A 16 year old young person is assessed as being able to make decisions about the proposed intervention. The primary purpose of the intervention is to provide medical treatment for mental disorder. The young person consents to treatment in hospital (and they do not need to be detained). The young person should be treated as an informal patient.

Example E

> A 17 year old young person is assessed as not having the capacity to make decisions about the proposed intervention. The MCA could be used to authorise treatment if the criteria for its use are met.

Example F

> A 15 year old is assessed as not being able to make decisions about the proposed intervention. The primary purpose of the intervention is not to provide medical treatment for mental disorder but to provide safety and protection. Consideration should be given to using section 25 of the Children Act.

ANNEX A
Key words and phrases used in this Code

Term	Definition
Absent without leave (AWOL)	When a **detained patient** leaves hospital without getting permission first or does not return to hospital when required to do so. Also applies to **guardianship** patients who leave the place their guardian says they should live and to **SCT patients** and **conditionally discharged restricted patients** who don't return to hospital when **recalled**, or who leave the hospital without permission after they have been recalled.
The Act	Unless otherwise stated, the Mental Health Act 1983 (as amended by the Mental Health Act 2007).
Advance decision to refuse treatment	A decision, under the **Mental Capacity Act**, to refuse specified treatment made in advance by a person who has capacity to do so. This decision will then apply at a future time when that person lacks **capacity** to consent to, or refuse the specified treatment.
Advocacy	Independent help and support with understanding issues and assistance in putting forward one's own views, feelings and ideas. See also **Independent mental health advocate**.
After-care	Community care services following discharge from hospital; especially the duty of health and social services to provide after-care under **section 117** of the Act, following the **discharge** of a patient from detention for treatment under the Act. The duty applies to **SCT patients** and **conditionally discharged restricted patients**, as well as those who have been fully discharged.
Application for detention	An application made by an **approved mental health professional**, or a **nearest relative**, under **Part 2** of **the Act** for a **patient** to be detained in a hospital either for **assessment** or for **medical treatment**. Applications may be made under section 2 (application for admission for assessment), section 3 (application for admission for medical treatment) or section 4 (emergency application for admission for assessment).
Appropriate medical treatment	**Medical treatment for mental disorder** which is appropriate taking into account the nature and degree of the person's **mental disorder** and all the other circumstances of their case.
Appropriate medical treatment test	The requirement in some of the **criteria for detention**, and in the **criteria for SCT**, that **appropriate medical treatment** must be available for the **patient**.

Term	Definition
Approved clinician	A mental health professional approved by the **Secretary of State** (or the **Welsh Ministers**) to act as an approved clinician for the purposes of **the Act**. Some decisions under the Act can only be taken by people who are approved clinicians. All **responsible clinicians** must be approved clinicians.
Approved mental health professional (AMHP)	A social worker or other professional approved by a **local social services authority (LSSA)** to carry out a variety of functions under the Act.
Assessment	Examining a **patient** to establish whether the patient has a **mental disorder** and, if they do, what treatment and care they need. It is also used to be mean examining or interviewing a patient to decide whether an **application for detention** or a **guardianship application** should be made.
Attorney	Someone appointed under the **Mental Capacity Act** who has the legal right to make decisions (eg decisions about treatment) within the scope of their authority on behalf of the person (the donor) who made the power of attorney. Also known as a "donee of lasting power of attorney".
Capacity	The ability to take a decision about a particular matter at the time the decision needs to be made. Some people may lack capacity to take a particular decision (eg to **consent** to treatment) because they cannot understand, retain, use or weigh the information relevant to the decision. A legal definition of lack of capacity for people aged 16 or over is set out in section 2 of the **Mental Capacity Act** 2005. See also **competence to consent**.
Care Programme Approach (CPA)	A system of care and support for individuals with complex needs which includes an assessment, a care plan and a care co-ordinator. It is used mainly for adults in England who receive specialist mental healthcare and in some CAMHS services. There are similar systems for supporting other groups of individuals, including children and young people (Children's Assessment Framework), older adults (Single Assessment Process) and people with learning disabilities (Person Centred Planning).
Carer	Someone who provides voluntary care by looking after and assisting a family member, friend or neighbour who requires support because of their mental health needs.
Child (and children)	A person under the age of 16.

Term	Definition
Child and adolescent mental health services (CAMHS)	Specialist mental health services for children and adolescents. CAMHS cover all types of provision and intervention – from mental health promotion and primary prevention and specialist community-based services through to very specialist care, as provided by in-patient units for children and young people with mental illness. They are mainly composed of a multi-disciplinary workforce with specialist training in child and adolescent mental health.
Children Act 1989	A law relating to **children** and **young people** and those with parental responsibility for them.
Commission	The independent body which is responsible for monitoring the operation of **the Act.** At the time of publication, this is the Mental Health Act Commission (MHAC). However, legislation is currently before Parliament which will abolish the MHAC and transfer its functions to a new body, the Care Quality Commission, which is to establish a new integrated health and adult social care regulator, bringing together existing health and social care regulators into one regulatory body. Subject to Parliament, it is expected that the new Commission will be established in April 2009.
Community treatment order (CTO)	Written authorisation on a statutory form for **the discharge** of a **patient** from **detention** in hospital onto **supervised community treatment**.
Competence to consent	Similar to **capacity** to **consent**, but specifically about children. As well as covering a child's inability to make particular decisions because of their mental condition, it also covers children who do not have the maturity to take the particular decision in question.
Compulsory measures	Things that can be done to people under **the Act** without their agreement. This includes **detention** in hospital, **supervised community treatment** and **guardianship**.
Compulsory treatment	**Medical treatment for mental disorder** given under **the Act** against the wishes of the **patient**.
Conditional discharge	The **discharge** from hospital by the **Secretary of State for Justice** or the **Tribunal** of a **restricted patient** subject to conditions. The patient remains subject to **recall** to hospital by the Secretary of State.
Conditionally discharged restricted patient	A **restricted patient** who has been given a **conditional discharge**.
Consent	Agreeing to allow someone else to do something to or for you. Particularly consent to treatment. Valid consent requires that the person has the **capacity** to make the decision (or the **competence to consent**, if a child), and they are given the information they need to make the decision, and that they are not under any duress or inappropriate pressure.

Term	Definition
Convey (and conveyance)	Transporting a patient under **the Act** to hospital (or anywhere else), compulsorily if necessary.
Court of Protection	The specialist court set up under the **Mental Capacity Act** to deal with all issues relating to people who lack **capacity** to take decisions for themselves.
Criteria for detention	A set of criteria that must be met before a person can be **detained**, or remain detained, under **the Act**. The criteria are different in different sections of the Act.
Criteria for SCT	A set of criteria that must be met before a person can become an **SCT patient** or remain an SCT patient.
Criminal Records Bureau	An Executive Agency of the Home Office, which provides access to criminal record information through its disclosure service.
Deprivation of liberty	A term used in Article 5 of the **European Convention on Human Rights (ECHR)** to mean the circumstances in which a person's freedom is taken away. Its meaning in practice has been developed through case law.
Deprivation of liberty safeguards	The framework of safeguards under the **Mental Capacity Act** (as amended by the Mental Health Act 2007) for people who need to be deprived of their liberty in their best interests for care or treatment to which they lack the **capacity** to **consent** themselves.[1]
Deputy (or Court-appointed deputy)	A person appointed by the **Court of Protection** under section 16 of the **Mental Capacity Act** to take specified decisions on behalf of someone who lacks **capacity** to take those decisions themselves. This is not the same thing as the **nominated deputy** sometimes appointed by the **doctor** or **approved clinician** in charge of a patient's treatment.
Detained patient	Unless otherwise stated, a patient who is **detained** in hospital under **the Act**, or who is liable to be detained in hospital but who is (for any reason) currently out of hospital. In **chapters 23** and **24**, detained patients has a more specific meaning, explained in **paragraphs 23.7-23.8**.
Detention (and detained)	Unless otherwise stated, being held compulsorily in hospital under **the Act** for a period of **assessment** or **medical treatment**. Sometimes referred to colloquially as "sectioning".
Detention for assessment (and detained for assessment)	The **detention** of a person in order to carry out an **assessment**. Can normally only last for a maximum of 28 days. Also known as "section 2 detention".

[1] These safeguards are expected to be in force from April 2009.

Term	Definition
Detention for medical treatment (and detained for medical treatment)	The **detention** of a person in order to give them the **medical treatment for mental disorder** they need. There are various types of detention for medical treatment in **the Act**. It most often means detention as a result of an **application for detention** under section 3 of the Act. But it also includes several types of detention under **Part 3** of the Act, including **hospital directions**, **hospital orders** and **interim hospital orders**.
Diagnostic over-shadowing	A risk for everyone with a **mental disorder**, but a particular danger for people with **learning disabilities**, that behavioural problems may be misinterpreted as symptomatic of mental disorder when they are in fact a sign of an underlying physical health problem.
Discharge	Unless otherwise stated, a decision that a **patient** should no longer be subject to **detention**, **supervised community treatment**, **guardianship** or **conditional discharge**. Discharge from detention is not the same as being discharged from hospital. The patient might already have left hospital on **leave of absence**, or might agree to remain in hospital as an **informal patient**.
Displacement (of nearest relative)	The provision under section 29 of **the Act**, under which the county court can order that the functions of the **nearest relative** be carried out by another person or by a **local social services authority**.
Doctor	A registered medical practitioner.
Doctor approved under section 12	A doctor who has been approved by the **Secretary of State** (or the **Welsh Ministers**) under the Act as having special experience in the diagnosis or treatment of mental disorder. In practice, **strategic health authorities** take these decisions on behalf of the Secretary of State in England. Some medical recommendations and medical evidence to courts under the Act can only be made by a doctor who is approved under section 12. (Doctors who are **approved clinicians** are automatically treated as though they have been approved under section 12.)
Electro-convulsive therapy (ECT)	A form of **medical treatment for mental disorder** in which seizures are induced by passing electricity through the brain of an anaesthetised **patient**; generally used as treatment for severe depression.
Emergency application	An **application for detention** for **assessment** made only one supporting **medical recommendation** in cases of urgent necessity. The patient can only be detained for a maximum of 72 hours unless a second medical recommendation is received. Also known as a "section 4 application".

Term	Definition
European Convention on Human Rights (ECHR)	The European Convention for the Protection of Human Rights and Fundamental Freedoms. The substantive rights it guarantees are largely incorporated into UK law by the **Human Rights Act 1998**.
GP	A patient's general practitioner (or "family doctor").
Guardian	See **guardianship**.
Guardianship	The appointment of a **guardian** to help and supervise patients in the community for their own welfare or to protect other people. The guardian may be either a **local social services authority (LSSA)** or someone else approved by an LSSA (a **private guardian**).
Guardianship application	An application to a **local social services authority** by an **approved mental health professional** or a **nearest relative** for a **patient** to become subject to **guardianship**.
Guardianship order	An order by the court, under **Part 3** of **the Act** that a **mentally disordered offender** should become subject to **guardianship**.
Guiding principles	The principles set out in **chapter 1** that have to be considered when decisions are made under the Act.
Habilitation	Equipping someone with skills and abilities they have never had. As opposed to **rehabilitation**, which means helping them recover skills and abilities they have lost.
Health action plan	A plan which details the actions needed to maintain and improve the health of an individual with a learning disability and any help needed to achieve them. It links the individual with the range of services and supports they need in order to have better health. It is part of their broader **person-centred plan**.
Holding powers	The powers in section 5 of **the Act** which allow hospital in-patients to be detained temporarily so that a decision can be made about whether an **application for detention** should be made. There are two holding powers: under section 5(2), **doctors** and **approved clinicians** can detain patients for up to 72 hours; and under section 5(4), certain nurses can detain patients for up to 6 hours.
Hospital direction	An order by the court under **Part 3** of **the Act** for the **detention for medical treatment** in hospital of a **mentally disordered offender**. It is given alongside a prison sentence. Hospital directions are given under section 45A of the Act.

Term	Definition
Hospital managers	The organisation (or individual) responsible for the operation of **the Act** in a particular hospital (eg an **NHS trust**, an **NHS foundation trust** or the owners of an **independent hospital**). Hospital managers have various functions under the Act, which include the power to **discharge** a patient. In practice, most of the hospital managers' decisions are taken on their behalf by individuals (or groups of individuals) authorised by the hospital managers to do so. This can include clinical staff. Hospital managers' decisions about discharge are normally delegated to a "**managers' panel**" of three or more people.
Hospital order	An order by a court under **Part 3** of **the Act** for the **detention for medical treatment** in hospital of a **mentally disordered offender**, given instead of a prison sentence or other form of punishment. Hospital orders are normally made under section 37 of the Act.
Human Rights Act 1998	A law largely incorporating into UK law the substantive rights set out in the **European Convention on Human Rights**.
Independent hospital	A hospital which is not managed by the NHS.
Independent mental health advocate (IMHA)	An advocate available to offer help to patients under arrangements which are specifically required to be made under **the Act**.[2]
Independent mental health advocacy services	The services which make **independent mental health advocates** available to **patients**. The Act calls patients who are eligible for these services "qualifying patients".
Informal patient	Someone who is being treated for a **mental disorder** and who is not **detained** under **the Act**. Also sometimes known as a "voluntary patient".
Interim hospital order	An order by a court under **Part 3** of **the Act** for the **detention for medical treatment** in hospital of a **mentally disordered offender** on an interim basis, to enable the court to decide whether to make a **hospital order** or deal with the offender's case in some other way. Interim hospital orders are made under section 38 of the Act.
Learning disability	In **the Act**, a learning disability means a state of arrested or incomplete development of the mind which includes significant impairment of intelligence and social functioning. It is a form of **mental disorder**.
Learning disability qualification	The rule which says that certain parts of **the Act** only apply to a **learning disability** if the learning disability is associated with abnormally aggressive or seriously irresponsible behaviour on the part of the person concerned.

[2] These arrangements are not expected to be in force until April 2009.

Term	Definition
Leave of absence	Permission for a **patient** who is **detained** in hospital to be absent from the hospital for short periods, eg to go to the shops or spend a weekend at home, or for much longer periods. Patients remain under the powers of **the Act** when they are on leave and can be **recalled** to hospital if necessary in the interest of the patient's health or safety or for the protection of other people.
Local social services authority (LSSA)	The local authority (or council) responsible for social services in a particular area of the country.
Managers	See **hospital managers**.
Managers' panel	A panel of three or more people appointed to take decisions on behalf of **hospital managers** about the **discharge** of patients from **detention** or **supervised community treatment**.
Medical recom- mendation	Normally means a recommendation provided by a **doctor** in support of an **application for detention** or a **guardianship application**.
Medical treatment	In **the Act**, this covers a wide range of services. As well as the kind of care and treatment given by **doctors**, it also includes nursing, psychological therapies, and specialist mental health **habilitation, rehabilitation** and care.
Medical treatment for mental disorder	**Medical treatment** which is for the purpose of alleviating, or preventing a worsening of, the **mental disorder**, or one or more of its symptoms or manifestations.
Mental Capacity Act	The Mental Capacity Act 2005. An Act of Parliament that governs decision-making on behalf of people who lack **capacity**, both where they lose capacity at some point in their lives, eg as a result of dementia or brain injury, and where the incapacitating condition has been present since birth.
Mental disorder	Any disorder or disability of the mind. As well as mental illnesses, it includes conditions like personality disorders, autistic spectrum disorders and **learning disabilities**.
Mental Health Act Commission	See **Commission**.
Mental illness	An illness of the mind. It includes common conditions like depression and anxiety and less common conditions like schizophrenia, bipolar disorder, anorexia nervosa and dementia.
Mentally disordered offender	A person who has a **mental disorder** and who has committed a criminal offence.

Term	Definition
Nearest relative	A person defined by section 26 of **the Act** who has certain rights and powers under the Act in respect of a **patient** for whom they are the nearest relative.
NHS	The National Health Service.
NHS com-missioners	**Primary care trusts (PCTs)** and other bodies responsible for commissioning NHS services.
NHS trust and NHS foundation trust	Types of NHS body responsible for providing NHS services in a local area.
Nominated deputy	A **doctor** or **approved clinician** who may make a report detaining a **patient** under the **holding powers** in section 5 in the absence of the **doctor** or approved clinician who is in charge of the patient's treatment.
Part 2	The part of **the Act** which deals with **detention, guardianship** and **supervised community treatment** for civil (ie non-offender) patients.
	Some aspects of Part 2 also apply to some patients who have been detained or made subject to guardianship by the courts or who have been transferred from prison to detenton in hospital by the **Secretary of State for Justice** under **Part 3** of **the Act**.
Part 2 patient	A civil patient – ie a patient who became subject to **compulsory measures** under **the Act** as a result of an **application for detention** or a **guardianship application** by a **nearest relative** or an **approved mental health professional** under **Part 2** of the Act.
Part 3	The part of **the Act** which deals with **mentally disordered offenders** and defendants in criminal proceedings. Among other things, it allows courts to **detain** people in hospital for treatment instead of punishing them, where particular criteria are met. It also allows the **Secretary of State for Justice** to transfer people from prison to detention in hospital for treatment.
Part 3 patient	A patient made subject to **compulsory measures** under **the Act** by the courts or by being transferred to detention in hospital from prison under **Part 3** of the Act. Part 3 patients can be either "restricted" (ie subject to special restrictions on when they can be **discharged**, given **leave of absence**, and various other matters) or "unrestricted" (ie treated for the most part like a **Part 2 patient**).
Part 4	The part of **the Act** which deals mainly with the **medical treatment for mental disorder** of detained patients (including **SCT patients** who have been **recalled** to hospital). In particular, it sets out when they can and cannot be treated for their mental disorder without their **consent**.
Part 4A	The Part of the Act which deals with the **medical treatment for mental disorder** of **SCT patients** when they have not been **recalled** to hospital.

Key words and phrases used in this Code

Term	Definition
Part 4A certificate	A **SOAD certificate** approving particular forms of **medical treatment for mental disorder** for an **SCT patient**.
Part 4A patient	In **chapters 23** and **24** means an **SCT patient** who has not been **recalled** to hospital.
Patient	People who are, or appear to be, suffering from a **mental disorder**. This use of the term is not a recommendation that the term "patient" should be used in practice in preference to other terms such as "service users", "clients" or similar terms. It is simply a reflection of the terminology used in **the Act** itself.
Person-centred plan	An individual plan for each person with a **learning disability**, tailored to their needs and aspirations, which aims to help them to be a part of their community and to help the community to welcome them.
Place of safety	A place in which people may be temporarily detained under **the Act**. In particular, a place to which the police may remove a person for the purpose of assessment under section 135 or 136 of the Act. (A place of safety may be a hospital, a residential care home, a police station, or any other suitable place.)
Primary care trust (PCT)	The NHS body responsible, in particular, for commissioning (arranging) NHS services for a particular part of England. PCTs may also provide NHS services themselves.
Private guardian	An individual person (rather than a **local social services authority**) who is a patient's **guardian** under **the Act.**
Qualifying patients	**Patients** who are eligible for support from **independent mental health advocacy services**.
Recall (and recalled)	A requirement that a **patient** who is subject to **the Act** return to hospital. It can apply to patients who are on **leave of absence**, who are on **supervised community treatment**, or who have been given a **conditional discharge** from hospital.
Regulations	Secondary legislation made under **the Act**. In most cases, it means the Mental Health (Hospital, Guardianship and Treatment) (England) Regulations 2008.
Rehabilitation	See **habilitation**.
Remand to hospital (and remanded to hospital)	An order by a court under **Part 3** of **the Act** for the **detention** in hospital of a defendant in criminal proceedings. Remand under section 35 is for a report on the person's mental condition. Remand under section 36 is for **medical treatment for mental disorder**.
Responsible clinician	The **approved clinician** with overall responsibility for a patient's case. Certain decisions (such as renewing a patient's **detention** or placing a patient on **supervised community treatment**) can only be taken by the responsible clinician.

Term	Definition
Responsible hospital	The hospital whose managers are responsible for an **SCT patient**. To begin with, at least, this is the hospital in which the patient was detained before being discharged onto **supervised community treatment**.
Responsible local social services authority (LSSA)	The **local social services authority (LSSA)** responsible for a **patient** who is subject to **guardianship** under the Act. The responsible LSSA is normally the LSSA for the area where the patient lives. But if the patient has a **private guardian**, it is the LSSA for the area where the guardian lives.
Restricted patient	A **Part 3 patient** who, following criminal proceedings, is made subject to a restriction order under section 41 of **the Act**, to a limitation direction under section 45A or to a restriction direction under section 49. The order or direction will be imposed on an offender where it appears that it is necessary to protect the public from serious harm. One of the effects of the restrictions imposed by these sections is that restricted patients cannot be given **leave of absence** or be transferred to another hospital without the consent of the **Secretary of State for Justice**, and only the **Tribunal** can discharge them without the Secretary of State's agreement. See also **Unrestricted Part 3 patient**.
Revocation (and revoke)	Term used in **the Act** to describe the rescinding of a **community treatment order (CTO)** when an **SCT patient** needs further treatment in hospital under the Act. If a patient's CTO is revoked, the patient is **detained** under the powers of the Act in the same way as before the CTO was made.
SCT patient	A patient who is on **supervised community treatment**.
Second opinion appointed doctor (SOAD)	An independent **doctor** appointed by the **Commission** who gives a second opinion on whether certain types of **medical treatment for mental disorder** should be given without the patient's **consent**.
Secretary of State	Cabinet ministers in the Government. In the Act, either the Secretary of State for Health or the Secretary of State for Justice, depending on the context.
Secretary of State for Health	The **Secretary of State** who is responsible, among other things, for the NHS and social services for adults. The Secretary of State for Health is supported by the Department of Health.
Secretary of State for Justice	The **Secretary of State** who is responsible, among other things, for courts, prisons, probation, criminal law and sentencing. The Secretary of State for Justice is supported by the Ministry of Justice.
Section 4 application	See **emergency application**.
Section 57 treatment	A form of **medical treatment for mental disorder** to which the special rules in section 57 of the Act apply, especially neurosurgery for **mental disorder** (sometimes called "psychosurgery").[3]

---

[3] It is possible that other forms of treatment may be added to section 57, section 58 or section 58A by regulations.

Term	Definition
Section 58 treatment	A form of **medical treatment for mental disorder** to which the special rules in section 58 of the Act apply, which means medication for **mental disorder** for detained patients after an initial three-month period.[3]
Section 58A treatment	A form of **medical treatment for mental disorder** to which the special rules in section 58 of the Act apply, especially **electro-convulsive therapy**.[3]
Section 117	See **after-care**.
SOAD certificate	A certificate issued by a **second opinion appointed doctor (SOAD)** approving particular forms of medical treatment for a patient.
Strategic health authority (SHA)	NHS body responsible for overseeing all NHS services in a particular region of England.
Supervised community treatment (SCT)	Arrangements under which patients can be discharged from detention in hospital under **the Act**, but remain subject to the Act in the community rather than in hospital. Patients on SCT are expected to comply with conditions set out in the **community treatment order** and can be **recalled** to hospital if treatment in hospital is necessary again.
Tribunal	A judicial body which has the power to discharge patients from **detention, supervised community treatment, guardianship** and **conditional discharge**. At the time of publication, this means the Mental Health Review Tribunal (MHRT). However, subject to Parliament, the MHRT is intended to be replaced in England by a new First Tier Tribunal established under the Tribunals, Courts and Enforcement Act 2007.
Unrestricted Part 3 patient	A patient subject to a **hospital order** or **guardianship order** under **Part 3** of **the Act**, or who has been transferred from prison to detention in hospital under that Part, who is not also subject to a restriction order or direction. For the most part, unrestricted patients are treated in the same way as **Part 2 patients**, although they cannot be discharged by their **nearest relative**. See also **Restricted patient**.
Voluntary patient	See **informal patient**.
Welsh Ministers	Ministers in the Welsh Assembly Government.
Young person	A person aged 16 or 17.

[3] It is possible that other forms of treatment may be added to section 57, section 58 or section 58A by regulations.

ANNEX B
List of policies and procedures

This annex contains a summary of the policies, procedures and guidance which the Code says should be put in place locally by hospital managers, local social services authorities (LSSAs) and others.

Paragraph of Code	Policy, procedure or guidance
2.44	**Information policy** Hospital managers should have in place policies to ensure that all detained and supervised community treatment (SCT) patients and their nearest relatives are given information about their legal situation and rights in accordance with the legislation.
4.46	**Police assistance for people undertaking assessments with a view to applications under the Act** There should be locally agreed arrangements for the circumstances in which the police should be asked to provide assistance to approved mental health professionals (AMHPs) and doctors undertaking assessments.
8.16	**Displacement of nearest relatives** LSSAs should provide clear, practical guidance to help AMHPs decide whether to make an application to the county court for the appointment of an acting nearest relative for a patient and how to proceed.
8.19	**Displacement of nearest relatives** LSSAs should provide clear practical guidance to help AMHPs decide who to nominate when making an application to displace a nearest relative.
10.7	**Warrants under section 135 of the Act** LSSAs should ensure that guidance is available to AMHPs on how and when to apply for a warrant under section 135 to permit the police to enter premises.
10.16	**Sections 135 and 136 of the Act** LSSAs, NHS bodies, police forces and ambulance services should have an agreed local policy in place governing all aspects of the use of section 135 and 136 (police powers and places of safety).
11.9-11.12	**Conveyance of patients under the Act** Relevant authorities, including NHS bodies responsible for hospitals, ambulance services and the police, should agree joint local policies and procedures for conveying patients under the Act, setting out clearly the respective responsibilities of the different agencies and service providers.
13.8	**Receipt of applications for detention** Hospital managers should provide a checklist for the guidance of people delegated to receive detention documents.

Paragraph of Code	Policy, procedure or guidance
13.15	**Receipt of guardianship applications** LSSAs should prepare a checklist for the guidance of those delegated to receive guardianship applications on their behalf.
14.3	**Allocation of responsible clinicians** Hospital managers should have local protocols in place for allocating responsible clinicians to patients.
15.6	**Management of disturbed or violent behaviour** All hospitals should have a policy on the recognition and prevention of disturbed, challenging or violent behaviour, including the use of de-escalation techniques, enhanced observation, physical intervention, rapid tranquillisation and seclusion.
15.21	**Restraint and physical interventions** Hospital policies on management of disturbed behaviour should include clear written policies on the use of restraint and physical interventions, including provisions for post-incident reviews.
15.31	**Mechanical restraint** If any forms of mechanical restraint are to be used, there should be a clear policy in place governing their use.
15.36	**Training for staff exposed to aggression or violence** All hospitals should have a policy on training staff who work in areas where they may be exposed to aggression or violence or who may need to become involved in the restraint of patients.
15.42	**Observation** All hospitals should have clear written policies on the use of observation.
15.47-15.59	**Seclusion** Hospital policies should include clear written guidelines on the use of seclusion and set requirements for recording, monitoring and reviewing the use of seclusion and any follow-up action.
15.66	**Longer-term segregation** Hospitals proposing to allow long-term segregation should have a policy in place which sets out when it is to be used and how it is to be kept under review.
16.5-16.6	**Mobile phones** Hospital managers should have a policy on the possession and use of mobile phones by patients and their visitors.
16.7	**Internet access** Hospital managers should have guidance on patients' access to e-mail and the internet using the hospital's own IT infrastructure.
16.10	**Searching** Hospital managers should ensure that there is an operational policy on searching detained patients, their belongings and surroundings and their visitors.

Paragraph of Code	Policy, procedure or guidance
16.33	**Accommodation with enhanced levels of security** Hospitals offering accommodation with enhanced levels of security should have written guidelines, setting out the categories of patients for whom it is appropriate to use physically secure conditions and those for whom it is not appropriate.
16.39	**Entry and exit from wards** Wards should have a written policy that sets out precisely what the arrangements are for entry to and exit from the ward.
19.9	**Visits to patients in hospitals** Hospitals should have a policy on the circumstances in which visits to patients may be restricted.
19.17	**Visits by and to children and young people** All hospitals should have written policies and procedures regarding the arrangements for children and young people who visit patients in hospital and for visits to patients who are children or young people.
22.10	**Patients absent without leave from hospital** Hospital managers should ensure that there is a clear written policy about the action to be taken when a detained patient, or a patient on SCT, goes missing. This policy should be agreed with other agencies such as the police and ambulance services.
22.12	**Guardianship patients absent without leave** LSSAs should have policies for the action to be taken when they, or a private guardian, become aware that a guardianship patient is absent without leave (AWOL) from the place they are required to live.
25.46	**Supervised community treatment – concerns of carers and relatives** The managers of responsible hospitals should ensure that local protocols are in place to cover how concerns raised by carers or relatives about SCT patients' health or compliance with the conditions of their community treatment orders are addressed and taken forward.
26.15	**Guardianship** Each LSSA should have a policy setting out the arrangements for the way in which it will discharge its responsibilities in relation to guardianship.
29.5	**Renewal of detention** Hospital managers should determine local policies on the selection of the second professional required to agree to the renewal of a patient's detention.
30.33	**Inspection and withholding of correspondence** The managers of high-security psychiatric hospitals should have a written policy for the exercise of their power to withhold both the incoming and outgoing post from patients in certain circumstances.

Index

Mental Health Act Code of Practice

E

education access, 36.68, 36.77
electro-convulsive therapy (ECT) (under section 58A), 2.16, 20.6, 23.6, 23.22, 23.52, 24.12, 24.18–24, 24.26
    patients aged under 18 years, 24.18–24, 36.14, 36.55–62
    section 58A, 20.12, 23.5–6, 23.9–10, 23.20, 23.26, 24.4t, 24.28–31, 24.76, 24.79t
    urgent cases where certificates not required, 24.33
emergency applications for detention (under section 4), 5.1–13, 7.13, 20.5, 21.24, 23.7–10, 23.8t, 23.52, 26.34, 33.28
emergency resuscitation techniques, 15.37
enhanced observation interventions, 15.6, 15.8, 15.40–2
European Convention on Human Rights, 2.32, 4.60, 16.2, 18.2, 30.15, 30.40
    treatment without consent and, 23.39–41
European Court of Human Rights, 23.40, 36.9

F

Family Law Reform Act 1969, 36.3, 36.27–30
family members of patients, 1.5, 2.5, 4.5, 4.66–8, 24.55
    after-care (under section 117) and, 27.12, 27.13
    confidentiality and, 18.10–13
    guardianship patients and, 2.46
    information to children, 2.43
    information to nearest relatives, 2.27–33
    learning disabilities, patients with, 34.11, 34.12
    reviews of detention/SCT and, 31.29, 31.32
    SCT patients and, 25.19, 25.20, 25.46, 25.60
    see also nearest relatives
force, reasonable, use of, 11.17
    searches and, 16.21, 16.22, 16.25
friends of patients, 2.5, 18.10–13, 25.60, 31.32, 34.11

G

gender identity, 6.11
gender/sex, segregation of facilities by, 16.9
General Practitioners (GPs), 4.78, 4.103, 24.55, 25.17, 26.25, 27.12
Gillick competence, 23.30, 36.38–50, 36.66, 36.78
guardianship, 2.46, 4.4, 25.79, 28.3
    absence without leave and, 22.2, 22.6
    AMHPs and, 7.1–2, 8.10, 13.14, 26.3, 26.8–10
    assessments for, 26.7–14
    attorneys/deputies and, 9.3, 9.6
    care planning, 26.19–25
    criminal justice system and, 33.7
    documents, 13.14–15, 13.18–20
    guardianship orders (under section 37), 26.36–7
    hospital care and, 26.31–4
    IMHAs and, 20.4, 20.12
    learning disabilities and, 34.6
    LSSAs and, 2.46, 22.6, 22.12, 26.15–25, 26.30, 26.34, 26.35, 26.36, 30.24–5

376

LSSAs and applications for, 13.14–15, 13.18–20, 26.15
MCA and, 26.10, 26.11, 26.30, 26.32, 28.10
medication and, 26.10, 26.11, 26.30, 26.32, 28.10
nearest relatives and, 8.6, 8.10
patients resisting authority of guardian, 26.35
power to decide where patients should live, 26.3, 26.8, 26.12–13, 26.26–30, 26.32
purpose of, 26.2–26
SCT as alternative, 28.6t
transfers to, 30.24–5
Tribunal and, 2.46, 9.6, 26.15, 26.37, 32.2, 32.5, 32.16, 32.24

H

habilitation, 6.2, 23.2
hearing impairments, 2.3, 4.41–2, 15.24, 16.16, 32.36
    deaf patients, 4.106–10, 15.24
High Court, applications to, 36.66
high security psychiatric hospitals, 2.23, 30.33
holding powers
    of doctors and approved clinicians (under section 5(2)), 12.2–20
    nomination of deputies (under section 5(3)), 12.11–17
    of nurses under section 5(4), 12.21–34, 12.35–40
hormones to reduce male sex drive, surgical implantation of, 23.6, 24.6–9
hospital directions (under section 45A), 33.18, 33.21, 33.23
hospital managers
    admission powers and duties, 30.11–12
    after-care (under section 117) and, 27.7–9
    children and young people and, 30.42
    criminal justice system and, 33.14
    detained patients and, 3.14–16, 30.7, 31.2, 31.10–16, 31.18–22, 31.23–47
    discharge criteria, 31.14–22
    discharge power, 30.7, 31.2–10, 31.14, 31.18–22, 31.36–47
    discharge reviews, 31.10–13, 31.23–44
    exercise of functions of, 30.7–10
    identification of, 30.2–6
    information for patients and relatives, 30.28
    managers' panels and, 30.5–6, 30.7, 31.3–9, 31.12–13, 31.14–22, 31.23–47
    patients' correspondence and, 2.23, 30.32–3
    SCT patients and, 3.14, 25.71–4, 30.7, 30.26–7, 31.2, 31.10–14, 31.18–22, 31.23–47
    second professionals and, 29.8–9
    Secretary of State for Health and, 30.39–41, 32.9
    statutory duties, 2.44, 20.12–15, 25.37, 25.74, 30.11–42, 32.5, 32.9–10, 36.71, 36.76
    transfers of patients between hospitals, 30.13–23
    transfers to guardianship, 30.24–5
    Tribunal and, 30.34–8, 32.5–8, 32.9, 32.10, 32.16, 32.24, 32.25, 32.32–6, 32.37
    victims of crime and, 30.29–31
hospital orders (under section 37), 33.8, 33.13, 33.15, 33.18, 33.21–2, 33.25
Human Rights Act 1998, 1.7, 23.39, 31.23, 36.3, 36.33, 36.43

I

L

LSSAs and, 32.5, 32.10, 32.16, 32.24, 32.25, 32.36, 32.37
medical examinations, 32.22
private visits to patients and, 19.5–8, 32.22
purpose of, 32.2–4
reports to, 32.10–21
representation rights, 32.25
SCT patients and, 25.15, 25.77, 30.39–41, 32.2–4, 32.5–8, 32.14, 32.25
Secretary of State for Health and, 30.39–41, 32.9, 32.21, 32.23
withdrawal of applications, 32.23–4
Ministry of Justice, 33.34
Mental Health Unit, 4.97, 32.12, 33.36
mobile phones, hospital policy on, 16.5–6
monitoring
of certificates, 24.37, 24.78
conveyance of patients, 11.4, 11.10
of disturbed behaviour, 15.27, 15.37, 15.47, 15.56, 15.65
of hospital visitors, 19.15–16
places of safety and, 10.17, 10.42–4
of SCT, 25.38–40, 25.71
section 4 and, 5.9
section 5 and, 12.37
of transfers of prisoners to hospital, 33.31
see also record keeping

N

National Assistance Act 1948, 4.89
National Health Service (NHS)
independent hospitals and, 31.45–7
NHS foundation trusts, 30.2, 31.5–6
NHS trusts, 30.2, 31.6
National Institute for Health and Clinical Excellence (NICE), 15.2
nearest relatives, 8.1–23
acting nearest relative appointed by county court, 8.5, 8.6–7, 8.18–19, 8.23
after-care (under section 117) and, 27.12
AMHPs and, 4.56–65, 8.5, 8.9–23
applications for detention in hospital by, 4.28, 4.30, 4.80, 7.7, 11.13, 11.15, 30.12
attorneys/deputies and, 9.8–10
AWOL patients and, 22.11, 22.18
conflicts of interest and, 7.7
delegation of functions, 8.4, 8.8
displacement of (section 29 of Act), 4.65, 8.6–23
guardianship patients and, 26.16, 26.37
identification of, 8.2–3
IMHAs and, 20.13–15, 20.18
information to, 2.27–33, 2.44, 30.28
no nearest relative, 8.5, 8.6, 8.11
powers of discharge, 29.18–22, 31.31
reviews of detention/SCT and, 31.28
SCT patients and, 2.28–30, 2.44, 25.17, 25.50, 25.77–8
SOADs and, 24.55